the *New* Rational Therapy

Elliot D. Cohen, Ph.D.

With a Foreword by ALBERT ELLIS

the *New* Rational Therapy

Thinking Your Way to Serenity, Success, and Profound Happiness

ROWMAN & LITTLEFIELD PUBLISHERS, INC.

Lanham • Boulder • New York • Toronto • Plymouth, UK

ROWMAN & LITTLEFIELD PUBLISHERS, INC.

Published in the United States of America
by Rowman & Littlefield Publishers, Inc.
A wholly owned subsidiary of The Rowman & Littlefield Publishing Group, Inc.
4501 Forbes Boulevard, Suite 200, Lanham, Maryland 20706
www.rowmanlittlefield.com

Estover Road
Plymouth PL6 7PY
United Kingdom

British Library Cataloging in Publication Information Available

Library of Congress Cataloging-in-Publication Data

Cohen, Elliot D.
   The new rational therapy : thinking your way to serenity, success, and profound
happiness / Elliot Cohen.
     p. cm.
   Includes bibliographical references and index.
   ISBN-13: 978-0-7425-4733-9 (cloth : alk. paper)
   ISBN-10: 0-7425-4733-7 (cloth : alk. paper)
   ISBN-13: 978-0-7425-4734-6 (pbk. : alk. paper)
   ISBN-10: 0-7425-4734-5 (pnk. : alk. paper)
   1. Philosophical counseling. 2. Conduct of life. I. Title.
BJ1595.5.C63 2006
158—dc22
                                               2006016928

Printed in the United States of America

This book is dedicated to my friend and mentor, Albert Ellis, who has supported, taught, and inspired me in countless ways.

CONTENTS

FOREWORD

Elliot Cohen's *The New Rational Therapy* is an excellent follow-up to his *What Would Aristotle Do?* Like the latter book, it shows in great detail how you—and billions of other people—erroneously think and, by doing so, largely create what we call "emotional" disturbance. More importantly, he indicates what you can do to correct your dysfunctional thinking, feeling, and behaving.

Rational-Emotive Behavior Therapy (REBT), which I started formulating in 1953 and practicing in January 1955, is the first of the major cognitive-behavior therapies. It hypothesizes, as Elliot shows in this book, that you are born and reared to easily upset yourself but that you are also a constructivist who has the ability to think, feel, and act more functionally to stop upsetting yourself and to lead a happier life. Unlike most of the other cognitive-behavior therapies that started up in the 1960s, REBT stresses that you are an unusual thinking animal who develops several basic philosophies—that also have strong emotional and behavioral elements—that make you and keep you dysfunctional. Moreover, you are often unaware of your core philosophies, and when you become aware of them, you dogmatically believe that they are true or factual. As the Buddhists said some 2,500 years ago, they are actually illusions.

REBT therefore shows you how to look for and uncover your leading philosophies; to dispute them forcefully, emotionally, and actively; and to change them to effective new philosophies, or rational coping philosophies. How did I originate REBT? Mainly, by being devoted to philosophy (and not merely psychology) and using it successfully on my own practical and emotive problems—as I show in my recent book *Rational Emotive Behavior Therapy—It Works for Me, It Can Work for You.*

As Cohen accurately shows in this book, you and other people have a number of special false or illusory philosophies that often lead you astray. These include demanding perfection, damning yourself and others, "awfulizing," and "I-can't-stand-it-itis." REBT shows you how to discover and dispute these destructive attitudes. But Cohen adds a few more idiocies, such as jumping on the bandwagon, manipulation, "the world revolves around me," and "thou shalt upset yourself."

Cohen also shows, since he has been adept at practicing REBT and has been professionally trained in it at the Albert Ellis Institute in New York for several years, that just about all your philosophical mistakes stem from your innate and socially acquired tendencies, especially from your tendencies to make healthy desires into unhealthy and absolutistic shoulds, oughts, musts, and demands. He shows how many famed philosophers had antidotes for your "musturbation," and he adds some antidotes of his own.

All told, this is an amazingly profound book. It distills the wisdom of many outstanding philosophers as only a professional philosopher-therapist like Elliot Cohen can do. Be grateful for his combined talents and happy for the unusual self-help material that he has included in this book.

ALBERT ELLIS, PH.D.,
founder, Rational-Emotive Behavior Therapy

PREFACE

Speaking here of a new rational therapy is somewhat like speaking of a new oil reserve. The oil was in the ground for millions of years, but only recently has it been tapped and processed. The great body of wisdom amassed by the great sages throughout recorded history is obviously not a new kid on the block. What's profoundly new, however, is processing it as a central component of rational psychology. This is what I have attempted in this book, and it portends nothing less than a psychological revolution.

About a half century ago, a man with a vision looked to the teachings of the ancient Stoic philosophers to develop a rational approach to psychology. The result was a type of therapy that has radically changed the face of contemporary psychology. I speak here of one of the most influential psychologists of the past century, Albert Ellis, founder of the popular therapy known as Rational-Emotive Behavior Therapy (REBT). Ellis tapped into an enormously valuable reserve, but there is an incredibly vast sea of such knowledge that still remains untapped. The strides made in this book to harness the wisdom of the ages mark a new beginning in the endeavor to make rational therapy more profoundly rational.

Much of the past work of rational psychology has been in helping people identify their irrational thinking and to provide behavioral techniques for overcoming their self-destructive tendencies. In contrast, this book focuses on providing philosophical *antidotes* to people's irrational thinking. Philosophy can be an amazingly powerful guide to overcoming the most dangerous types of irrationality that lead people to live in severe distress. But it is much more than this. Not only is it curative. Its deep insight into human existence can help transform a miserable life into one of *profound* happiness. That is, its methods and ideas can guide you from distress at the mundane struggles of everyday living to a life pregnant with insight, meaning, value, and purpose.

Of course, this must be coupled with the usual disclaimers. No self-help book can responsibly claim to substitute for the services of a competent therapist. Nor can *any* single modality legitimately claim to be suitable for *everyone*. Some people suffering from major depression, bipolar disorder, and other psychological disorders may also require drug therapy before they can satisfactorily work through their problems.

There is also not just one royal route to happiness. Indeed, the philosophical map has been paved with a myriad of inroads to human prosperity. Some antidotes may suit you better than others. For example, if you are inclined toward Western religious ideas, St. Thomas Aquinas might hit the spot; if you are an atheist or an agnostic, you might be more comfortable with Nietzsche. But you can be confident that there are philosophical antidotes that address virtually every human challenge from multiple perspectives. I hope you will enjoy your ascent into some of the most profound insights ever conceived. May they yield a welcome boost toward your serenity, success, and profound happiness!

ACKNOWLEDGMENTS

I wish to express a warm debt of gratitude to my editor, Ross H. Miller, Ph.D., for his unwavering support and creative intuition; to my colleagues, Shlomit Schuster, Ph.D., James Sterba, Ph.D., and Samuel Zinaich Jr., Ph.D., for their kind comments on this book; to my beloved wife and professional confidant, Gale S. Cohen, LMHC; and to the person to whom this book owes its essence, Albert Ellis, Ph.D.

Introduction

THE NEW RATIONAL THERAPY

Depression can envelop your life in darkness, swallowing up your hope, crushing your spirit, thwarting talents and creativity, and leaving you in a state of destitution as seemingly real as a forest wilted and depleted by some alien canker. Guilt can gnaw at your psyche, hovering over you like a dark cloud, belittling your dignity, and drowning out sound judgment amidst a moralistic, inner voice. Anxiety can drape your present in ruminations about your future, turning your existence into a dark tunnel in which you perceive ominous danger lurking at every life juncture. Anger can swell up and consume your spirit like a tornado sweeping aimlessly through a peaceful city, leaving devastation in its path, lamented after the storm subsides, only to blow up again when the conditions seem right.

Saying you *can't*—when you really just *won't*—can *can't*stipate your creative potential. Perceiving through stereotypes can stifle your ability to resonate with others. Blind conformity to social injunctions having neither rhyme nor reason can gobble up your individuality until you no longer recognize yourself. Patriot fervor fired up by demagoguery and deception can defeat your resolute devotion to freedom and democracy. Resorting to threats and deceit to get what you want can deliver much less than what you've bargained for. Seeing things only from *your* perspective can leave you shipwrecked in your own subjective universe. Perceiving a duty to woefully ruminate, overrating or underrating the probabilities, wishfully thinking, fatalistically giving in and up—these common tendencies can leave you feeling flat and dead.

Let me be blunt right from the start. I'm speaking here about *human* tendencies, yours *and* mine. It won't do to say, "No flies on me! These are the other guy's foibles and not mine." Of course, your issues and vulnerabilities may not be mine, and mine may not be yours. You might be struggling

1

with something unfortunate that happened in your life. I might be anxious about confronting an unsung future. Your Achilles' heel might be my strength and vice versa. But neither you nor I are immune from what is distinctively human.

There are many *psychological* approaches that try to help us humans deal meaningfully with our emotional and behavioral problems. For example, some therapies view intense and destructive emotions as bodily states requiring medication. Some attempt to provide a warm, caring, nonjudgmental environment as the primary vehicle of constructive change. Others bid us to become our emotions in attempting to take responsibility for them. Others apply systems analysis to address interpersonal dysfunctions. Others try to uncover self-destructive unconscious motivations. Others stress free will in confronting the human condition. Others stress living in concert with practical realities of life. Others focus primarily on helping you to modify self-destructive behavior, while others also try to help change irrational thinking. Variations of these and sundry combinations provide the vast secular landscape of contemporary counseling and psychotherapy, not to mention approaches that attempt to provide spiritual guidance from a theological perspective.

The breadth of psychological approaches from which to choose can leave you in a tizzy about which is right for you. The truth is that all these approaches have focused on something of value in promoting emotional growth and adjustment. But at the same time, each has embedded itself within a *narrow philosophical perspective*. For example, some perceive human beings as essentially biological machines so that medication becomes the preferred treatment, and some perceive human beings as essentially subjective entities so that "talk" therapy becomes the treatment of choice.

All these approaches have grown out of a much broader philosophical tradition. The study of the mind was originally the province of *philosophy*, well before psychology became a separate branch of human inquiry. In becoming grounded in empirical research, psychology managed to amass a useful body of practical scientific knowledge. Through trial and error, clinicians and researchers have discovered many techniques to help people overcome their behavioral and emotional problems. But at the same time, when the study of the human mind took to the laboratories and clinics, it also left behind the lion's share of its rich philosophical heritage.

Intrinsically, many problems of everyday life are philosophical. They stem from lack of clarity and insight into a wide range of abstract subjects ordinarily broached by philosophers. For example, as you will see, some are rooted in questions about the nature of morality and about good and evil;

some are about human dignity, autonomy, freedom, and democracy; some are about the nature of knowledge; some about beauty; others are about the nature of reality itself; still others are about the existence of God and of miracles; and still others are about what counts as justified belief. In short, so much of what we humans stress and distress over belongs to the province of philosophy.

Human beings, said Aristotle, are "social animals." They live in families, cities, states, nations, and the world. The psychological health of an individual cannot therefore be divorced from its broader social context. Thus, a nation that stifled its citizens' free speech and expression would likely take its toll on individual happiness. Such is the turf of social and political philosophy, and the psychological problems growing out of this soil are also grist for the philosophical mill.

In the past twenty years or so, a new movement has been growing primarily among philosophers to use philosophy in helping ordinary folks address their behavioral and emotional problems. This movement is also beginning to gain support from some psychologists working on the cutting edge of their discipline. The word is out that there is much more that can be gained from a systematic investigation into the ways philosophy can help people live happier, more productive lives. Unfortunately, most therapists who work in the trenches are still relying largely on traditional psychological approaches in treating their clients.

This book is part of this new philosophical venture in counseling and psychotherapy. Much of what I have to say you won't hear from the average clinician. Why? Not because she is trying to keep a secret from you, nor is it necessarily because she considers it to be irrelevant or just not useful. Rather, much of what I have to tell you falls outside the traditional venue of most clinicians.

My philosophical approach began to take shape in the mid-1980s when I realized that we philosophers could effect a psychological revolution by helping to reunite psychology with its philosophical roots. These were the early days when very few of my colleagues were thinking about getting into the trenches to help fellow humans grapple with problems of ordinary life. My philosophical approach did not originate in a psychological vacuum, however. No one has done more to influence the course of its development than my mentor, psychologist Albert Ellis, the founder of the school of psychology known as Rational-Emotive Behavior Therapy (REBT).

But can turning to philosophy in the midst of a life crisis bear fruit? Can philosophy, a subject that has long been considered by many to be an obscure and esoteric study, *really* help soothe the psyches of average folks?

Can the contributions of philosophers like Aristotle, Plato, Epicurus, Aquinas, Spinoza, Kant, and a host of others bring serenity to the unsettled mind racked with emotional pain? Can it help you become more prudent and successful in your life pursuits? Can it take you from being depressed, anxious, guilt ridden, and angry to a state of profound happiness?

Paradoxically, it may be precisely because so many of us do not heed the wisdom of great minds that we persist in irrational emotions and self-destructive behavior in the first place. It is the mission of this book to help you, the reader, attain a deep and enduring happiness through the use of philosophy, its methods and theories, in overcoming the destructive force of the most irrational, *un*philosophical ideas endemic to humankind.

What is evident about our most destructive emotions is that *they tend to be sustained by faulty reasoning.* The bleak shroud of depression is typically sustained by thinking that unrealistically conceives the world in all-or-nothing, black-or-white terms; that globally damns the *entire* universe on the basis of singular events; and that exaggerates an unfortunate turn of events, elevating it to gloom and doom. Debilitating guilt often berates the self, classifying it as *totally* worthless for a perceived (but not necessarily real) moral transgression. Self-stultifying anxiety tends to magnify risks, proceeding down a mental slippery slope that dead-ends in catastrophic predictions not backed by empirical evidence. Anger catapulted to the level of rage commonly sustains by demanding perfection of fallible human beings in an imperfect universe.

From interpersonal relations sullied by bullying and deceit to the waging of unjust wars by nations, faulty reasoning has managed to promote a tidal wave of destructive and regrettable patterns of behavior. The history of humankind attests to abundant pain, anguish, and bloodshed directly traceable to bad logic.

HOW FAULTY THINKING CAN WRECK YOUR LIFE

Philosophers, from antiquity, have warned against relying on irrational patterns of thought in conducting the affairs of your life. The ancient Greek philosophers were among the first to perceive a clear connection between faulty reasoning—so-called fallacies—and destructive emotions. It was, in fact, Aristotle who explicitly pointed out the connection. Said this sage,

> Outbursts of anger and sexual appetites and some other such passions, it
> is evident, actually alter our bodily condition, and in some men even

produce fits of madness. . . . It turns out that a man behaves incontinently [has such outbursts of emotion] under the influence (in a sense) of a rule and an opinion.[1]

Aristotle here made use of a form of reasoning he called "practical syllogism." This reasoning has two premises and one conclusion.[2] One of these premises is a "rule" and the other an "opinion." The *rule* includes (or implies) an "ought," "should," or "must" and accordingly tells a person what to do or how to feel, whereas the opinion is a statement of particular fact, a *report*, that is filed under the rule.[3] What's so special about this kind of reasoning is that its conclusion is not just another statement but instead an action or an outpouring of emotion.

Take these premises, for example:

> Emotional Rule: If a person does something that you strongly dislike, then this person is totally worthless and should be damned.
> Report: Jack did something I detest—he lied to me!

What do you think would happen if you accepted these two premises? You guessed it. Ordinarily, you would "deduce" anger, even rage.[4] This emotion would be the practical conclusion of your reasoning, and it would include not *just* other thoughts—like, "Jack should be damned"—but also bodily changes associated with anger, like increased adrenal activity, respiration, and heart rate.[5]

In addition, changes in your overt behavior would also accompany these cognitive and internal visceral changes. This is because rules piggyback on other rules, and some of these rules also prescribe *actions*. For example, these action-yielding premises ride on the prior ones:

> Behavioral Rule: If someone is totally worthless, then he should be put in his place.
> Report: Jack is totally worthless.

Just how you'd put Jack in his place would also depend on other *behavioral rules* you accept. For example, these additional rules could prescribe putting people in their place by calling them names, threatening them, harming them, or even killing them. Did you ever think about what it takes for a soldier to learn how to kill another human being? Indoctrinate him to perceive "the enemy" as less than human, and the rest is history.

THE ELEVEN CARDINAL FALLACIES

I hope you are beginning to see that your personal and interpersonal happiness—as well as that of your significant others, friends, coworkers, and associates—depends largely on the *premises* behind your emotions and behavior. This is the first big way in which philosophy comes home to roost in psychological practice. Philosophers look at things in terms of *reasoning from premises to conclusions.* They look at your premises to see if your reasoning is sound.

In contrast, traditional psychology tends to see things in terms of *cause and effect.* For example, a therapist might tell you that what caused you to get angry at Jack was some *event*—for example, that he lied to you—together with what you thought about it. Just as, under certain conditions, striking a match can cause a flame, many psychologists also think we can discover the scientific laws that cause people to lose their tempers and act in certain destructive ways.

Instead of looking for causal laws, a philosophical approach attempts to identify and catalog the various types of *fallacious premises* in destructive patterns of reasoning. For this reason, I have referred to my philosophical approach as *Logic-Based Therapy (LBT)*. This changes the mission of psychology. Instead of looking for the causes of our self-destructive behavior and emotions, LBT examines our reasoning for dangerous premises.[6]

On the basis of clinical observations and studies over the past two decades,[7] I have identified eleven of the most common and virulent offenders, the eleven cardinal fallacies. Unchecked, each of these fallacies has the potential to substantially impair your personal and interpersonal happiness. Here's the hit list:

Fallacies of Behavioral and Emotional Rules
1. Demanding perfection: Perfect-a-holic addiction to what you can't have in an imperfect universe.
2. Awfulizing: Reasoning from bad to *worst*.
3. Damnation: Shit-ification of self, others, and the universe.
4. Jumping on the bandwagon: Blind, inauthentic, antidemocratic and parrot-like conformity.
5. *Can't*stipation: Obstructing your creative potential by holding in and refusing to excrete an emotional, behavioral, or volitional *can't*.
6. Thou shalt upset yourself: Dutifully and obsessively disturbing yourself and significant others.

7. Manipulation: Bullying, bullshitting, or well poisoning to get what you want.
8. The world-revolves-around-me thinking: Setting yourself up as the reality guru.

Fallacies of Reporting

9. Oversimplifying reality: Pigeonholing reality or prejudging and stereotyping individuals.
10. Distorting probabilities: Making generalizations and predictions about the future that are not probable relative to the evidence at hand.
11. Blind conjecture: Advancing explanations, causal judgments and contrary-to-fact claims about the world based on fear, guilt, superstition, magical thinking, fanaticism, or other anti-scientific grounds.

Each of these fallacies will be addressed in a separate chapter.[8] The first eight usually occur as rules in the premises of people's emotional reasoning (fallacies of behavioral and emotional rules). This kind of rule *prescribes* destructive behavior and emotions. For example, demanding perfection tells you that the world *must* be perfect or near perfect and that, therefore, you must never settle for anything less. In subscribing to this rule, you become a *perfect-a-holic*, craving perfection, going through the DTs (demandingness tremens) when you inevitably come up short. Under the influence of this unrealistic intoxicant—the demand for perfection—you can deduce debilitating emotional stress ranging from severe depression to extreme anger.

In contrast, the last three fallacies I've listed—oversimplifying reality, distorting probabilities, and blind conjecture—usually occur in the reports you file under your emotional rules (fallacies of reporting). These tend to give false and misleading *descriptions* of reality. For example, one popular way of jumping to conclusions is to fatalistically insist that things *must* go wrong in the future because they've gone wrong in the past. Such a fatalistic description of reality typically leads to a self-fulfilling prophecy. You simply give up on trying and remain in the same negative situation.[9]

I have elsewhere defined a fallacy as a "way of thinking or reasoning that has a proven track record of frustrating personal and interpersonal happiness."[10] This definition captures the practical significance of calling something a *fallacy* in the first place. Why else should you be on guard against certain ways of thinking other than that they present dangerous roadblocks to your personal and interpersonal happiness?

It's safe to say that, on any philosophical theory of human happiness with which I'm familiar, every one of the fallacies on the previous list have been implicated in the destruction of human happiness. If you agree with Epicurus[11] that happiness means maximizing your pleasure, these fallacies are likely to defeat your goal, at least in the long run. If, like Aristotle,[12] you think happiness is living virtuously; like Jean-Paul Sartre,[13] autonomously; like Augustine,[14] according to God; like Buddha, in overcoming "dukka";[15] or, like Kant,[16] according to the dictates of "pure reason," then you are not likely to live happily if you also live according to these fallacies.

As you'll see, a common strand of all eleven of these cardinal fallacies is that they involve *extreme* thinking, for example, overrating, underrating, absolutizing, pigeonholing, overdoing, and underdoing. As Aristotle stressed, rational solutions to life problems typically lie somewhere in the middle between such extremes.[17] For example, things needn't be perfect to be worthwhile. You needn't have certainty to have reasonable odds. You don't have to worry about everything in order to make reasonable efforts to deal with your problems. You don't have to be a blind conformist to have social cooperation. Things aren't always black or white—there are also shades of gray. An unfortunate turn of events doesn't *have* to be catastrophic.

Fallacies hide rational alternates to problems behind a cloud of false or unrealistic absolutes. As you'll also see, once you clear the air of these fallacies—identify and refute them—at your disposal is an abundant, diversified stock of philosophical wisdom for helping you define and attain your own profound sense of human happiness.

YOU SUPPRESS FALLACIES, YOU DON'T REPRESS THEM

So, where do you look to find these destructive bugs?

When you make practical decisions, the rules you apply are not usually clearly articulated. In fact, they are not usually articulated at all. Instead, they are *assumed*. These rules are not repressed, hidden somewhere in the unconsciousness pit. Nor are they forgotten.

People assume premises whenever they fail to state what is needed to "validate" their reasoning. Take, for example, this incomplete reasoning:

> Report: I screwed up at work today.
> Conclusion: I'm a screw-up.

Clearly, my reasoning assumes the rule of damnation, which goes something like this:

Rule: If I screw up at something, then I'm *myself* a screw-up.[18]

Without the rule of damnation, your conclusion would not "follow" from your premises. In such cases, we philosophers say the rule in question is a *suppressed premise*, not a repressed belief. The fallacious rules in practical reasoning are ordinarily suppressed, not repressed.

The suppressed rule is not buried in your unconscious. It's simply unstated or unexpressed even though accepted. It is *implicit* in what you say or think, even though you are not (explicitly) saying or thinking it to yourself when you apply it. Nevertheless, you would agree if someone were to say, "So you think that if you screw up at something, then that makes you a screw-up."

The often-cited mark of a *repressed* thought is that you would be inclined to *reject* it, if called to your attention, and may even feel uncomfortable at its suggestion. Since a repressed thought is one you are supposed to be trying to hide from yourself—tucking it away in your unconscious—you would be unwilling to admit it on a conscious level.

In contrast, people tend to *stubbornly insist* on their *suppressed* rules when these are called to their attention. Indeed, people generally respond as though these rules were "self-evident," sensing no need whatsoever to prove them. "Of course, screwing up at something makes that person a screw-up! Isn't that obvious?" Beware the obvious.

This is what can be so insidious about these cardinal fallacies. You can be assuming them in your reasoning, not think to question them, make yourself miserable as a result, and not even have a clue as to what's wrong.

REFUTING YOUR FAULTY PREMISES

This gives good sense to Socrates' old saw that "the unexamined life is not worth living." In this context, it means that, unless you *question, question, and question* your premises, instead of just assuming them, you're likely to saddle yourself with destructive premises and not even know it. For example, instead of just assuming that screwing up *automatically* makes you a screw-up, you can ask yourself what grounds you have for thinking this.

Once you question a premise, you're in a position to try to *refute* it. If it's unreasonable and you think it through carefully, then you are likely to uncover its flaw. In fact, as you'll see, all the fallacies on my list can be refuted.

Are you assuming that what's true of the part is always true of the whole? Refutation: that would mean that a complex machine with simple parts is itself simple, which is self-contradictory. Likewise, do the logic: a bad deed doesn't make an *entire* human existence bad.

Are you demanding that the world or some part of it be *perfect*? Refutation: there's simply no evidence to show that the world is a perfect place but abundant evidence to show how imperfect it truly is. Have you ever met the perfect—or even the almost perfect—person? Only in your dreams.[19]

This is how philosophers think—carefully. If you tend to accept things unquestioningly, cultivating a philosophical habit of looking carefully at your own premises before acting on them can be a royal route to your salvation.

FINDING PHILOSOPHICAL ANTIDOTES TO THE ELEVEN CARDINAL FALLACIES

In order to repair something, you need to know what's broken. The refutation of a premise shows you what's wrong with it. Refutation sets the stage for finding a correction because it provides a functional analysis of what needs to be corrected.

For example, consider again the damnation rule: "If you screw up, then you are, *yourself*, a screw-up." You have already seen a simple refutation of this rule. But there can be alternative lines of refutation of an irrational rule. So, in the refutation stage, you can be creative. For example, the damnation rule can also be refuted because it turns *all* humans into worthless screw-ups. This is because all of us, yes *all* of us, inevitably screw up. Since the rule in question has the absurd consequence of rendering all of us worthless, it should be rejected. Doing something worthless doesn't make *you* worthless! As human beings we are all imperfect. Making mistakes is part of the human scene, but so too is learning from them. An *antidote* to the damnation rule might accordingly be an instruction such as the following one:

> You should accept responsibility for your mistake, learn from it, construct a new plan of action, and try to achieve it.

This new rule can provide a rational "should" to counter the *irrational* "should." It argues *against* the irrational rule. On the one hand, *self*-damnation prescribes self-contempt.[20] On the other hand, its antidote counters self-contempt with *constructive, forward-moving* action. Here is an example of these two rules in conflict:

Fallacious Reasoning
Self-Damnation: If I screw up, then I'm a screw-up
Report: I screwed up at work today—I forgot to show up for that important meeting.

Antidotal Reasoning
Antidote to Self-Damnation: You should accept responsibility for your mistake, learn from it, construct a new plan of action, and try to achieve it.
Report: I screwed up at work today—I forgot to show up for that important meeting.

Notice that the conclusion you deduce will depend on whether you file your report under self-damnation or under its antidote. If the former, you'll deduce self-contempt. If the latter, you may experience dissatisfaction with your conduct but avoid self-denigrating emotion. The difference between these two states can be far-reaching from the perspective of human adaptation and happiness. Since totally worthless persons cannot have prosperous futures, the first tends toward depression and self-destructive stagnation. On the other hand, since you can change your behavior, the latter gives you the opportunity to make constructive changes and to do better in the future.

Now this antidote can be strengthened by examining its more profound, *philosophical* significance. For example, the idea that a human being is without future recourse runs counter to the philosophy known as *existentialism*. According to the French existentialist Jean-Paul Sartre, human beings are never without a choice. They are "condemned to be free."[21] People who give up on their futures have freely sealed their own fate by not accepting responsibility for it—they have freely chosen to define themselves negatively "as a disappointed dream, as miscarried hopes, as vain expectations."[22] In calling yourself worthless, you have made a conscious choice not to try to learn from past mistakes and not to try to do better. According to Sartre, in hiding this freedom from yourself, you behave cowardly, whereas to live responsibly means to accept your freedom.

Sartre's philosophical view of human freedom and responsibility is useful here because it provides antidotal insight into a self-destructive rule. As you will see, the wisdom of the ages can, in this way, contain many useful antidotes for overcoming the eleven cardinal fallacies.

EXERCISING WILLPOWER

The state of tension that exists between a fallacious rule and an antidote is known as "cognitive dissonance." In such a state, you are filing your report under two conflicting rules.[23] For example, a state of cognitive dissonance exists if you are filing the above report under *both* of the above rules.[24]

Cognitive dissonance is an important sign of progress because it means that you are beginning to resist a fallacious premise with an antidote. But *overcoming* such a premise often takes a special effort. Knowing an antidote doesn't mean you will *act* on it. You may still need to overcome the physical desire to behave irrationally. Anyone who has stopped herself from reaching for that additional slice of chocolate cake (or another nacho chip or whatever your favor) knows what I mean. This can take considerable willpower.

Aristotle asked, "How can a man fail in self-restraint when believing correctly that what he does is wrong?" He answered that it was due to a kind of *weakness of will.* Under the influence of strong bodily "desire," you might be led to resolve your cognitive dissonance by acting on an irrational rule instead of a rational one so as to deduce self-destructive emotions and behavior.[25]

The self-restrained person is able to withstand the opposing bodily influences and to act according to the rational rule. So, what does the self-restrained person have that the unrestrained person lacks?

The answer is cultivation of *willpower*—"cultivation" since such rational constraint is not an innate biological capacity that arises full blown. As Aristotle made clear, it is a product of practice and effort.[26]

In fact, the idea of willpower can usefully be conceived on the analogy of a *muscle* that requires development through practice before it can carry the weight of rationally resolving cognitive dissonance.[27] Inasmuch as muscle building proceeds carefully and incrementally, so too does the cultivation of willpower. You would not expect a beginning bodybuilder to lift the same amount that an experienced bodybuilder lifts. While there will undoubtedly be varying capacities among different people, it is necessary to work up to it. In like manner, it would not be reasonable to expect a person to possess great willpower without having worked up to it. For example, a person who is easily agitated by small inconveniences is not likely to tolerate greater ones without first having learned to manage the smaller ones.[28]

From this practical perspective, human freedom is the human's ability to harness this internal muscle to overcome irrational premises backed by bodily inclinations. You can perceive this freedom as an internal *feeling* of power that arises when you make decisions, especially when you are in a state of cognitive dissonance.

Some philosophical antidotes will require greater willpower and present a greater challenge than others. Once you successfully "swallow" one antidote, however, you may find yourself ready for a more challenging one. I hope you will build up your willpower and accept the challenge.

APPLYING PHILOSOPHICAL ANTIDOTES

Philosophy alone will not change your life unless you make the necessary effort to *apply* it to your life. Here, then, is an important proviso to whatever wisdom you carry off from this book. Don't just nod your head in agreement with the great philosophers discussed here. Put your willpower muscle to work to overcome your fallacious premises, put your actions where your philosophy is, and treat yourself to a greater, more profound happiness.

In applying philosophical antidotes, don't feel obliged to buy *wholesale* a philosopher's view. In fact, don't expect to find here a thorough treatment of *all* aspects of a philosopher's thinking. This would take many volumes and is well beyond the practical purposes of this book. Instead, I have used key aspects that seem most useful in addressing the fallacies at hand. For example, I have emphasized important contributions of determinist philosophers, such as Epictetus and Spinoza, in addressing the *demand for perfection* without assuming the truth of determinism.

The "philosophic counsel" presented here is more systematic and structured than any previously undertaken insofar as it is developed within a consistent therapeutic framework in the construction of specific antidotes for specific fallacies. No other systematic amalgamation of philosophy and therapy of this nature has been developed before. Nevertheless, this treatment is not intended as exhaustive of the wide range of possibilities in extracting antidotes from philosophical literature. You should therefore feel free to explore other useful implications of the philosophical views discussed as well as others that may not have been broached in this book.

Under each fallacy, I discuss several different antidotes that are relevant to the fallacy in question. By *relevant*, I mean that each of them has the potential to help you overcome the irrational thinking it addresses. To be relevant, each must at least repair the "hole" in the thinking it was intended to fix, but just *how far* a certain antidote takes you in "overcoming" a fallacy is a matter of degree. This is because an antidote can be more or less potent.

THE POTENCY OF AN ANTIDOTE

A *potent* antidote will have potential to guide you in constructive directions and to help you not only feel and do all right but also feel and do excellent. The measure of an antidote's potency is therefore a measure of how constructive it can be in helping you to prosper. For example, instead of simply helping you to cope, an antidote that helped you perceive an unfortunate situation as an opportunity for growth and advancement would be more potent.

Don't confuse potency with being positive. Some psychologists have stressed "positive thinking" as though it meant the same as "constructive thinking." In one sense, positive thinking means optimistic thinking. However, some fallacies, such as wishful thinking and terrificing,[29] are *over*optimistic and can lead to self-destructive actions and emotions. An antidote that told you to smile and whistle a happy tune instead of getting out of the way of a Mack truck would be positively stupid. On the other hand, as you will see, it can sometimes be quite realistic to be *pessimistic* about a future outcome. You should therefore take care not to confuse being positive with being realistic. Sometimes being positive (in the sense of being *over*optimistic) may be unrealistic and self-defeating.

Just *how* constructive (and potent) an antidote is can depend on how *ambitious* it is. Philosophers sometimes distinguish between the *morality of duty* and the *morality of aspiration*.[30] The former makes *minimum* demands on a person. For example, you have a duty not to kill or steal. If you do neither of these things, you have satisfied this type of morality.

In contrast, the morality of aspiration is a morality of striving for excellence. It is the type of morality discussed in detail by ancient Greek thinkers like Plato and Aristotle. This morality speaks in the language of virtues and not in terms of requirement. This sort of morality doesn't rest on meeting minimum standards. For example, you are not *required* to be courageous. In contrast to killing or stealing, no one puts you in jail simply for failing to be courageous. Nevertheless, you are to be congratulated for being courageous.

Similarly, philosophical antidotes have the potential for helping you attain your higher human aspirations. Philosophy, by its nature, can lead you up the ladder of achievement. It is visionary and creative and encourages striving. It is this idealism that gives it great potency when harnessed as antidotes.

Philosophical antidotes are recipes for *virtue*. The philosophical antidotes presented here do not merely help you overcome irrational thinking. They aim at helping you *transcend* it. This means they aim at helping you live up to your *higher* human potentials.

These higher human potentials are defined by a set of eleven *transcendent virtues*. These virtues are metaphysical security, courage, respect, authenticity, temperance, moral creativity, empowerment, empathy, good judgment, foresightedness, and the ability to think scientifically (scientificity). These virtues paint a robust picture of what LBT means by *happiness*.[31] According to the theory of LBT, the royal route to such happiness is philosophy. It is what ultimately makes it *profound*. Philosophy nourishes your rational soul. It gives you insight. However, which specific philosophical antidotes you take help define and personalize the profundity of your happiness and give your personal happiness its own unique character. According to LBT, attainment of the eleven transcendent virtues is essential for human happiness or flourishing,[32] but the philosophical antidotes (the rules of happiness) you take largely define these virtues.[33] For example, your idea of self-respect will be different if you take a theological perspective like that of St. Thomas than if you take a humanistic one like that of Nietzsche. But, regardless of what approach you take, your happiness will depend on having self-respect.

The first eight of the transcendent virtues can properly be called *behavioral and emotional virtues* because they redress and transcend fallacious behavioral and emotional rules. Part 1 of this book will show you how to cultivate these eight virtues.

The last three of the eleven virtues—having good judgment in practical matters, foresight in assessing probabilities, and the ability to apply the scientific method to solve problems of living—can properly be called *cognitive virtues* because they redress and transcend cognitive errors made in reporting on reality. As Aristotle would tell you, these three virtues are themselves fundamental ingredients of the more general virtue known as *practical wisdom* (or prudence). A person with this "crowning" cognitive virtue possesses the cognitive skills requisite to filing rational reports under rational behavioral and emotional rules. Part 2 of this book will help you cultivate these skills.

Each philosophical antidote given in this book helps define or flesh out at least one of the eleven transcendent virtues. These antidotes can help you go from doom and gloom to sanguinity and inner peace. They can help you

Table 1.1.   The Eleven Transcendent Virtues

Cardinal Fallacy	Transcendent Virtue
Demanding perfection	Metaphysical security (security about reality)
Awfulizing	Courage (in the face of evil)
Damnation (of self, others, and the universe)	Respect (for self, others, and the universe)
Jumping on the bandwagon	Authenticity (being your own person)
Can'tstipation	Temperance (self-control)
Thou shalt upset yourself	Moral creativity
Manipulation	Empowerment
The world revolves around me	Empathy (connecting with others)
Oversimplifying reality	Good judgment
Distorting probabilities	Foresightedness (in assessing probabilities)
Blind conjecture	Scientificity (in providing explanations)

Note: Unshaded area = behavioral and emotional fallacies/virtues; shaded area = cognitive fallacies/virtues.

move from an existence marred by continual despair over perceived moral dilemmas to a healthy, life-affirming outlook on life. Yes, philosophy can be *that* potent.

In calling these virtues "transcendent," I mean that each transcends (takes you above and beyond) a particular cardinal fallacy. For each of the eleven cardinal fallacies, there's a virtue that transcends it. Table 1.1 shows you which virtue transcends which fallacy.

SNAPSHOTS OF THE ELEVEN TRANSCENDENT VIRTUES

Aristotle said that "moral virtues" arise as a result of habit and that habits are themselves formed through practice.[34] This is also the sense in which each of the eleven transcendent virtues can be called a "virtue." For example, a few good judgments won't make you a *person* of good judgment, but the more you succeed at making such judgments, the more it becomes a habit or disposition of character. So, the way to attain these virtues is to practice them. This means overcoming your cognitive dissonance by realizing your fallacies, refuting them, and exercising sufficient willpower in applying an appropriate philosophical antidote. Of course, you'll never be perfect. There's always going to be room for improvement, and backsliding is always possible. Practicing virtue is therefore a lifelong commitment.

Here is a brief description of the primary ingredients of each of these virtues:

1. *Metaphysical security* refers to the ability to accept imperfections in reality.[35] The metaphysically secure person accepts his *human* fallibility and limitations as well as those of others and does not expect the world to be perfect. He remains hopeful about realistic possibilities, is humble in the face of the uncertainty of the universe, and has a strong desire for knowledge but is not frustrated by his inability to know all. Such a person does not attempt to control what is beyond his ability to control but stays focused on excelling in what he *can* control.

2. *Courage* means confronting adversity without under- or overestimating the danger. It means fearing things to the extent that it is reasonable to fear them and, in the face of danger, acting according to the merits of the situation. The courageous person perceives evil as a *relative* concept according to which things could always be worse and are never *absolutely* bad (the worst thing in the world). Such a person tends to learn from and derive positive value from his misfortunes and is willing to take reasonable risks in order to live well.

3. *Respect* transcends the tendency to rate reality, including human reality, as utterly worthless or totally shitty and instead looks for goodness and dignity. Global respect avoids rating the whole according to the part and looks favorably on the larger cosmic picture. Self-respect involves unconditional self-acceptance based on a deep philosophical understanding of human worth and dignity. Respect for others consistently extends this profound respect for unconditional human worth and dignity to other human beings.

4. *Authenticity* is being your own person. This means autonomously and freely living according to your own creative lights as opposed to losing yourself on a bandwagon of social conformity. An authentic person is no cog in a social establishment. She values her individuality, cherishes a democratic life style and its inherent personal freedoms, and does not hide her responsibility for life choices behind deterministic excuses.

5. *Temperance* (self-control) involves *rational* control over your actions, emotions, and will. By telling yourself you *can't* do otherwise, you can defeat your own prospects for happiness. For example, you easily lose your temper, cave to pressure, eat or drink to excess, and keep yourself from advancing by refusing to try. In contrast, in becoming temperate, you can take control of your life (body, mind, and spirit) by cognitively and behaviorally overcoming such self-stultifying *can'ts*.

6. *Moral creativity* transcends the self-defeating idea that you have a moral duty to obsess over perceived problems and to drag your significant others along with you. It involves a philosophical grasp of morality and moral standards; tolerance for the ambiguity and uncertainty of moral choices; an ability to frame life in constructive, unproblematic ways; a willingness to try out novel ways of resolving concerns; and a consideration for the welfare, interests, and needs of others.

7. *Empowerment* means treating others as rational, self-determining agents in contrast to trying to get what you want through power plays, intimidation, and deceit. This means advising rather than goading, using rational argument to convince rather than making threats, recognizing the right of others to informed consent, and respecting the right to just treatment, even when serious conflicts arise.

8. *Empathy* amounts to transcending your own ego-centered universe by connecting (cognitively, emotionally, and spiritually) with the subjectivity of others. It means giving up the self-defeating idea that only your values, interests, preferences, and beliefs carry import and validity. It is a condition of such other virtues as beneficence, friendship, and gratitude.

9. *Good judgment* is the ability to make objective unbiased discernments in practical matters. In cases of judging other human beings, it means equitable and sympathetic judgment in contrast to stereotypical and prejudicial judgment. A person with good judgment is realistic, perceptive, open-minded, creative, and constructive.

10. *Foresightedness* (in assessing probabilities) is the ability to make generalizations about the material world and predictions about the future that are probable relative to the facts as known. A person who has this virtue is able to use it successfully in making life decisions. Such a person is able to cope effectively in this material universe, where there are degrees of probability, not certainty.

11. *Scientificity* (in providing explanations) is the ability to apply a critical, scientific method in accounting for the whys and wherefores of existence. A scientific person recognizes that scientific and religious explanations can be compatible but is disinclined toward superstition, magical thinking, religious fanaticism, and other antiscientific ways of accounting for reality. Such a person tends to rely on confirmatory evidence rather than on personal emotional reactions (like fear and guilt).

CONSTRUCTING PHILOSOPHICAL ANTIDOTES

In the following chapters, I provide you with a stock of antidotes that can be quite potent in promoting the eleven transcendent virtues. Some may suit your circumstances better than others. If you are confronting a midlife crisis, then Epicurus can help you gain a fresh, life-affirming perspective instead of stewing fruitlessly in your mortality. If you have come to see the world as depraved, evil, or destitute of value, then Buddha can help you transcend your own narrow, ego-centered perspective by having compassion for others in similar situations.

Some antidotes may fit your worldview better than others. If you believe in God and in objective standards of goodness and beauty, then a theological philosophical perspective like that of St. Augustine might bode well for you. Alternatively, if you think beauty is subjective, "merely in the eyes of the beholder," then David Hume's theory might work better for you.

Which philosophical route you take is up to you. You can set sail aboard the good ship Hume, St. Thomas, and so many other sundry and diverse seaworthy vessels docked in this book. Each can take you far on your voyage to profound happiness, but each may take a different route to get you there. If you want to find dignity in self or others as a way of turning your gloom and doom into profound happiness, then Kant or Buber can take you there. If you want to find meaning through God, then you best not get aboard the good ship Nietzsche, but the St. Thomas might be a welcome choice. In the end, all these philosophical views can make potent contributions to the transcendent virtues and therefore to your profound happiness. But which philosophical ship you choose to board is at your discretion.

Philosophical antidotes are not necessarily consistent with *each other.* This is because the great philosophers of antiquity have *rationally* agreed to disagree about the most basic questions of human existence, from the existence of God to the nature of the material world. Each is rational because each is *internally* consistent; clearly and carefully conceived, developed, and justified; and in tune with empirical reality. In addition, each is rational because it provides a useful tool for correcting, overcoming, and transcending one or more of the eleven cardinal fallacies addressed in this book.

This means that LBT is at bottom a *practical* therapy. It rests its case on how *effective* philosophical antidotes can be in helping you go from emotional and behavioral discord to profound happiness. It is therefore *constructive* in the sense that it can help you transcend your unhappiness.

LBT is also constructivist in the distinct sense of approving alternative constructions of reality. The postmodernist philosopher Michael Foucault spoke of "games of truth," by which he meant alternative ways of constructing reality.[36] As in the case of other games, the rules of such games do not merely *describe* reality. Rather, they *prescribe* valid moves within the confines of the given game. Following Foucault's usage, you could say (if you want) that the philosophical antidotes given in this book define some highly therapeutic games of truth. These rules can be said to prescribe the valid moves—*oughts* and *shoulds*—for constructing reality within the contexts of diverse philosophical theories. But don't allow this use of the word *game* to distract you from the fact that these moves, unlike most "games," are moves made *in vivo*. They can have profound implications for the quality of your everyday life.

In drawing a comparison between the rules of language and those of game playing, philosopher Ludwig Wittgenstein added, "Is there not also the case where we play and—make up the rules as we go along? And there is even one where we alter them—as we go along."[37] It is in this sense that philosophical antidotes can be considered rules of games. You are not bound by everything in a philosophy, and, as you proceed, you can "alter" the rules or "make them up" by bringing in rules from a related philosophical theory. Here, then, is another sense in which LBT is constructive. It gives you a measure of autonomy by allowing you to be *creative*. As you'll see, in constructing philosophical antidotes from philosophical theories, I have myself exercised such creative license by eclectically combining views from several philosophers. I have also added some of my own insights. This should give you a useful model to emulate in being creative. And I encourage *you* to *be* creative.

Each of the antidotes I have provided is presented in the form of a rule given under the fallacy it addresses. After the rule, I have parenthetically listed the names of the philosophers I used in building the rule. Each rule is then followed by a discussion. You should not read the rule apart from the discussion. The discussion fleshes out and gives substance to the formulation. But once you have grasped this meaning and substance, you should be good to go. Onward to serenity, success, and profound happiness!

NOTES

1. Aristotle, *Nicomachean Ethics*, in *The Basic Works of Aristotle*, ed. Richard McKeon (New York: Random House, 1941), bk. 7, chap. 3, 1041.

2. Whenever a person makes a decision, he or she draws a conclusion from a set of premises. This process of drawing an inference is known as *reasoning*. You make an inference when you try to justify one statement in terms of another. The set of statements you give as reasons for a further statement is known as your premises. In all reasoning, there must be at least one premise. As you will see, there is usually more than one. The further statement that you justify with your premises is known as your *conclusion*. All reasoning has *one* conclusion. If you have more than one conclusion, then you have made more than one inference. If I tell you that I hate Jane because she is stuck up, I am attempting to justify my dislike for her in terms of my contention that she is stuck up. My premise is that she is stuck up, and the conclusion I draw from this is that I dislike her.

3. The most common, basic layout of practical reasoning has this pattern:

Rule: If X happens, then you should (ought, must) respond in way Y.
Report: X happened.
Conclusion: You respond in way Y.

This pattern can be combined with other layers of rules and reports to form a complex network of premises in which rules are derived from further, more general rules and reports are derived from further, more general reports. Sometimes these more intricate patterns form syndromes of fallacies. I will talk later about these.

4. I say "ready to deduce" and not simply "deduce" because, as Aristotle informed us, there can be things that happen that prevent the deduction from going through. As you will see, one way to stop the deduction is to oppose it with a further set of premises that directs you to think, feel, or act differently.

Some logicians would not consider practical syllogisms to be deductive inferences because they think that only statements, not emotions or actions, can be deduced. Nevertheless, I will retain the terminology of deductive logic. Even if there are some features of practical inferences that don't square with deduction strictly so called, as you will see, there are practical advantages of applying the techniques and concepts of deductive logic to psychotherapy.

5. Some psychological theories (such as REBT) hold that such physiological aspects of emotion are *caused* by beliefs rather than *logically deduced* from premises. A more precise account of this position would be that these bodily changes are caused by what is deduced from premises. Thus, from premises A and B, I might deduce C, which, in turn, *causes* visceral changes in me. Notice, however, that even on this understanding, these changes depend on my inference from premises and is therefore an effect of my reasoning. And this is precisely the main contention of a logic-based approach.

6. Insofar as psychology has quested for the natural laws that determine human behavior, it has treated you (and me) as chunks of biological matter whose behavior and emotions are determined according to laws of nature. In contrast, LBT allows the possibility that human beings have *free will* in the sense of *not* being subject to such causal determination.

7. In compiling this list, I have also used artificial intelligence software known as Belief-Scan 4.1 for Windows. This program, which I have invented, scans people's thinking for fallacies, as expressed in personal essays. The program refines its search by rigorously asking the person Socratic questions designed to determine whether the fallacy in question has been committed. It then compiles a list of fallacies that have been confirmed.

8. Several fallacies listed represent *classes* of fallacies in that they include different types. For example, there are different types of manipulation, and there are different ways to distort probabilities.

9. Several fallacies listed are treated by classical rational psychotherapy and their dangerous implications for human happiness have been well documented in the annals of clinical research. For example, REBT emphasizes demanding perfection, awfulizing, and damnation, while cognitive-behavior therapy emphasizes certain types of fallacies of reports. However, a number of fallacies on the list are more often treated by philosophers who work in informal logic; these have therefore received scant attention by psychologists, for example, jumping on the bandwagon, thou shalt upset yourself, manipulation, and the world revolves around me. See Albert Ellis, *A New Guide to Rational Living* (Hollywood, Calif.: Wilshire Book Company, 1975), and Aaron Beck, *Cognitive Therapy and the Emotional Disorders* (New York: Penguin, Books, 1979).

10. See, for example, Elliot D. Cohen, *Caution: Faulty Thinking Can Be Harmful to Your Happiness* (Mason, Ohio: Thomson Custom Publishing, 2003).

11. Epicurus, *Letter to Menoeceus*, in *From Plato to Derrida*, 4th ed., ed. Forrest E. Baird and Walter Kaufmann (Upper Saddle River, N.J.: Prentice Hall, 2003), 250–53.

12. Aristotle, *Nicomachean Ethics*.

13. Jean-Paul Sartre, Existentialism, in *Philosophers at Work: Issues and Practice of Philosophy*, ed. Elliot D. Cohen (Fort Worth, Tex.: Harcourt, 2000), 444–49.

14. St. Augustine, *City of God*, in Baird and Kaufmann, *From Plato to Derrida*, 305–15.

15. This term refers to unhappiness due to sickness, old age, and death. See E. A. Burtt, ed., *The Teachings of the Compassionate Buddha* (New York: Penguin Books, 1991), 28.

16. Immanuel Kant, *Groundwork of the Metaphysics of Morals*, trans. H. J. Paton (New York: HarperCollins, 1964).

17. Aristotle, *Nicomachean Ethics*, bk. 2, chap. 6.

18. You could be assuming a more specific rule such as, "If I screw up at something important, then I am a screw-up," or one even more specific like, "If I screw up at work, then I am a screw-up." In the first case, you would also be assuming, in your report, that your work is "something important."

19. A refutation of each of the eleven cardinal fallacies is provided in the chapter in which it is discussed.

20. I take "self-contempt" to be a form of intense anger waged on oneself. Later, in chapter 3, I distinguish between self-damnation and damnation *of others*.

21. Sartre, Existentialism, 446.

22. Sartre, Existentialism, 447.

23. I do not claim that one is simultaneously filing a report under two conflicting rules since it appears to be impossible to (consciously) accept two inconsistent rules at once. I suspect that the truth is more that of vacillation between both rules rather than simultaneous acceptance.

24. The act of filing a report under a rule amounts to the agent's perception that the antecedent ("if" clause) of the rule is true. If the agent accepts the rule under which the report is filed, then the agent will also accept its consequent ("then" clause). In my use of the term "filing a report under a rule," I am assuming that the rule in question is one that is accepted by the agent.

25. "In a practical syllogism, the major premise is an opinion, while the minor premise deals with particular things, which are the province of perception. Now when the two premises are combined, just as in theoretic reasoning the mind is compelled to affirm the resulting conclusion, so in the case of practical premises you are forced at once to do it. For example, given the premises 'All sweet things ought to be tasted' and 'Yonder thing is sweet'—a particular instance of the general class—you are bound, if able and not prevented, immediately to taste the thing. When therefore there is present in the mind on the one hand a universal judgment forbidding you to taste and on the other hand a universal judgment saying 'All sweet things are pleasant,' and a minor premise, 'Yonder thing is sweet' (and it is this minor premise that is active), and when desire is present at the same time, then, though the former universal judgment says 'Avoid that thing,' the desire leads you to it (since desire can put the various parts of the body in motion). Aristotle, *Nicomachean Ethics*, bk. 7, chap. 3, 1041.

26. "The virtues on the other hand we acquire by first having actually practised them, just as we do the arts." Aristotle, *Nicomachean Ethics*, bk. 2, chap. 1, 952.

27. Aristotelis Santas, Willpower, *International Journal of Applied Philosophy* 42 (fall 1988): 9–16.

28. See Elliot D. Cohen, *What Would Aristotle Do? Self-Control through the Power of Reason* (Amherst, N.Y.: Prometheus Books, 2003).

29. See Cohen, *What Would Aristotle Do?*

30. See especially Lon L. Fuller, *The Morality of Law* (New Haven, Conn.: Yale University Press, 1974), chap. 1.

31. This broad definition appears to be consistent with many theories of happiness, for example, those of Aristotle, Plato, Epicurus, Bentham, Mill, and Kant, among others.

32. I say "essential" rather than "sufficient." However, in addressing the eleven cardinal fallacies, LBT addresses the most prevalent and stubborn roadblocks to human happiness. The transcendent virtues replace these deficits with virtues. It therefore seems reasonable that realization of these virtues is also *sufficient* for human happiness. However, the empirical evidence for this hypothesis is largely anecdotal. I suspect that future empirical studies will confirm this hypothesis.

33. This is sometimes called an "intrinsic theory of virtues." See, for example, Elliot D. Cohen and Gale S. Cohen, *The Virtuous Therapist* (Belmont, Calif.: Wadsworth, 1999).

34. Aristotle, *Nicomachean Ethics*, bk. 2, chap. 1.

35. Paradoxically, demanding perfection is so prevalent among human beings, yet there is no English world to refer to its opposing virtue. The first step in striving to attain this virtue is to give it a name.

36. For an application of this idea to philosophical counseling, see James Tuedio, A Post Modern Basis for Narrative Realism in Philosophical Counseling, *International Journal of Philosophical Practice* 2, no. 1 (spring 2004), online at http://www.aspcp.org/ijpp/Tuediov2n1.pdf.

37. Ludwig Wittgenstein, *Philosophical Investigations*, trans. G. E. M. Anscombe (New York: Macmillan, 1968), 83.

I

HOW TO BUILD BEHAVIORAL AND EMOTIONAL VIRTUES

1

FEELING SECURE IN AN
IMPERFECT UNIVERSE

Are you a perfect-a-holic? This means habitually *demanding perfection* about some aspect of your life. I am speaking here of one of the most destructive and commonplace forms of irrational thinking. This is a psychological addiction, a perceived (and misconceived) *need* for the absolute.

In rational therapy, this fallacy (referred to as "demandingness," or "*mus*turbation") has been deemed to be the source of most emotional and behavioral disturbances in humans.[1] My own clinical experience has confirmed that this fallacy is, in fact, *the* most frequently occurring fallacy of rules and also perhaps the most fundamental.

Demanding perfection can be formulated more explicitly as follows:

> If the world fails to conform to some state of ideality, perfection, or near perfection, then the world is not the way it absolutely, unconditionally *must* be, and you cannot and must not ever have it any other way.

The most salient feature of this rule is its use of the term *must* to indicate a demand, not just a wish, that the world conform to some absolutistic ideal. It is this "*mus*tabatory" aspect of the rule that leads its adherents (who are many) to deduce extreme frustration ranging from depression to rage when the world fails to conform to the ideal. Since the world cannot realistically be expected to be perfect, perfect-a-holism inevitably leads to the *demandingness tremens*: the painful emotional and behavioral withdrawals of demanding what you can't rationally require in an imperfect universe—perfection.

Some common forms of this fallacy occur when you demand that such things as these *must never* happen:

- Someone doesn't approve of you, or someone special doesn't approve of you.

- You make a mistake or fail to perform perfectly.
- Things don't go your way or exactly the way you want them to go.
- You are not treated fairly.
- Something bad happens to you or to a significant other.
- You can't control everything or something important to you.
- You can't get what you want.
- You do not succeed at something, or you are less successful than you want to be.
- You lose something of substantial value to you.
- Your body has some perceived imperfection or flaw.

Inevitably, as you go through life, you will encounter adversity. Things will not always turn out the way you want; others from whom you seek approval may scoff at you; people you trust may betray you; freakish accidents may take away someone or something you cherish; or the natural lottery may not always yield a desired outcome. So, the refutation of this rule is really quite straightforward:

> The assumption that ideality, perfection, or even near perfection is humanly possible in this earthly universe is false to fact.

Being ready to confront the vicissitudes of an imperfect universe can, therefore, prove to be of substantial value. In fact, philosophers throughout the ages have given the concept of perfectionistic demands careful consideration and have bequeathed to us a fund of insight that can provide useful antidotes to self-destructive, human, perfect-a-holic tendencies. These philosophical antidotes can help you feel secure—that is, comfortable—in being a fallible human being in a far-from-perfect universe.

ANTIDOTES TO DEMANDING PERFECTION

Antidote 1
Accept your fallible human nature and therewith the endless challenge of becoming more and more self-actualized; instead of ruminating about what is negative in your life, recognize also what is positive and good and seek to attain more of the same. (Augustine, Aquinas)

The pre-Socratic Greek philosopher Heraclitus was the first to emphasize change as the basic feature of the world. Things, he thought, were in a state of constant change such that one could never "step into the same river twice." The idea of an absolute unchangeable reality was absent from this worldview. Even Plato, in his quest for perfection, could not find this on earth. Accepting Heraclitus' idea that the world existing in space and time was one of "becoming" rather than of "Being," he turned to a "heaven of Ideas," apart from the world of particular things, in order to satisfy his desire for perfection. In short, the idea that human earthly existence is an imperfect one is woven into the fabric of ancient philosophy, and this theme has persisted in Western philosophy ever since.

Plato's famous distinction between the realm of *Being*, which is a perfect place, and that of *becoming*, which is an imperfect place, provided metaphysical fodder for much of Christian theology that followed, including Augustine's famous distinction between the Kingdom of God and the Kingdom of Earth. According to the latter distinction, as residents of Earth, it is shear arrogance for human beings to assume that they can live a perfect existence. Indeed, such an existence is reserved for God, not for God's creatures. So spoke Augustine:

> This I know, that the nature of God can never and nowhere be deficient in anything, while things made out of nothing can be deficient.[2]

The human demand for perfection is accordingly confused. As humans, we are inherently deficient. This does not mean that we can't try to be like God by seeking to overcome many of our deficiencies. As St. Thomas Aquinas said, "The last end of things is to become like unto God,"[3] "although they are able to attain this likeness in a most imperfect manner."[4] Accordingly, Aquinas would distinguish between human excellence and perfection. Only God is perfect. Further, he recognizes that there is a fundamental difference between "shooting for the stars" as a method of self-improvement and *demanding* that you land on them.[5] As such, he would encourage you to shoot for the stars (to become like God). At the same time, he would admonish you against *demanding* that you reach them.

In fact, traditional Western metaphysics, beginning with Plato, is extremely optimistic. It holds that reality and goodness are exchangeable terms. Insofar as something is real, it is also good and vice versa. Further, insofar as something lacks reality, it is bad and vice versa. Badness is the absence of reality, while goodness is its actuality. The proverbial glass is half full. The more reality a thing has, the better it is. Thus, a totally self-actualized being—what we call God—is an absolutely good being. There is therefore no evil in God and no God in evil. Such deficiencies in being necessarily belong to mortal, earthly existence. For example, human ignorance is a deficiency in knowledge. Omniscience (all-knowingness) is reserved for God and is therefore not humanly possibility. Consequently, human beings are necessarily and inescapably *fallible* beings.[6]

In giving up the demand for the absolute, you are free to concentrate on realizing your *human* potential. This human potential has no ceiling since there will always be room for self-improvement. For example, no matter how much wisdom you acquire, there is always more to learn. When the Greek Oracle pronounced Socrates the wisest man in Athens, Socrates interpreted this to mean that he alone knew how little he really did in fact know. That is, the more you learn, the more you see how much more there is you don't know. This is an eye-opener. In accepting your fallible, imperfect nature, you always have room for learning more and more and for becoming more and more self-actualized. This is also a wakeup call to take more seriously what is good (real) in your life instead of seizing on what is wrong (missing) as though this too had a positive reality ranking.

Again, since God is the only totally actualized being, God alone is the only supremely perfect being. There is nothing bad about God since God lacks nothing in being. Accordingly, in an attempt to prove God's existence by appealing to God's status as a perfect being, the Benedictine monk St. Anselm spoke to God:

> You [God] alone . . . of all things . . . possess existence to the highest degree; for anything else . . . possesses existence to a lesser degree.[7]

Humans are not totally actualized like God. To be human is to be *imperfect*. Give yourself permission to be human. After all, that is precisely what you are.

But not even a perfect being could perfect what is inherently imperfect. In my youth, I used to bother myself with the blemishes of human existence that somehow seemed to me to deface and destroy the inherent value and beauty of material things. For example, working in wood, building a cabinet, I frustrated myself over trying to get rid of every imperfection in the wood I could find. On some occasions, I intentionally destroyed my work because it just didn't meet up.

My problem was not in the wood. Nor could a carpentry class have been of much use in addressing it. No, the antidote here was a more philosophically enlightened metaphysic. As Plato emphasized, matter is, by its very nature, *im*perfect. The nicks and chips of wood, the soiled carpet, the crabgrass on my front lawn that keeps growing back no matter how many times I try to eradicate it, the scratch on my car door caused by a scratch-and-run motorist in a congested mall parking lot—these imperfections are what makes these things precisely what they are: material things, that is, perishable and changeable things existing in time and space. I know now that the ideal cabinet (or lawn or whatever) is, if anywhere, in Plato's heaven, not anywhere on earth. In this perishable, changeable realm of imperfection, things will be as they are—imperfect—and they will be distinguished by what they are not as well as by what they are. Again, that's what it means for things to be material. Seen in this light, the blemishes of materiality are less likely to become a wasteful obsession and to detain you from attaining more positive goodness in your own life and in the lives of others whom you touch.

This isn't to say that I am "cured" of my own tendency to demand perfection. No, I am still a perfect-a-holic. Once a perfect-a-holic, always one. Like any addiction, once you deny that you have a problem, that's when you are most likely to fall off the wagon. Yes, my name is Dr. Elliot D. Cohen, and I am a perfect-a-holic. But I am also *in recovery*. This is the way I suggest *you* look on all the fallacious tendencies discussed in this book. No matter how far you may go in overcoming them, you are still subject to backsliding. This is because we are—you and me both—only human.

Antidote 2
Seek truth through rational inquiry, undemandingly, and with an open mind. (Socrates)

I spoke a moment ago about the quest for knowledge being a bottomless pursuit. Not only can you not know everything, but much of what you think you know will be only tentative, relative, probable, but not certain and absolute.[8]

Some philosophers, however, have held that the objects of true knowledge are eternal and unalterable. Socrates himself thought that eternal and unalterable reality (for example, the essences of Truth, Goodness, and Beauty) could be pursued through rational inquiry. Yet when he set his sights on grasping these ideas, he often found good logical reasons to deny that he had discovered what he was seeking. In the end, for Socrates, it was the careful, rational inquiry itself that was most fruitful, for what he ultimately came to know was what he didn't know. Thus, for example, at the end of a careful dialogue with a young student, Theaetetus, about the correct definition of knowledge, Socrates concluded,

> Then supposing you should ever henceforth try to conceive afresh, Theaetetus . . . if you remain barren, you will be gentler and more agreeable to your companions, having the good sense not to fancy what you do not know. For that, and no more, is all that my art can affect.[9]

In not *demanding* that he attain absolute knowledge, Socrates was the wiser. For in his humility, he was free to question and refute the popular misconceptions of his times. In contrast, when you demand absolute certainty, you either end in frustration or placate yourself with dogmatic, destructive rationalizations. You fill your ears with cotton and close your mind to disconfirming evidence and counterexamples. And, when, if ever, you finally test these dogmatic convictions by acting on them, you wind up acting blindly and regretfully.

Many bloody wars and mass genocide have occurred as a result of blind faith in the absolute. Slavery, Nazism, apartheid, and other forms of racial oppression have been anchored in "the superiority of the white race" as though this were really the truth. Even today, there are people who blindly and tenaciously cling to such dangerous and dogmatic convictions in the name of truth.

Waging holy wars in the name of the Prince of Peace strikes a dissonant chord and carries the stench of religious hypocrisy. Yet many atrocious and brutal acts have been committed with the cocksure conviction that they were pious acts. "What is pleasing to the gods is pious, and what is not pleasing to them is impious," said the theologian Euthyphro to Socrates in attempting to defend why he had just pressed charges against his own father for murdering a murderer.[10] But the gods, argued Socrates, are not always pleased and displeased by the same things, which would make the same thing both pious and impious. In the end, Socrates helped Euthyphro discover that he really didn't even know what piety was—not a small gain since the life of Euthyphro's father hung in the balance.

The times I have told myself I knew for certain all that I needed to know have usually been the times I have fallen flat on my face. I am much less cocksure these days since I have had my face in the mud long enough to have learned. The truth will set you free only if it is not stagnant but pursued with an open mind. If you demand more, you are setting yourself up for the fall.

Can you really know anything about the outside world *for certain*? Maybe you can know abstract, arithmetical propositions for certain, such as

"2 + 2 = 4," but you cannot know for certain *applied* arithmetical propositions, that is, ones about external reality. If you add two drops of water to
two more drops, you'll *necessarily* count four drops, right?

Wrong! For one, water coalesces and becomes one body, and even if
you could still redivide and remeasure it, some of it might have evaporated
or otherwise have been lost. In addition there is always the possibility of bad
vision, counting errors, and sundry other contingent factors of an imperfect, material universe. Yet, for us mortals, it's *this* universe that *really* counts.

Maybe you can be certain of truths like "All red dogs are red" and "All
bachelors are unmarried." But as empirical philosophers like John Locke
and David Hume have stressed, such statements are trivial and provide no
useful information about the material world.[11]

Many unhappy folks are disappointed absolutists. But it's not necessarily the quest for the absolute that is the source of this distress. It's instead
the *demand* for absolute truth. If you want, like Socrates, to look for absolute truth, then you should be prepared not to find it. Better to be like
Socrates. Embrace the rational ride and be grateful for finding out what you
really don't know.

✳Antidote 3

*Stop scrutinizing your body, looking for defects, and degrading it according to subjec-
tive, cultural ideals. Instead, celebrate the beauty in the function and harmony of your
natural endowment. (Augustine, Hume)*

Even if, as Socrates believed, there's an eternal, changeless idea of
beauty, you're not going to find it here on earth. When it comes to your
physical beauty, Socrates would be the first to remind you that your *body* is
a material thing and is therefore imperfect.

Did you ever see a face or a torso that you couldn't improve on? Even
if you insist that you have beheld such a heavenly form here on earth, it
would only be "perfect" according to the norms you are applying, but this
hardly means that these standards are, themselves, indisputably perfect.

The upshot is this. If you demand *physical* perfection (of yourself or
others), you are not likely to find it, at least in this mortal existence of ours.
The more flaws you fix, the more you are likely to find. And as you continue to age, the likelihood is that you will find many. But that shouldn't
deter you from taking pride in your body.

From Augustine's perspective, your *body* does not have to be perfect to
be good or beautiful. "All natures," says Augustine, "are good simply because they exist and, therefore, have each its own measure of being, its own

beauty, even in a way, its own peace."[12] And Plato contends that the beauty and goodness of any living creature is in its conformity to the use for which it is designed by nature.[13] For the physical malcontent, who scrutinizes her body, looking for defects to repair, it is useful to remember this admonition: instead of looking for defects in your body, rejoice in the goodness and beauty of your natural bodily endowments.

What of being overweight, having an exceptionally large nose, having brown eyes instead of blue, or having another physical condition that you would personally prefer to change? Augustine answers that no "blemish" in a thing should be "blamed" unless it interferes with its specific function. "For example, when we say that blindness is a defect of the eyes, we imply that it is the very nature of the eyes to see, and when we say that deafness is a malady of the ears, we are supposing that it is their nature to hear."[14]

Does your "blemish" preempt your body (or some part of it) from functioning properly? For example, does the size of your nose prevent you from breathing well? Does the state of your stomach prevent you from properly digesting your food? Does your eye color prevent you from seeing well? If your answer to this functionality query is no, then there is no *real* bodily defect and accordingly no impediment to the goodness and beauty of your body.

This does not mean that you should not exercise your body, eat healthy foods, and otherwise maintain your body. Such are fundamental prerequisites of human happiness. So said the ancient Stoic Epicurus, "The necessary desires are for the health of body and peace of mind; if these are satisfied, that is enough for the happy life."[15] But this simple formula nowhere implies that you must have a perfect body to be happy.

So, what does Augustine's antidote portend for the bodily integrity and beauty of one who really does have a bodily defect, for example, blindness or deafness? There is extreme need for caution here not to infer the defectiveness of the body *as a whole* from the defectiveness of a part of it. Augustine says that we may "fail to perceive the beauty of a total pattern in which the particular parts, which seem ugly to us, blend in so harmonious and beautiful a way."[16] The deaf and the blind can thus be beautiful. One who has lost a limb or has suffered severe burns still can possess bodily integrity and beauty in a "blending of parts in so harmonious and beautiful a way" as in the warm, poignant smile that spreads gracefully across a delicate, innocent oval face, radiantly transforming lesions in the skin, penetrating through to even the coldest of hearts, or in the demeanor of a well-proportioned, muscular physique that functions so healthily that the absence of limb makes it all the more splendid.

In this light, aesthetic judgment is squandered by picking yourself or others apart instead of looking globally for beauty. If the beautiful were merely a function of a selected part of a thing, then none of us would be beautiful since none of us have entirely "perfect" features. From Augustine's perspective, the parts are beautiful insofar as they are functional. But the beauty of the whole is not reducible to the beauty of the individual parts.

On the other hand, the eighteenth-century British philosopher David Hume thought that judgments about beauty were variable and subjective. So said Hume,

> Beauty is no quality in things themselves: It exists merely in the mind which contemplates them; and each mind perceives a different beauty. One person may even perceive deformity, where another is sensible of beauty; and every individual ought to acquiesce in his own sentiment, without pretending to regulate those of others. To seek the real beauty, or real deformity, is as fruitless an enquiry, as to pretend to ascertain the real sweet or real bitter.[17]

Should you be taller or shorter, be thinner or fatter, or have more hair or less? According to Hume, the answer to such questions cannot be found in nature. Nor must your judgment be constrained by a common idea of beauty like one you might find promoted in a fashion magazine. You are, in this way, the legislator of your own beauty, an autonomous measure and purveyor of your own beauty.

In Hume's view, it is *nowhere* written that *your* aesthetic judgment is any less valid than that of another. And, as Voltaire remarked, "the beautiful is often quite relative, so that what is decent in Japan is indecent in Rome, and what is fashionable in Paris is not so in Peking."[18]

The point is that you can be beautiful so long as *you* permit it. So, stop scrutinizing your body, looking for defects, and degrading it according to subjective, cultural ideals. If you insist on "objective" standards by which to judge your physical endowment, then use Augustine's standards. Accept the goodness and integrity inherent in your bodily existence. Affirm the beauty of your healthfulness, the harmony and balance of your body's relational properties and its awesome capacity to function like a well-designed machine, one that is able to serve you in so many crucial ways from keeping your blood circulating to helping you to think profound thoughts. When you reflect on it, this is really quite beautiful in its own right and not worth degrading for the sake of some arbitrary set of cultural standards.

Antidote 4
Change your absolutistic, unrealistic, musts and shoulds to preferences. (Spinoza)

In Hume's aesthetic subjectivism is the rejection of a perfect, objective form of beauty existing as Plato saw it, in a "heaven of ideals." More generally, Hume conceived the idea of perfection itself to be relative and subjective.[19] In fact, Hume did not believe that *any* abstract ideas, including that of God, could be demonstrated to exist outside the mind.

But you don't have to be as skeptical as Hume to see just how nonsensical it is to demand perfection. The view that the human demand for perfection arises from a prejudicial, self-imposed preference rather than from some objective, absolute necessity is also suggested by Baruch Spinoza, a seventeenth-century Dutch philosopher.

Metaphysically, Spinoza, like Hume, rejected the Platonic dualism inherent in Christianity, but unlike Hume, he embraced a pantheistic perspective instead. All reality, thought Spinoza, follows necessarily from one universal substance, none other than God. There are no separate kingdoms of God and of earth, of heaven and earth, of soul and body, of being and becoming. It is not that there is nature here and God there but instead nature is just one way of looking at one solitary unitary God. This is an impersonal deity, not one that answers prayers or works miracles. In bringing the curtain down on heaven apart from earth, Spinoza also abandoned the idea of a realm of perfect reality that provides ultimate ends or purposes to which to strive. God or Nature is not purposive at all, nor is it perfect. In fact, the idea of perfection is a human artifact arising as a result of turning preferences into demands. Spinoza explains,

> After men began to form universal ideas, and devise models of houses, buildings, towers, and the like, and to *prefer* some models of things to others, it came about that each one called perfect what he saw agreed with the universal idea he had formed of this kind of thing, and imperfect, what he saw agreed less with the model he had conceived. . . . Nor does there seem to be any other reason why men also commonly call perfect or imperfect natural things, which have not been made by human hands . . . when they see something happen in Nature which does not agree with the model they have conceived of this kind of thing, they believe that nature itself has failed or sinned, and left the thing imperfect. We see, therefore, that men are accustomed to call natural things perfect or imperfect more from prejudice than from true knowledge of those things.[20]

For Spinoza, perfectionistic demands simply mask the fact that perfection is not inherent in nature itself but instead in the mind of the person seeking it. This is a clear reminder to see through the thin veneer of perfectionistic language of "musts" and "needs" and to realize instead your own role in imposing these demands on yourself. For example, the demand that your significant others approve of you is based on your own concept of what you deem to be a perfect interpersonal relationship with significant others (friend, mate, family, and so on). This model of human relatedness does not exist in the mind of God, in the universal order of nature, or in some supreme first principle of human relating. It is nowhere written in eternal reality but consists rather in your own subjective preference for such relatedness. QED: it is not *really* a necessity, not truly a "must." Changing this "must" to the preference that it really is can thereby help you avoid the stress you impose on yourself by living in a world that is not likely to actualize your preference, at least not as a matter of necessity. Kicking and stamping your feet or howling at the moon won't elevate your preference to supreme reality. The likely consequence instead is painful and intolerant relating to the ones whom you love.

Antidote 5

Don't sweat the things you can't directly control. Expend your efforts instead on what you can control. (Spinoza, Epictetus)

In fact, according to Spinoza, it's futile to demand that things be otherwise than what they are since no external events are subject to human control in the first place. For him, whatever happens, happens of necessity, and the more rational insight we can attain into the genesis of our emotions, the more control we are able to exert over them. For example, he tells us,

> We see that sadness over some good which has perished is lessened as soon as the man who has lost it realizes that this good could not, in any way, have been kept.[21]

The free person, as opposed to a person enslaved by his emotions, is accordingly one who clearly understands and accepts what is necessary and outside his means of control. "Insofar as the mind understands all things as necessary, it has a greater power over the affects, or is less acted on by them."[22]

While Spinoza's view is based on a rigid determinism according to which all things happen of necessity, you don't have to be a determinist to agree that some (indeed many) things are beyond human control. For example, while death is not theoretically an absolute certainty, it is unreasonable to demand immortality. Knowing that death is inevitable is not likely to fully ease the pain of losing a beloved one, but there can be considerable consolation in knowing that this person has lived a relatively long life given natural biological constraints.

This idea that you can avoid substantial emotional distress by appreciating the limits of human control is a key aspect of ancient Stoic philosophy, notably that of Epictetus.[23] He advises,

> Some things are under our control, while others are not under our control. Under our control are conception, choice, desire, aversion, and in a word, everything that is our own doing; not under our control are our body, our property, reputation, office and, in a word, everything that is not our own doing. . . . Remember, therefore, that if what is naturally slavish you think to be free, and what is not your own to be your own, you will be hampered, will grieve, will be in turmoil, and will blame both gods and men; while if you think only what is your own, to be your own, and what is not your own to be, as it really is, not your own, then no one will ever be able to exert compulsion upon you, no one will hinder you, you will blame no one, will find fault with no one, will do absolutely nothing against your will, you will have no personal enemies, no one will harm you, for neither is there any harm that can touch you.[24]

Simply stated, by trying to exert control over things that are not directly conformable to your will, you are setting yourself up for considerable emotional stress. On the other hand, by tending instead to what you can directly control, namely, your own "conception, choice, desire, aversion," and whatever else answers directly to your will, you can avoid considerable emotional stress.

I would add this qualification, however. You are not likely to avoid emotional stress by *demanding* that you form the right conceptions, make the right choices, take up the correct desires, and fear only what should be feared. Even things that are directly subject to your willful control are not so utterly controll*able* that you can demand perfection about them. You are still likely to experience considerable stress if you demand that you never experience irrational emotions, desire only rational things, or make only wise choices. As imperfect beings, it is irrational for us human beings to demand perfection even in this sphere of willful things no less than in things outside our direct control.

Still, Epictetus' general admonition to devote your efforts to controlling what is within your direct control and to treat with indifference that which is not can be a helpful antidote to the demand for perfection. For example, in discussing the relevance of Epictetus' admonition to insult and offense, William Ferraiolo astutely observes,

> Sticks and stones may assuredly break our bones, but neither spoken nor written word can ever hurt us if we develop an impregnable indifference to events and phenomena that we cannot command. All of us would do well to regularly remind ourselves to focus our efforts on self-discipline and self-improvement rather than wasting energy in worrying about how we are perceived by others.[25]

In discussing the manner in which people make themselves anxious over things not in their direct control, Ferraiolo cites Epictetus:

> When I see anyone anxious, I say, what does this man want? Unless he wanted something or other not in his own power, how could he still be anxious? A musician, for instance, feels no anxiety while he is singing by himself; but when he appears upon the stage he does, even if his voice be ever so good, or he plays ever so well. For what he wishes is not only to sing well, but likewise to gain applause. But this is not in his own power.[26]

On this view, anxiety arises from our desire to control the external world rather than to control what directly conforms to our will, for "we are anxious about this paltry body or estate of ours, or about what Caesar thinks, and not at all about anything internal" (Epictetus). As long as the musician does not *demand* that he sing perfectly, he can avoid considerable anxiety by focusing his energies on singing well and not on getting the approval of the audience, for it is the former, not the latter, that is within his direct control.[27] More generally, by not sweating those (external) things that are outside your direct control and by focusing your effort on those (internal) things that are largely conformable to the human will, you can not only avoid considerable emotional stress but also attain greater inner peace and tranquillity. You can also live more creatively and happily by performing better at those things that *are* within your power of control.

Rational-Emotive Behavior Therapy (REBT), which is closely aligned with Epictetus' philosophy, has taken this admonition very seriously in its common prescription of "shame-attacking exercises" designed to help clients cultivate an attitude of indifference toward external affairs such as attaining the approval of others. For example, REBT's founder, Albert Ellis, once recommended pulling a banana on a string down a busy city street. In giving up caring about what others might be thinking of you (as you tote your banana), you can even find amusing what others bent on external approval might find stressful.

Antidote 6

Drop the practically absurd demand for a perfect universe and accept instead the possibility of a better one. (James)

In contrast to Spinoza and Epictetus, the famous contemporary American philosopher William James looked at human control of external reality from a pragmatic perspective. Instead of trying to adduce "proof" that human beings have free will, he chose to change the subject and ask what practical difference it made in the first place whether you believed in free will. The practical difference was indeed for him immense. On the one hand, the doctrine that human beings have free will and control over the external world is a

> melioristic doctrine. It holds up improvement as at least possible; whereas determinism assures us that our whole notion of possibility is born of human ignorance, and that necessity and impossibility between them rule the destinies of the world.[28]

In a wholly deterministic universe, there is also no point in talking about what *ought* to be since such talk assumes that there are genuine possibilities in the universe, which determinism forecloses. In such a universe in which all happens of necessity, there is no room for regret at great atrocities (such as, for example, the Holocaust or the recent 9-11 attacks in the United States), and you must therefore accept the universe as "afflicted with an incurable taint, an irremediable flaw."[29]

On the other hand, for James, the demand for perfection, the demand that there be no regrettable events is likewise a demand for a deterministic universe that forecloses genuine possibilities:

> Freedom in a world already perfect could only mean freedom to be *worse*, and who could be so insane as to wish that? To be necessarily what it is, to be impossibly aught else, would put the last touch of perfection on optimism's universe. Surely the only *possibility* that one can rationally

claim is the possibility that things may be *better*. That possibility, I need hardly say, is one that, as the actual world goes, we have ample grounds for deciderating.[30]

Herein is James's reduction to the absurd of the popular human demand for perfection. If the world were perfect, you might as well give up the idea of freedom altogether since what then would it mean but the opportunity to do worse? James's antidote: Give up the pragmatically absurd concept of a perfect universe. Hold out instead the rational possibility of things being better or of doing better in the future should the world fall short of your dreams, hopes, goals, or expectations.

In a universe in which things are not perfect and are subject to the possibility of improvement, you can learn from your mistakes and vow not to repeat them in the future. In such a universe, there is ample opportunity for growth and change. On the other hand, in a perfect universe, you are not afforded any opportunity for growth or change. This is not a very exciting universe, and it is not worth destroying your current happiness over. Says James, "Elation at mere existence, pure cosmic emotion and delight, would, it seems to me, quench all interest in those speculations, if the world were nothing but a luberland of happiness already."[31]

Undoubtedly, the world is not one in which justice is always served and good deeds are always rewarded. Disease, natural disasters, accidents, murder, rape, poverty, and the general vicissitudes of life provide obstacles to human happiness, and it is understandable how one might long for a perfect universe in which such obstacles to happiness are absent.

The existence of these "evils" of earthly living has long challenged religious thinkers to justify and defend the existence of a God who would permit them.[32] For how, one might query, could an all-good, all-knowing, and all-powerful God (the God of the Judeo-Christian tradition) permit such things? Wouldn't such a God have created a universe that was without them? Wouldn't a perfect being have created a perfect universe?

But, as James reminds us, this would be a stagnant universe in which there would be no room for human improvement, and it would be one in which the concept of freedom would be empty. It would be a universe in which there could be no courage because there would be no danger; no heroic feats; no self-sacrificing acts; no great breakthroughs in medical science that save many lives; no innovative ways to improve life; no opportunity to "live dangerously," to fail miserably, and learn to from it; no right to be wrong; and no freedom to choose between right and wrong (except in the trivial sense in which you always choose rightly).[33]

If this is the world you would want to inhabit, then you are welcome to keep perfection as your ideal of human existence. But if you are not convinced that inhabiting such a universe would be all that it might have seemed, then it is preferable to surrender the demand that things here on earth conform to this ideal. Better, then, to lighten up on the pursuit for perfection in this imperfect universe. Better, then, to accept as inevitable the obstacles of human existence—the not-always-hospitable, sometimes antisocial, inconsiderate, or downright nasty behavior of your fellow humans, the regrettable outcomes of life decisions and rolls of the dice. Better to do this than to kick and scream for want of perfection when reality falls short.

Antidote 7
Dedicate yourself, but amidst all your dedication, be still human. (Hume)

There are some who think that perfectionism stands behind prosperity. Fortunes are earned, science is advanced, athletic records are set, and contributions of sundry varieties are made by those who single-mindedly strive for perfection with unwavering and relentless dedication to their causes. Still, while it is probably true that many with high achievements are motivated by an ideal, it is not true that those who *demand* perfection live happily. Nor does the demand for perfection make success more likely. To the contrary, emotional stress—a corollary of demanding perfection—is notoriously destabilizing, tending to thwart creative thinking.

It can sometimes be difficult to tell the difference between a healthy devotion to a cause and an unhealthy addiction, between being a vigilant and determined worker and a workaholic. Nevertheless, there is a salient difference between the latter and the former. The workaholic sacrifices other meaningful and important aspects of living—friendship, family, recreation, and so forth—to the point of virtual exclusivity. There is a "must," an unequivocal imperative that drives a workaholic to work. It summons her even in her sleep. It is an obsessive and compulsive demand that is easily frustrated by any distraction from the work, and virtually everything, save for some special circumstances, is perceived as an impediment to fulfilling this unconditional imperative to work.

It may appear that there are many miles between the "social butterfly"—whose categorical commandment is to socialize—and the workaholic. In reality, there is a common thread, namely, the exclusivity by which each lives life. While the former sees work, at worst, as an impediment to socializing and, at best, as an opportunity to socialize, the latter sees socializing as an expendable distraction to work. To be sure, the respective activities are distinct, but their devotees have similarly adopted unconditional commands—absolute "musts"—that rule (dominate) their lives. To these "musts" each is in bondage, uncomfortably at war with the rest of life.

British philosopher David Hume has provided a suitable antidote to such polarizing demands. A prolific philosopher himself, he still found time for socializing. Sociable and witty, he enjoyed the company of colleagues and friends. Said he, "Be a philosopher, but amidst all your philosophy, be still a man."[34]

To be "a man," to be human, was, for Hume, to live a "mixed life" in which no human dimension was conspicuously absent, in which no one dimension trumped another. He says,

> Man is a reasonable being; and as such, receives from science his proper food and nourishment: But so narrow are the bounds of human understanding, that little satisfaction can be hoped for in this particular, either from the extent or security of his acquisitions. Man is a sociable, no less than a reasonable, being: But neither can he always enjoy company agreeable and amusing, or preserve the proper relish for them. Man is also an active being, and from this disposition as well as the various necessities of life, must submit to business and occupation: But the mind requires some relaxation, and cannot always support its bent to care and industry. It seems, then, that nature has pointed out a mixed kind of life as most suitable to the human race, and secretly admonished them to allow none of these biases to draw too much, so as to incapacitate them from other occupations and entertainments.[35]

The "mixed kind of life" to which Hume refers is logically preempted by the demand for perfect devotion to just one of these aspects of living. The philosopher who lives chronically atop the ivory tower may well defeat his purposes by having limited exposure to the ideas and influences of others. The businessperson who "lives" at her office will relinquish the opportunity to forge a family life. Given a mixed rational, social, and active human nature, the absolutistic demand to dedicate yourself exclusively is a recipe for unhappiness.

Aristotle's doctrine of the "golden mean" may be especially useful here. While there is no formula for overdoing or underdoing your level of dedication, there are surely recognizable breaches and extremes. Keeping yourself destitute of knowledge (refusing to read or otherwise adequately inform yourself) is one extreme, while attempting to live the contemplative life, to the exclusion of necessities (eating, sleeping, and so on), is another. So says Aristotle: "Being a man, one will also need external prosperity; for our nature is not self-sufficient for the purpose of contemplation, but our body also must be healthy and must have food and other attention."[36]

What is the mean for you may not be the mean for someone else since, as Aristotle tells us, the mean is relative to the individual. So I cannot speak to your particular mean in balancing rational, social, and active aspects of living. Some people are more social, others more cerebral, and still others more physical. Not every temperament is compatible with the life of a philosopher. Not every temperament is suitable for being an athlete. But there is no doubt that our mixed nature renders no single dimension self-sufficient.

Antidote 8
Instead of demanding lavish things, take pleasure in the simpler things in life. (Epicurus)

There are those who are motivated not by a desire to acquire knowledge, the good company of others, or to do good works but instead by a desire for luxurious things—exquisite food, drink, clothing, dwelling, and all else that wealth and good fortune can purchase. Attainment of these things is exalted to a *requirement* of happiness.

The self-defeating nature of this route to human happiness was well understood by the Greek Stoic, Epicurus, who prescribed enjoyment of the simpler things in life as a more effective route. Epicurus said, "The truest happiness does not come from enjoyment of physical pleasures but from a simple life, free from anxiety, with the normal physical needs satisfied." And "indeed, simple sauces bring a pleasure equal to that of lavish banquets if once the pain due to *need* is removed."[37] Ironically, it is the person who regards luxuries as "least needed" who takes the greatest pleasure in them if they should have good fortune enough to attain them. Since "vain pleasures are hard to obtain," the person who demands luxuries for happiness often ends up dissatisfied, while the person who demands no more than the simpler things in life—good wholesome food, a comfortable dwelling, and so on—is content without luxuries and appreciates them all the more if he should have the good fortune to acquire them. This, says Epicurus, renders such a person "fearless against fortune."[38]

This would also apply to demanding pleasure from your daily activities. For example, if you demand that everything you eat taste good, you will defeat your own purposes. I have found that some of my most enjoyable experiences dining out have been in restaurants that served mediocre food. This is because I did not come to dinner with the expectation of having the gustatory sensation of my life. I would prefer to be pleasantly surprised than to be unpleasantly disappointed. When the company and the ambiance are agreeable, you can easily overlook the food as well as the service.

On the other hand, I once dined out at a conference with a group of colleagues. One of them wasted his time (and mine) ranting and complaining over the poor service. The experience was extremely unpleasant, but not because of the service or the food, which was mediocre.

Epicurus is right. When you give up the demand for perfection, you're more likely to enjoy yourself, even if what you enjoy isn't the greatest.

What about sex? Epicurus spoke: "Neither continual drinking and dancing, nor sexual love, nor the enjoyment of fish and whatever else the luxurious table offers brings about the pleasant life; rather it is produced by the reason which is sober."[39] Overindulgence and obsessive desire for physical pleasures, thought Epicurus, can produce a state of continual anxiety about attaining pleasure, which is not pleasant.

Such excessive desires enslave rather than delight you. This is because they are driven by a demand rather than a preference. You tell yourself that you *must* have continual sex or that you *must* have *great* sex. In either case, in thinking of sex as a *need* instead of a preference, as not just desirable but mandatory—indeed even as a duty—you put undue stress on yourself. So having sex, which can be an occasion for intimacy, can become a time of intense anxiety. In fact, many people, both male and female, fail to reach orgasm because of stress, in particular, fear of not performing as they *must*.[40] However, when these individuals change their demand to a preference, their sexual performance often significantly improves. In such cases, giving up the demand for perfection can be a fine aphrodisiac.

NOTES

1. Albert Ellis and Robert A. Harper, *A New Guide to Rational Living* (Chatsworth, Calif.: Wilshire Book Company, 1975).

2. St. Augustine, *City of God*, bk. 12, chap. 8, in *From Plato to Derrida*, 4th ed., ed. Forrest E. Baird and Walter Kaufmann (Upper Saddle River, N.J.: Prentice Hall, 2003), 313.

3. St. Thomas Aquinas, *Summa Contra Gentiles*, in *Introduction to St. Thomas Aquinas*, ed. Anton C. Pegis (New York: Random House, 1948), chap. 19.

4. Aquinas, *Summa Contra Gentiles*, chap. 25.

5. Kevin FitzMaurice, cited in Albert Ellis, *Feeling Better, Getting Better, Staying Better* (Atascadero, Calif.: Impact Publishers, 2001), 105.

6. St. Thomas Aquinas, *Summa Theologica*, in Pegis, *Introduction to St. Thomas Aquinas*, question 5, art. 3.

7. St. Anselm, The Ontological Argument, in *Philosophy: History and Problems* (5th ed.), ed. Samuel Enoch Stumpf (New York: McGraw-Hill, 1994), 664.

8. This is discussed carefully in chapters 7 and 11.

9. Plato, *Theaetetus*, in *Plato: The Collected Dialogues*, ed. Edith Hamilton and Huntington Cairns (Princeton, N.J.: Princeton University Press, 1961), 919.

10. Plato, *Euthyphro*, in Hamilton and Cairns, *Plato*, 174.

11. Hume called such statements "relations of ideas." He contrasted them with "matters of fact," such as "The sun will rise tomorrow." Unlike the former, the latter make claims about the material world, but they aren't certain and can conceivably be false. For example, it's impossible that some red dogs are not red. However, it's at least possible that the sun doesn't rise tomorrow because the earth is destroyed by a giant meteor that collides with it. See David Hume, *Inquiry concerning Human Understanding*, sec. 4, pt. 1, in Baird and Kaufmann, *From Plato to Derrida*.

12. St. Augustine, *City of God*, bk. 12, chap. 5, in Baird and Kaufmann, *From Plato to Derrida*, 310.

13. Plato, *The Republic*, bk. 10, in Hamilton and Cairns, *Plato*.

14. St. Augustine, *City of God*, bk. 12, chap. 1, 307. This functional or "teleological" perspective has a long-standing tradition in ancient Greek philosophy beginning with Plato and well articulated in Aristotle. According to this tradition, not only do the individual parts of the body have functions or purposes, but human beings *as such* also have purposes. For example, Aristotle thought that the controlling purpose of a human being as such was to live rationally. However, nothing said here requires you to assume that human beings as such have purposes.

15. Epicurus, *Letter to Memoeceus*, in Baird and Kaufmann, *From Plato to Derrida*, 249.

16. St. Augustine, *City of God*, bk. 12, chap. 4, 310.

17. David Hume, *Of the Standard of Taste*, sec. 7, retrieved March 7, 2006, from http://www.csulb.edu/~jvancamp/361r15.html.

18. Voltaire, The Philosophical Dictionary, in *Voltaire Selections*, ed. Paul Edwards (New York: Macmillan, 1989), 128.

19. David Hume, *Of the Dignity or Meanness of Human Nature*, retrieved August 30, 2006, from http://www.fordham.edu/halsall/mod/hume-dignity.html.

20. Spinoza, *Ethics*, pt. 4, Of Human Bondage or the Power of the Affects, in *A Spinoza Reader*, ed, and trans. Edwin Curley (Princeton, N.J.: Princeton University Press, 1994), 198.

21. Spinoza, *Ethics*, pt. 4, 249.

22. Spinoza, *Ethics*, pt. 4, 249.

23. Like Spinoza, Epictetus is a determinist. But, as just mentioned, you needn't be a determinist in order to appreciate the limits of human control.

24. Epictetus, *Encheiridion*, in Baird and Kaufmann, *From Plato to Derrida*, 259.

25. William Ferraiolo, Stoic Counsel for Interpersonal Relations, *International Journal of Philosophical Practice* 2, no. 1 (spring 2004): 7, available at http://www .aspcp.org/ijpp/html/vol2no1.html.

26. Ferraiolo, Stoic Counsel for Interpersonal Relations, 7–8.

27. Strictly speaking, it is the expending of an *effort* to sing well that is in a person's power, not the actual outcome of this effort.

28. William James, Some Metaphysical Problems Pragmatically Considered, in *William James: Pragmatism*, ed. Ralph Barton Perry (New York: Meridian Books, 1955), 84.

29. William James, The Dilemma of Determinism, in *Philosophy: History and Problems*, 3rd ed., bk. 2, ed. Samuel Enoch Stumpf (New York: McGraw-Hill, 1983), 61.

30. James, Some Metaphysical Problems, 85.

31. James, Some Metaphysical Problems, 84.

32. For example, Aquinas advances his "five ways" of proving God's existence partly in response to the existence of such evils. See, Aquinas, Five Ways of Proving God's Existence: The A Posteriori Approach, in *Philosophers at Work: Issues and Practice of Philosophy*, ed. Elliot D. Cohen (Fort Worth, Tex.: Harcourt, 2000), 528–30.

33. See, for example, John Hick's soul building argument in The Problem of Evil: The Free-Will and Soul-Building Arguments, in *Philosophers at Work*, ed. Cohen, 544–46.

34. Hume, *An Enquiry concerning Human Understanding*, sec. 1, 716.

35. Hume, *An Enquiry concerning Human Understanding*, sect. 1, 716.

36. Aristotle, *Nicomachean Ethics*, bk. 10, chap. 8, trans. W. D. Ross, in Richard McKeon, *The Basic Works of Aristotle* (New York: Random House, 1941), 1107.

37. Epicurus, *Letter to Menoeceus*, 252 (emphasis added).

38. Epicurus, *Letter to Menoeceus*, 252.

39. Epicurus, Letter to Menoeceus, in Baird and Kaufmann, *From Plato to Derrida*, 252.

40. Albert Ellis, *Reason and Emotion in Psychotherapy* (New York: Citadel Press, 1962), chap. 13.

2

CONFRONTING EVIL,
GROWING STRONGER

L et's face it. In this imperfect world of ours, shit does happen. Untimely
death and wanton cruelty are facts of life. The holocaust happened.
Unjust wars have been fought. Slavery existed and still does in some parts
of the world. Rape, murder, and natural disasters are realities. On a shitti-
ness scale, all this would ordinarily be ranked high, at least by most people.
They are what would be thought terrible, horrible, and awful by most people. But there are also other unfortunate things that many people would add
to the list:

- Your spouse divorces you.
- You get fired from your job.
- You don't get a chance to say "I love you" before a beloved dies.
- You are scammed out of all or much of your money.
- You ask someone out and this person laughs at you.
- Someone you trust lies to you.

This list could obviously be expanded ad nauseam. But how bad does something have to get before you can rightly call it terrible, horrible, and awful?
Are all the things on this list really awful? Is there any rational basis for
adding or subtracting from it?

The answers to these probing questions depend in the first place on
what you mean by calling something terrible, horrible, and awful. In one
sense, these terms signify a *relatively high degree of badness*. That is, there is a
badness threshold past which bad things become awful. Just where this
marker is located depends on the person who is doing the rating. Thus,
some people would not ordinarily consider it awful if someone whom you

asked out laughed at you, whereas most would contend that the sexual molestation and murder of a child crosses well into the territory of the awful.

In another sense, *terrible, horrible,* and *awful* refer to anything that is undesirable or disappointing. In this sense, you might say something like "It would be awful if it rained and we couldn't go swimming." This is a rather innocuous sense, and people rarely seriously disturb themselves with this usage.

Yet, in another sense, *terrible, horrible,* and *awful* are nonrelative and nonnegotiable. In this sense, they refer to what is *absolutely bad,* that is, the *worst* thing that could conceivably happen. This is the fallacy that rational psychologists have appropriately termed *awfulizing.*

The irrational rule in question gives the following instruction:

> Awfulizing: If something shitty happens or might happen to you or to a significant other, then it's *totally* terrible, horrible, and awful—by far the worst and shittiest thing that could possibly ever happen.

In yielding to this rule, you can send yourself into a tailspin of self-destructive emotions. In following this rule, when something perceivably shitty happens or might happen, you overreact to just *how* shitty it really is. *In your mind,* it is catapulted to the absolute worst thing in the universe. Accordingly, you deduce intense anxiety about the mere possibility of getting fired, depression about your wife having divorced you, and anger, even rage, about having been lied to. Terrified over the possibility of losing your job, you make it harder to respond efficiently on the job. Wallowing in the awfulness of your divorce, your keep yourself from moving on. Aghast at being lied to, you wish the perpetrator hell and damnation and later come to regret it.

The irrationality here lies in the inference you make from the *relatively bad* to the *absolutely bad.* Here is the easy refutation:

> There are increasing degrees of badness in the universe, and they can increase ad nauseum, but the idea of the *absolutely worst* is a fiction for which there is no evidence.

You need not deny that the things in the previous list are bad to see the fallacy in the inference from *bad* to *worst.* The divorce could have been worse. Your spouse could have poisoned you to death slowly instead of divorcing you. You could meet a fate worse than losing your job, such as losing your head (literally). Someone can do something to you much worse than lying to you. Just use your imagination.

Are there truly terrible, horrible, and awful things in which the inference from bad to (absolute) worst is justified? Not strictly speaking since, for whatever you can imagine, there is something else you can imagine that is even worse. Being flattened by a Mack truck is quite bad, but it's even worse for two people to be so flattened and even worse for three, four, or five and so on. In a relative sense, seriously bad things can cross over the badness threshold into the range of things that qualify as terrible, horrible, and awful. Tragic things do happen, but these things still have a *relative* negative worth, not an absolute one.

In the previous chapter, you have seen how traditional metaphysics conceived of bad as the absence of good. For Plato, goodness was real, and things were bad to the extent that they were lesser goods. An *absolutely* bad thing would therefore be something that lacked existence (and goodness) altogether.

The Neoplatonist philosopher Plotinus referred to such absolute badness as "Evil." This, he said, "is not in any and every lack; it is in absolute lack. What falls in some degree short of the Good is not Evil. . . . Mere lack brings merely Not-Goodness: Evil demands the absolute lack." And he added,

> We are not to think of Evil as some particular bad thing—injustice, for example, or any other ugly trait—but as a principle distinct from any of the particular forms in which, by the existence of certain elements, it becomes manifest.[1]

So, for Plotinus, the bad things on our list are not absolutely bad ("Evil"). They are not the worst things since they still have some degree of goodness.[2] For Plotinus, absolute badness is something abstracted from all that is good in existence. But something like a divorce assumes living human beings as well as the existence of the institution of marriage. Losing your job assumes the existence of industry; telling lies requires the truth. So these things are not absolutely bad in any philosophical sense after all.

Plato himself thought that anything on earth was imperfect. So the concept of *perfectly* evil things was really a fiction for him. "Evils," he said, "must needs haunt this region of our mortal nature."[3] Perfect depravity would have to be like perfect goodness, something divine, not of this earth. But this is just the opposite of what Plato thought.

Bottom line: Both empirically and philosophically speaking, don't drive yourself crazy about things that are absolutely and unequivocally terrible, horrible, and awful. These things just don't exist in this mortal region of ours.

So how do you keep yourself from this abyss of insanity? Aristotle believed that it was a mark of a person with courage to "feel and act according to the merits of the case." In the least, this means not making things out to be absolutely evil. But even in the face of serious evils—things that are terrible in a relative sense—the courageous person, says Aristotle, will still face them "as he ought and as the rule directs."[4] So what rules to this purpose can be gleaned from the wisdom of the sages? What antidotes are there for confronting the appreciably bad things that happen to us?

ANTIDOTES TO AWFULZING

Antidote 1
Instead of whining about your misfortune, triumph over it by turning your suffering into something positive. (Nietzsche)

It is easy enough to focus your attention on what's wrong with your life while overlooking what's good. In the face of adversity, we often retract and lament what has befallen us: the loss of money in a business venture; a theft or a rape; a contested divorce or separation; the death of a beloved; a painful, irremediable, or terminal illness; paralysis; dismemberment; an inoperable cancer or other irrevocable condition. Forlorn, withdrawn, and depressed, we perceive only the evil face of our condition, and so we bleed and suffer. Like animals caught in a hunter's leg trap, the more we struggle, the more we bleed, the more mutilated we become, the more disease we suffer, and the more hopeless and desperate we become.

But this painful subjectivity is not the only response to adversity. Philosopher Friedrich Nietzsche had a more constructive response. So spoke Nietzsche: "The tendency of a person to allow himself to be degraded, robbed, deceived, and exploited might be the diffidence of a God amongst men."[5]

Indeed, for Nietzsche, it is through human suffering that we can learn and grow stronger:

> that by virtue of his suffering he *knows more* than the cleverest and wisest could possibly know, and that he knows his way and has once been "at home" in many distant, terrifying worlds of which "*you* know nothing."[6]

"Profound suffering," said Nietzsche, "makes noble" and "separates" the sufferer from the uninitiated.[7] The sufferer who withstands his suffering has created an opportunity to become courageous. Indeed, in confronting and standing up to his suffering, he *is* courageous. And the adversity of the sufferer, which can so easily be perceived as an impediment, can alternatively become a spur to cultivation of new and inventive modes of living. Indeed, it is in times of adversity that societies advance, whereas times of tranquility are often quite unproductive:[8]

> The discipline of suffering, of *great* suffering—do you not know that only *this* discipline has created all enhancements of man so far? That tension of the soul in unhappiness which cultivates its strength, its shudders face to face with great ruin, its inventiveness and courage in enduring, preserving, interpreting, and exploiting suffering, and whatever has been granted to it of profundity, secret, mask, spirit, cunning, greatness—was it not granted to it through suffering, through the discipline of great suffering?[9]

Through suffering, new meanings and directions, new missions in life, emerge that would never have otherwise come to pass:

> Man, as the animal that is most courageous, most accustomed to suffering, does not negate suffering as such: *he wants* it, even seeks it out, provided one shows him some *meaning* in it, some *wherefore* of suffering.[10]

Recently, I attended a luncheon honoring caseworkers for a victim advocacy program. The keynote speaker was herself a survivor of a violent assault. Years prior, while driving on a congested South Florida highway en route from her job as an insurance adjuster, another driver drove up alongside her and shot through her window, wounding her in the eyes. Blinded by the gunshot wound, she still managing to pilot her car to the roadside until a Good Samaritan knocked on her window offering assistance. When she allowed this man into her car, he abducted her and brutally beat and raped her, leaving her for dead. Her abductor was none other than the driver who had originally shot her.

Still this remarkable woman survived. Permanently blinded, her husband abandoned her for another woman, leaving her three children in her custody. But were it not for all her suffering, it is doubtful that this woman would have chosen to help others who were similarly brutalized. Ironically, it was this senseless, heinous crime that became a source of new positive meaning in her life. Remarried to a coworker, she jested how she met her new husband on a blind date. Clearly, she could laugh about her own disability, but I could also see moist clouds form in her eyes when she told her life story. As Nietzsche would attest, this woman's vision was profoundly superior to many sighted persons who hadn't suffered as she did.

But Nietzsche also proclaimed that suffering makes you "hard" and that it's noble to be so. "Only the noblest is altogether hard. This new tablet, O my brothers, I place over you: *become hard!*"[11]

I admonish you not to take this prescription to "become hard" too literally, however. In doing so, you risk oversimplifying his meaning and the merits of his antidote, for what it means to be "hard" is itself a relative matter. The woman of whom I have just spoken could still feel and could still cry, and it was precisely her ability to feel and to empathize that gave her the power to help others in similar circumstances. True, she did not wallow in self-pity, but neither did she become callous. If she had, she would never have had the acumen to help others in their time of crisis. She modeled courage, perseverance, endurance, and creativity by virtue of having turned her suffering into progress. But in the process, her compassion became an important dimension of her strength.

Having confronted the fragility of her own life through the brutal assault that left her for dead, this woman might have simply given up on life and died a thousand deaths. Instead, it made her stronger. She did not give up on life, I submit, because she was not afraid to live in the face of her own mortality.

Antidote 2
Concern yourself not with dying but with living well. (Epicurus, Wittgenstein, Sartre, Socrates, Aristotle, Santayana, Aurelius, Bacon)

Human beings, all of us, will die at some future time. It is uncertain only in respect of the time of death, not of the certainty of death itself. How you deal with this fact can make the difference between your personal happiness and existence rife with anxiety and even depression. If you perceive death as something utterly horrible, the worst thing that could possibly happen to anyone, then it will hang over you like a dark cloud, stifling your ability to live contentedly.

On the other hand, as Epicurus believed, if you don't fear death, you'll live happily since "there is no reason why the man who is thoroughly assured that there is nothing to fear in death should find anything to fear in life." And what reason is there to dread dying in the first place? "Death," says Epicurus, "the most dreaded of evils," should not concern us, for while we exist death is not present, and when death is present we no longer exist. It is therefore nothing either to the living or to the dead since it is not present to the living, and the dead no longer are.[12]

Epicurus explains that it is irrational to make yourself upset in anticipation of something that doesn't cause you any pain when it arrives. Since death is devoid of pain, it is irrational to upset yourself in anticipation of it.

Along these same lines, Ludwig Wittgenstein wrote, "Death is not an event in life. We do not live to experience death."[13] Nevertheless, people typically dread death because they assume that they will somehow be alive to experience their own death. But this is logically impossible. You can't be dead when you are alive. So, such a basis for dreading death is illogical.

Still, perhaps what most folks find abhorrent is precisely what Epicurus finds consoling: that death is a state of nonbeing. As such, you will never again be able to love, laugh, think profound thoughts, and experience joy. And isn't that a reason to upset yourself about your future death?

Upset yourself? Make yourself unhappy? The irrationality of this is glaring, for what's the point of spending your precious time making yourself miserable over not being able to have positive experiences? How self-defeating can you get? If you care about being happy, then why mope about and defeat your happiness? As existential philosophers like Sartre and Heidegger would remind us, our awareness of death should be our wake-up call to do something with our lives instead of mope.

So, it's all about happiness. Living well, says Epicurus, is not necessarily to live long because you can live a long unhappy existence:

> The wise man neither renounces life nor fears its end; for living does not offend him, nor does he suppose that not to live is in any way an evil. As he does not choose the food that is most in quantity but that which is most pleasant, so he does not seek the enjoyment of the longest life but of the happiest.[14]

Go for quality and stop defeating your purposes by worrying about dying.

Let me illustrate. I know someone who spends a good portion of her life researching health hazards and typically finds "cogent" reasons not to indulge in many things she otherwise finds desirable. There are risks in flying, so she curtails much of her travel. Before she tries a new food, she researches to see if it contains any hazardous ingredients; she eats out in the same "tried-and-true" restaurants, checks for biohazards in her environment and household products, and avoids buying clothing from "Third

World nations" where certain diseases are endemic. By the time she decides to "take the plunge," the experience has been sanitized, cleansed of its spontaneity. At the end of the day, she is safe but oh so very bored.

Moral: You aren't going to live forever. Don't destroy the quality of your life by getting hung up on your mortality.

But maybe Epicurus is too secular for your blood. You should know that he thought the mind was just part of your body—like your brain. When your body dies, so does your mind (or soul). On this view, there's no possibility of survival after the death of your body.

In contrast is Socrates' very poignant statement expressed from his prison cell just before he took the fatal dose of hemlock. Sentenced to death by the Athenian court on bogus charges, Socrates had the opportunity and means to escape from prison. However, not persuaded that death was the worst of evils, he chose instead to maintain his dignity by obeying the law and accepting the punishment meted out to him. Said Socrates,

> Now as you see there has come upon me that which may be thought, and is generally believed to be, the last and worst evil. . . . Let us reflect in another way, and we shall see that there is great reason to hope that death is a good, for one of two things:—either death is a state of nothingness and utter unconsciousness, or, as men say, there is a change and migration of the soul from this world to another. Now if you suppose that there is no consciousness, but a sleep like the sleep of him who is undisturbed even by the sight of dreams, death will be an unspeakable gain. . . . Now if death is like this, I say that to die is gain; for eternity is then only a single night. But if death is a journey to another place, and there, as men say, all the dead are, what good, O my friends and judges, can be greater than this? . . . What would not a man give if he might converse with Orpheus and Musaeus and Hesiod and Homer? . . . Above all, I shall be able to continue my search into true and false knowledge; as in this world, so also in that. . . . The hour of departure has arrived, and we go our ways—I to die, and you to live. Which is better God only knows.[15]

Far from being an evil, Socrates has given reason to think death might even be a good—either an eternal state of nonconsciousness akin to an undisturbed night's sleep or a flight of the soul to another world offering new opportunities for growth.[16] Socrates' antidote was to provide some *positive* ways to look at death, ways that can help you overcome the angst of awfulizing human mortality, ways that you are bound to miss by shrouding death in its classic black robe.

The image of Socrates preferring death to surrendering his principles is one that has served as a perennial example of courage. It is important to realize that Socrates is not telling you to check out on a whim. For Socrates, life was precious and not to be taken with a grain of salt. But loving life does not demand dreading death. As Epicurus would tell you, if you truly love life, you won't squander you personal happiness on fear of death. Viewed from this perspective, Socrates was able to act courageously in the face of death. He was not afraid of dying, as this would have made him cowardly. As Aristotle says, "He will be called brave who is fearless in face of a *noble* death, and of all emergencies that involve death."[17] Notice that Aristotle says *noble* death. Neither Aristotle nor Socrates would tell you to *needlessly* throw your life away. This would not in the least be noble.

Face it. Death is a necessary dimension of human existence. Birth and death are its boundaries, wherefore "there is no cure for birth and death save to enjoy the interval."[18] It is a natural part of life: "Despise not death, but welcome it, for nature wills it like all else."[19]

The British thinker Thomas Hobbes believed that all human behavior is self-aggrandizing and aims at survival as its final end. But life as such without happiness is an empty vessel. Life holds out the possibility of happiness, but its point is undermined if we fail at filling this vessel with anything of value. As St. Thomas surmised, if a shipowner wanted simply to play it safe, he would keep his ship in port. But venturing out to sea turns dead life into a living adventure.

As Sartre perceived, a person who speaks only of what he could have or should have done merely defines himself as "a disappointed dream, as miscarried hopes, as vain expectations."[20] Such a negatively defined existence is life without meaning. You can't begin to *live* without living life, and this means *doing* things that are conducive to your happiness. What these activities are is for you to decide, but however you define them, these are what make life so precious. An empty, boring existence is already a corpse. In letting death dictate your life, you are already dead.

The dread of death, its awfulized hue, can be stripped away when seen in the light of the wisdom of the ages: death is but a natural boundary of human life that is no more inherently evil than an uninterrupted night's sleep. Yet this essential condition of human existence has been dressed in a black robe and given a dark name: the Grim Reaper. With a "life" of its own, this dark-cloaked, skeletal figure on black horse with scythe in hand is said to cut off your life as though he were harvesting grain. How much more *mortifying* could we get in portraying an image of death. To die is made to sound like being ripped by Jack the Ripper.

But death is not a person. It does not ride a horse, carry a weapon, knock at your door, or have a face. Nor is it an animate thing. It is not even a *thing* at all. Death is the negation of being, the state of *not* being.

In his classic work *Novum Organum*, Sir Francis Bacon spoke of "idols of the human mind," by which he meant misconceptions that undermine rationality. Some of these idols ("idols of the marketplace") he said involve "ill and unfit choice of words."[21] Such idols arising from the misuse of words include "names which result from fantastic suppositions and to which nothing in reality corresponds."[22] For example, "Fortune," he said, was such a word. And here's another for Sir Francis's list: "the Grim Reaper."

Fear not this toothless idol, as the dangerousness is in the fear itself.

Antidote 3
In confronting adversity, view it from the disinterested perspective of a "pure subject of will-less knowledge." (Schopenhauer)

If you tell yourself that death *must* never befall you or the ones you hold dear, then it will seem dreadful to you, and even imagining the death of a beloved will be painful to consciousness. If you crave the love or approval of a certain person, telling yourself that you *must* have it, then the realization or even the suggestion that you can't have it will seem terrible to you. If you tell yourself that you must never be treated unjustly or unfairly, then it will seem utterly horrible if you are so treated. But the awfulness of these same objects of thought dissolves when you look on them "free from their relation to the will . . . without personal interest, without subjectivity, purely objectively . . . so far as they are ideas, but not insofar as they are motives."[23] So said philosopher Arthur Schopenhauer.

According to Schopenhauer, as long as we are in the throngs of desires, hopes, and fears, we will not enjoy happiness and peace. But we have the ability to chill out, to transcend the pangs of our everyday desires, and to look at the objects of our consciousness with a sort of detached appreciation for their beauty or their sublimity. Did you ever look at a shark through a glass, gazing as its colossal jaws, thinking dispassionately how it might be for you to be behind the glass with the shark? Since the glass protects you, you do not feel threatened, so you can detach yourself from your own will.

On the other hand, the absence of any perceived insulation between you and the world of everyday life feels more threatening, more serious, more in need of your control. Here you are inside the tank with the shark, and you are filled with the anxieties, fears, guilt, anger, depression, and anguish of wrestling in vivo with reality. But Schopenhauer reminds us that we can turn off our personal engagement and look at the objects of thought with a disinterest similar to the way we view the shark through the glass. In this way, we can gain aesthetic appreciation for what is sublime[24] in life's vicissitudes and peace of mind otherwise lost in the throngs of emotion.

Schopenhauer explains:

> A man of sublime character will accordingly consider men in a purely objective way, and not with reference to the relations which they might have to his will; he will, for example, observe their faults, even their hatred and injustice to himself, without being himself excited to hatred; he will behold their happiness without envy; he will recognize their good qualities without desiring any closer relations with them; he will perceive the beauty of women, but he will not desire them. His personal happiness or unhappiness will not greatly affect him.[25]

If you suddenly found yourself swimming in the tank with the shark, it would hardly be irrational to try to get out as quickly as you could. In fact, your sympathetic nervous system would automatically sound the alarm, increase your respiration and heart rate, and release adrenalin into your bloodstream, thereby preparing you for fight or flight. This response to danger is prewired and probably the result of an evolutionary process adapting human beings for survival. But this alarm often goes off precipitously and unnecessarily in many of us. We stand ready to defend our lives and limbs even when there is no real danger. A nasty look or a mean-spirited action may be awfulized and the agent demonized, catapulting us into intense anger, even rage.

It is in such cases that Schopenhauer's advice can become a useful antidote to destructive emotions. Stand back, objectify, and uninvolve yourself; look at the object of your perception as pure idea abstracted from personal motives, surrendering your interests to "pure contemplation" and becoming a "pure subject of will-less knowledge."[26]

For example, from this perspective, the hateful words of a significant other directed at you during a difficult time is not something awful to defend against but instead an occasion to contemplate human irrationality. So you simply listen as the hateful expression vents, listening not with an eye to respond but much as you would watch a shark through the glass partition, perceiving the fury behind the debasing language merely as a will-less spectator.

There are, of course, some cases of adversity in which practicing such detached constraint may present a greater challenge. For example, substantial loss of money and property is often catapulted to the status of terrible, horrible, and awful by the recipients of the loss. And, given the emphasis that popular culture places on material possessions, it is easy to see why so many of us become depressed and even suicidal over such loss. But the emotional detachment that Schopenhauer recommends is not without use even here.

I have myself recently experienced substantial personal loss of property. In the fall of 2004, two hurricanes struck the east coast region of Florida where I reside. The storms, which occurred within a few weeks of one another, succeeded in flooding my home, and, since it took several days to restore power, the house along with many of my personal possessions became infested with mold. All totaled, I lost about half my personal possessions because of mold or water damage, and many of these were irreplaceable, including photographs and personal memorabilia.

As I sifted through the devastation, I made myself, at times, detach emotionally. (It wasn't always easy.) It was an awesome power of nature that had accomplished this massive destruction. I perceived myself as helpless and powerless against this awesome force, a victim of chance, "a vanishing nothing in the presence of stupendous might." At the same time, I was "the eternal, peaceful, knowing subject"[27] of this sublime idea of the destructive force of nature. At these junctures, I perceived my loss not as something to lament or to try to replace or to rebuild but rather as the pure idea of this power against which I was so small and inconsequential.

For me, there was consolation in the aesthetic view. Naturally, I had to deal with the pragmatics of cleaning up the mess and restoring my home to living condition. But I had intermittent glimpses into the sublime, and it was this escape from the practical that helped me get through it.

I still keep the picture of some of the personal things I had to discard in my memory. I can picture a photograph I uncovered of a beloved dog that died several years ago. I can visualize the mold patches speckling the image of the small white figure of this deceased friend. It was an awesome reminder of the power of nature. I can recall placing the photo into the trash can, gingerly, almost like a burial. The experience was sublime. Unfortunately, I lost an irreplaceable photograph, but the experience was still a gain realized in the loss. I also keep it in my memory.

Antidote 4
Compare what seems awful to you to much worse things and content yourself with how much worse things could truly have been. (Epictetus)

Epictetus admonished, "Keep before your eyes day by day death and exile, and everything that seems terrible but most of all death; and then you will never have any abject thought, nor will you yearn for anything beyond measure."[28] You have already seen reason not to regard death as absolutely terrible. Still, compared to many other things that may *seem* terrible to us, the comparison can be an eye-opener. I do regard the destruction of my home and the loss of personal property resulting from the hurricanes as bad things. But I have only to consider the recent mass devastation in New Orleans from Hurricane Katrina or in Thailand as a result of the tsunami. Thousands of people lost their lives. I have only to consider these natural disasters to realize just how relative the assessment of awfulness can be.

And if you are thinking that there could have been nothing worse than what happened in New Orleans or in Thailand, then just use your imagination. Was the suffering of prisoners in the Nazi death camps even worse? What about the mass genocide in Rwanda? When you think about such grander evils, the hardship of going through a divorce or the loss of a job, among other mundane losses, seem *relatively* minor.

This relativity also calls attention to the fact that judgments about what is awful can't be verified. To see if something is red, you need only look at it. But to see if your divorce is terrible, there is no similar experiment that you can perform.

Nor is it ever a fact that something is terrible, horrible, or awful. This is because calling something terrible, horrible, or awful implies that you *should* be terrified, horrified, or awed by it. And this means that you are dictating to yourself to be terrified, horrified, or awed. There is no unshakable fact about the universe, no special property of awfulness, that automatically attaches to some things and not others. It is *you* who are the judge of this. You call the shots about what you ought to fear.

Antidote 5
Since the awfulness of something is not itself an unalterable fact but instead your own inference from the facts, stop inferring awfulness. (Hume)

Long ago, David Hume pointed out that you can't get *ought* or *should* from a set of facts no matter how many facts you heap up. Spoke Hume:

> In every system of morality, which I have hitherto met with, I have always remark'd, that the author proceeds for some time in the ordinary way of reasoning, and establishes the being of a God, or makes observations concerning human affairs; when of a sudden I am surpriz'd to

find, that instead of the usual copulations of propositions, is, and is not, I meet with no proposition that is not connected with an ought, or an ought not. This change is imperceptible; but is, however, of the last consequence. For as this ought, or ought not, expresses some new relation or affirmation, 'tis necessary that it shou'd be observ'd and explain'd; and at the same time that a reason should be given, for what seems altogether inconceivable, how this new relation can be a deduction from others, which are entirely different from it.[29]

For example, you can say how your spouse has cheated on you with your best friend, how they both lied and deceived you, how they betrayed your trust, and so on. But when you stop describing what you think happened and instead exclaim, "How horrible!" you have gone beyond the facts; you have said how you *should* feel; you have directed yourself to be horrified. It is you, not the facts, speaking. And here is another sense in which such judgments are relative. They are up to *you*.

Now as soon as you realize this relativity (subjectivity), the sting is out of your judgment. It is only when you tell yourself that reality is awful in some unyielding, stubborn factual sense that you will have problems dealing with it. On the other hand, if it is up to *you* whether something is to be ranked as awful, then you are much less likely to drive yourself crazy over events in your life that don't go the way you want them to go. You've got the power. You are the one who awfulizes, not the universe. There isn't anything awful about the universe unless you decide it is.

NOTES

1. Plotinus, *The Enneads*, trans. Stephen MacKenna (London: Faber & Faber, 1967), Eighth Tractate, "The Nature and Source of Evil," 70.

2. Along these lines, St. Augustine said that "absolutely bad things" can never exist because "even those natures that were vitiated at the outset by an evil will are only evil in so far as they are defective, while they are good in so far as they are natural." *City of God*, chap. 3.

3. Plato, *Theaetetus*, in *Plato: Collected Dialogues*, ed. Edith Hamilton and Huntington Cairns (Princeton, N.J.: Princeton University Press, 1961), 881.

4. Aristotle, *Ethics*, bk. 3, chap. 7.

5. Friedrich Nietzsche, *Beyond Good and Evil*, trans. Helen Zimmern, "What Is Noble?," 66, in *The Philosophy of Nietzsche* (New York: Random House, 1954), 451.

6. Nietzsche, *Beyond Good and Evil*, "What Is Noble?," sec. 270, 596.

7. Nietzsche, *Beyond Good and Evil*, "What Is Noble?," sec. 270, 596.

8. "Actually, every major growth is accompanied by a tremendous crumbling and passing away: suffering, the symptoms of decline *belong* in times of tremendous

advances." Friedrich Nietzsche, Notes (1887), retrieved June 15, 2006, from http://www.edmaupin.com/somatic/nietzsche_wtp_bk_i.htm.

9. Nietzsche, *Beyond Good and Evil*, "Our Virtues," sec. 225, in *The Philosophy of Nietzsche*, 530.

10. Nietzsche, *The Genealogy of Morals*, trans. Horace B. Samuel, "Ascetic Ideals," Essay 3, sec. 28, in *The Philosophy of Nietzsche*, 792.

11. Nietzsche, *Thus Spake Zarathustra*, trans. Thomas Common, Third Part, "Old and New Tables," sec. 29, in *The Philosophy of Nietzsche*, 240.

12. Epicurus, *Letter to Menoeceus*, in *From Plato to Derrida*, 4th ed., ed. Forrest E. Baird and Walter Kaufmann (Upper Saddle River, N.J.: Prentice Hall, 2003), 251.

13. Ludwig Wittgenstein, *Tractatus Logico-Philosophicus*, 6.4311, retrieved January 13, 2006, from http://www.gutenberg.org/dirs/etext04/tloph10.txt.

14. Epicurus, *Letter to Menoeceus*, 251.

15. Plato, *Apology*, trans. Benjamin Jowett, retrieved January 12, 2006, from http://classics.mit.edu/Plato/apology.html.

16. To the Christian who believes in eternal damnation, this is likely to seem an incomplete set of possibilities, but what most people dread about death is its finitude, the end it signifies to earthly being, not its prospect for burning in hell. For the believer, this latter possibility may be a spur to clean up his or her earthly act, now or in the future, but it is not why people typically think of death as the ultimate evil.

17. Aristotle, *Ethics*, bk. 3, chap. 6 (emphasis added).

18. George Santayana, *Soliloquies in England*, 1922, "War Shrines," retrieved January 12, 2006, from http://www.quotationspage.com/quote/572.html.

19. Marcus Aurelius, retrieved January 12, 2006, from http://www.brainyquote.com/quotes/authors/m/marcus_aurelius.html.

20. Jean-Paul Sartre, Existentialism, in *Philosophers at Work: Issues and Practice of Philosophy*, ed. Elliot D. Cohen (Fort Worth, Tex.: Harcourt, 2000), 447.

21. Francis Bacon, *Novum Organum*, Aphorisms (bk. 1), 43, retrieved January 12, 2006, from http://www.constitution.org/bacon/nov_org.htm.

22. Bacon, *Novum Organum*, Aphorisms, 60.

23. Arthur Schopenhauer, "The World as Will and Idea," in *Aesthetics: A Critical Anthology*, ed. George Dickie and Richard Sclafani (New York: St. Martin's Press, 1977), 716.

24. By the sublime, Schopenhauer means taking a disinterested stance toward objects that are perceived as terrible and threatening to the will, for example, a violent storm.

25. Schopenhauer, "The World as Will and Idea," 720–21.

26. Schopenhauer, "The World as Will and Idea," 716.

27. Schopenhauer, "The World as Will and Idea," 720.

28. Epictetus, *Encheiridion*, in Baird and Kaufmann, *From Plato to Derrida*, 261.

29. David Hume, *Treatise of Human Nature*, ed. L. A. Selby-Bigge (London: Oxford University Press, 1975), bk. 3: *Of Morals*, pt. 1, sec. 1.

3

BUILDING RESPECT

Some bad things happen of no fault of yours or anyone else's, such as a tsunami or a fatal disease. Other bad things may be of your own doing, such as forgetting to turn off the stove and burning down your house or driving recklessly and getting into a serious accident. Still other bad things are perpetrated by other people either on you or on others, such as when you are robbed, your spouse is sexually assaulted, an innocent man is found guilty in a court of law, or an elected official whom you believed in violates the public trust.

In the midst of something shitty, it's easy enough to become contemptuous and bitter, easy enough to damn yourself, another, or the universe, easy enough to explode in heated rage at that "no good piece of shit," to bleakly withdraw from "the sucky universe," or to wallow in dark depression over your worthless existence.

The fallacy here comes in three self-disturbing variations that can be distinguished according to the object damned:

- Global damnation ("Damn the universe!")
  If something shitty happens, then the world itself is shitty.
- Damnation of self ("Damn me!")
  If I screw up or do something shitty, then I am myself a worthless screw-up or shit.
- Damnation of others ("Damn you!")
  If someone else screws up or does something shitty, then he or she is a worthless screw-up or shit.

The second and third of these damnation rules can easily be shown to lead to absurdity:

> Refutation: Doing something worthless doesn't equate to *being* (totally) worthless. Otherwise, everyone would be worthless.

Do you know anyone who hasn't done any evil deeds or hasn't ever screwed up? Remember, as St. Thomas Aquinas emphasized, it's the nature of humans to err; otherwise, we would all be gods. The human *self* cannot be reduced without remainder to a bad deed.

Of course, philosophers have had conflicting views about the nature of the *self*. For example, according to René Descartes, a self is "a thinking thing," that is, an immaterial substance or soul that doubts, understands, affirms, denies, wills, refuses, imagines, and feels.[1] In contrast, for David Hume, what you call your self is "nothing but a bundle or collection of different perceptions" held together by your memories.[2] For Sartre, you are "a plan which is aware of itself" and that gets fulfilled over a lifetime. You are therefore nothing else than the totality of your acts, nothing else than your entire life.[3] For William James, you are the *sum total* of all that you *can* call yours, not only your body and your psychic powers but also your clothes, house, wife, children, ancestors, friends, reputation, works, lands, horses, yacht, and bank account.[4]

Notice that on none of these accounts would doing something worthless make your self entirely worthless. In Descartes' view, your soul would still continue to do what it's supposed to do, namely, think. In Hume's view, your self would simply include some more ideas in its bundle. For Sartre, you would still be defined by the *totality* of your actions over a lifetime. As for James, you would still have numerous things of value to call yours.

What of the world itself? Why isn't a world with tsunamis, Nazis, terrorists, child molesters, AIDS, Ebola, and a host of other shitty things itself a shitty world?

> Refutation: What's true of the part is not necessarily true of the whole. Otherwise, a machine with simple parts would itself be simple, a dish prepared with bitter ingredients (like pepper) would itself be bitter, water would be no wetter than the elements that compose it, a colony of ants would be just as benign as a single ant, you couldn't combine two colors to get a different color, and so on. The world does indeed have some bitter ingredients, but it can still be sweet.

Human misdeeds, natural disasters, and other perceived tragedies challenge our capacity for enduring happiness. Yet they present no impermeable impasses to cultivating self-esteem, a profound respect for others, and a deep-seated global reverence that transcends bitterness, contempt, and alienation.

GLOBAL DAMNATION

Antidotes to Global Damnation

Antidote 1
Instead of obsessing and whining about the evil shit, look toward the value, purpose, harmony, and beauty in the grander schema of things. (Leibniz, Rorty, Foucault, Derrida)

It is in this manner that the seventeenth-century philosopher Gottfried Leibniz saw the universe. For him, all things were composed of tiny life forces called monads (from the Greek meaning "unity"). These atomic building blocks of nature were not inert particles like those postulated by ancient Greek philosophers such as Democritus. Instead, they were active and alive, each doing their own thing in harmony with all the other monads in the universe, much like "several bands of musicians and choirs playing . . . perfectly together, by each following their own notes, in such a way that he who hears them all finds in them a harmony that is wonderful."[5]

If you just listened to a single note, you wouldn't hear the melody or the harmony. If you focused your attention on a dissonant chord, you would not see how it fit together with the rest of the notes and harmonies. Likewise, if you dwelled on the evil shit in isolation from the rest of the universe, you would miss the goodness and beauty in the coherent, harmonious, universal whole.[6]

So thought Leibniz. In fact, he went as far as to say that God created the best of all possible worlds. The stuff that seems evil are really necessary ingredients of a profoundly good whole since "an imperfection in the part may be required for a greater perfection in the whole," just as "the general of an army will prefer a great victory with a slight wound to a state of affairs without wound and without a victory."[7] So, if you discount the value of the grander things in life for that which is bleak, humdrum, or bland, you will have sold yourself short.

Now I don't say that you have to agree that every shitty thing is a blessing or that the world couldn't be improved. You can speculate all you want about these things, but just don't make the mistake of letting yourself get carried away by the shit so that you look no further beyond it.

The tragedies of life can be edifying. I learned a lot from the hurricane that destroyed my home and many of my personal treasures. The women about whom I spoke earlier who had her eyesight taken from her by an assailant in a seemingly pointless act of brutality ended up finding purpose and meaning through the ordeal.

Leibniz thought that the harmony of the universe was preestablished (by God), but you don't have to take this as truth. You might instead use your own creativity. Contemporary philosopher Richard Rorty said that we *make* worlds rather than *discover* them.[8] Similarly, as mentioned in chapter 1, postmodernists like Foucault have pointed to the possibility of interpreting reality through alternative "truth games." And so-called deconstructionists, like Jacques Derrida, have stressed the possibility of *de*constructing traditional systems of thought (dismantling them) in favor of new, creative ones.[9] You are free to construct your own worldview out of the notes and chords of the universe (or "monads" if you will) or to *de*construct your former interpretation. As in interpreting a work of abstract art, there can be different interpretations of the whole.[10]

You could, of course, choose to paint it black. You could interpret the world as dog-eat-dog and as rotten to the core, but what for? If you claim to be offering instruction, then you betray your point since instruction embodies knowledge, has positive merit, and seeks to improve the world. But it is futile to try to improve a universe that is rotten to the core. In the end, a bleak interpretation blocks your creative capacities and buries them alive.

On the other hand, painting reality using your full range of colors (instead of just black) releases your creative capacities and gives you a shot at profound happiness. The range of constructive interpretations is abundantly rich, and you have the power and intellect to paint it as beautifully as you want. That makes more sense.

Antidote 2

Embrace suffering and loss as universal truth instead of demanding what you can't have. Transcend self-pity with compassion for others in your same boat. (Buddha)

You also have the power to transcend universal evils and to live peacefully and serenely despite them. Such is the teaching of Buddha, who long ago realized the perils of demanding perfection. By virtue of being a finite human being in a universe in which all things are impermanent, it is unrealistic to crave more for yourself or your loved ones than what such a universe can offer. "Now this," said Buddha,

> is the noble truth of pain: birth is painful, old age is painful, sickness is painful, death is painful, sorrow, lamentation, dejection, and despair are painful. Contact with unpleasant things is painful. In short, the five groups of grasping [the body, feelings, ideas, volitions, and conscious awareness] are painful.[11]

In self-interestedly damning the universe for these inevitable conditions of life, you succeed only in defeating your own prospects for happiness. Instead of being at odds with the universe, better to acquiesce in it, better to accept and become one with it, better to let go of your blind craving for what you can never have, better to conceive suffering and loss as universal truth than to take it personally. So it is has been said that Buddha instructed a woman who was seeking medicine to revive her deceased little boy to fetch mustard seed from a house in which no one had died. In finding through her encounters that there was no such house, she relinquished her self-absorbed craving:

> Overcome with emotion, she went outside of the city, carried her son to the burning ground, and holding him in her arms, said: "Dear little son, I thought that you alone had been overtaken by this thing which men call death. But you are not the only one death has overtaken. This is a law common to all mankind. So saying, she cast her son away in the burning-ground."[12]

Casting off her self-pity, this woman was able to find peace. In Buddhist thinking, it is only through such self-transcendence and compassion (love) for others (and, ultimately, for all living things) that inner peace (nirvana) is attainable. Like the woman in the parable of the mustard seed, you do not stand alone in your suffering. It is the inevitable nature of the universe. Becoming one with the universe rather than declaring war on it is the way. Self-transcendent compassion is the way. This is a far cry from global damnation, which will only lead you to suffer more.

Don't get me wrong. Compassion for others can be a spur to action and change. No one is telling you to sit on your rump permitting evil to prevail when you can do something about it. But the important words here are "when you can do something about it." Remember Epictetus' antidote to demanding perfection: Don't sweat the stuff you can't do anything about.[13] Howling at the moon is a waste of time and energy. But there are many things you can do if you want to help change the world. You can change the world just by saying something polite to loved ones, like telling them that you love them. You can change the world by refusing to do things that hurt people, like being dishonest, violating their privacy, calling them names, or sundry other ways in which people commonly inflict pain. This is all part of what Buddha meant by having universal compassion. Resonate with the universe. It's a hell of a lot better than damning it.

Antidote 3
Instead of bemoaning your own misfortunes and shortcomings, embrace the goodness of others and of the world as your own. (James, Epictetus)

I mentioned earlier James's idea of the self. He says that it includes everything you *can* call yours. But according to James, you have considerable power over what you claim for yours. On the one hand, as just mentioned, Stoics like Epictetus tell you to concern yourself only with those things that are within your control. The Stoic approach, says James,

> proceeds altogether by exclusion. If I am Stoic, the goods I cannot appropriate cease to be *my* goods, and the temptation lies very near to deny that they are goods at all.[14]

For example, since you can't live forever, immortality is out of self-range. If you can't have the love, cooperation, or respect of certain people, then you can write them out of your life script and pay them no mind. By so narrowing your range of concern, you can make yourself invulnerable in the face of death or in the face of rejection and avoid considerable grief. But there is, says James, another, entirely opposite, positive way to proceed, namely, by way of expanding the self rather than contracting it:

> Sympathetic people . . . can feel a sort of delicate rapture in thinking that, however sick, ill-favored, mean-conditioned, and generally forsaken they may be, they yet are integral parts of the whole of this brave world, have a fellow's share in the strength of the dray-horses, the happiness of the young people, the wisdom of the wise ones, and are not altogether without part or lot in the fortunes of the Vanderbilts and the Hohenzollerns themselves. . . . He who, with Marcus Aurelius, can truly say, "O Universe, I wish all that thou wishest," has a self from which every trace of negativeness and obstructiveness has been removed—no wind can blow except to fill its sails.[15]

From this optimistic perspective, you can share in the joys of others as your own. Instead of looking on other people's good fortune with jealousy or envy, you can see them as part of your own world and delight in the goodness therein.

This is not inconsistent with Epictetus' approach, however. You can, after all, do both. You can refuse to disturb yourself over the things you can't control as well as find happiness in being an integral part of a universe that includes goodness. In James's terms, you can expand and contract your self to appropriately adjust for what you can and can't have. Now that's a double-edged antidote to a tendency to damn the universe.

Antidote 4

Say "Thou" to the universe instead of "It." Say "Thou" even to the "weeds" of the universe seamlessly bound up with it. (Buber)

Philosopher Martin Buber had a neat idea about how to resonate with the universe. He distinguished between I-Thou and I-It relationships.[16] When you look on something (say, a tree) as a separate existence (an object existing at a particular place and time) and having a specific use or function (for example, providing shade from the sun or a source of firewood), then you are in an I-It relation with that thing. Have you ever walked through a forest spraying yourself with insect repellent, watching your every step, and taking care that you don't get into some poison ivy, step on a snake, or get scratched by a tree branch? You are in an I-It mode.

I confess that I have had this unpleasant experience. On the other hand, there are three large queen palms that stand tall in my front yard. I have sometimes perceived them as they coalesced with themselves, the landscape, the sky, and with all else that fills this tropical vista. In my communion with nature, I have felt all partitions vanish. No longer was I separate from nature and nature from me, but I was in nature and nature in me. Weeds sprouting up beneath the palms were not things to get rid of but instead were seamlessly involved in a single, unified whole. I brought with me no agenda, no lawn mowers, no cutting tools. Nature ceased then to be It and reverently became Thou.

Now to the point: Thou canst be damned. It's only when the world becomes It that you can say damn It. Try damning Thou. You can't damn that which you are revering. Another antidote to global damnation is to revere the universe: I-Thou the world. As Buber admits, you must soon come back to practical reality. I have since sharpened my cutting tools and pulled out weeds in my front lawn. Nevertheless, having an I-Thou encounter with nature now and then can be a healthy reminder that the universe is one coherent, royal whole, seamlessly bound up with all else, including *you*. You are in that world, and that world is in you. Even the weeds of the world—and these are many and sundry in the mainstream of living—are seamlessly annexed to that same world and can still be called Thou. This should give you pause the next time you are inclined to damn the universe.

Antidote 5
Instead of whining about the shit in the world, do something to make it better. (Buddha, Kaplan)

I hope you will try "Thou-ing" the universe instead of damning it. But you don't have to revere the universe in order not to damn it. These are, after all, opposites, and between opposites there are other shades of reality just like between black and white there are many different colors. So, you say, maybe the universe doesn't suck altogether—it does indeed contain good things—but there are also some very bad things in it too. Suppose we say that. That still doesn't amount to damning the universe, right?

For example, the ancient Persian philosopher Mani taught that the world consisted of two opposing forces—good and evil. Evil is rooted in matter, while good is in the spiritual, rational nature of human beings. This became a basis of a religious perspective, Manichaeism, according to which the ultimate goal of human beings is to free themselves from the oppression of evil, which weighs down the soul.

This view was resurrected with less Platonic overtones more recently in Judaic reconstructivist thinking such as that of Mordecai Kaplan.[17] Like Mani, Kaplan thinks that good is to be identified with the rational, purposive elements in nature (and ultimately with God), while evil is irrational and chaotic. Since organized, purposive efforts usually win out of disorganized chaotic ones, Kaplan thinks that good will triumph over evil in the end: "We say: 'Where there is a will there is a way.' By that we record the experience that, despite the obstacles to a determined will presented by circumstance which are fortuitous, or which are less informed by purpose or plan, the determined will is bound to win out in the end." So it is up to you to make "the practical effort to reduce the amount of evil in the world, so as to leave the world the better for our having live in it."[18]

Here then is another antidote to global damnation. Instead of damning the universe, become active in the fight against evil. In damning the universe, you are simply giving up on the world, tossing any hope to the wind. If the universe is truly worthless, then there is nothing you can do about it. That's why this fallacy is so damn depressing. On the other hand, if you enlist yourself in the cause of world improvement, you aren't going to rid the world of all the evils, but you will at least make it better. That's really a good reason not to give up on the universe, right?

So how might you become an activist on the side of good? I already mentioned some of Buddha's ideas. And you can, of course, devote your time to constructive works (which you can define for yourself). But even if you stop whining about the shit in the world and kick back and enjoy a movie or a day at the beach, the world will be that much better. Make the world a better place. Stop damning the world and do something about it.

To make the world better, it is sometimes necessary to identify something to improve on. So, as I stressed before, I am not saying that you should turn a blind eye to evil—just as long as you don't obsess over the dirt at the expense of seeing the clean spots. Of course, you will need to say what is wrong before you can fix it. As long as you don't confuse "this or that is bad" with "the world itself is bad," you should be all right. Stick to rating things *in* the world rather than *the world* itself. "There is shit in world" and "The world is shit" do not express equivalent ideas. Don't confuse these two distinct levels of discourse.

A popular rejoinder to this rational prescription is, "Well maybe the (whole) world doesn't suck, but my (whole) life does." Here again, the statement "Something shitty happened to me" is not equivalent to "My (whole) life is shit." In inferring the second statement from the first, you are assuming that what's true of a single event in your life must also be true of your entire life. But, as Leibniz made clear, this is a fallacious inference. If your marriage ended in divorce after one year, that surely wouldn't mean that your life also ended in divorce after one year. So this rejoinder won't get you very far. You should instead stick to rating the events *in* your life, not your life itself.

DAMNATION OF SELF

The second form of damnation that is poison for the soul is damnation of self. Here you confound failure with *being a failure*, performing an unworthy act with *being unworthy*, making a mistake with *being a mistake*, and doing something shitty with *being shitty*.

This fallacy prophetically leads to further screwing up. If you tell yourself that you are a totally worthless screw-up, you will set yourself up for further failure, for if you are a total failure, then you will functionally lack the capacity for success. Screw-ups are expected to screw up. Isn't that what makes them screw-ups?

The more you denigrate yourself, the less you are likely to perform well. This is because you are effectively prescribing failure to yourself. In calling yourself worthless, you are telling yourself that you *must* screw up. That is, after all, what screw-ups do.

When I was a young boy of about seven, my teacher invited us students to wear costumes to school on Halloween. One little boy dressed up like a tiger. When a little girl went up to him and began to pet him, he attacked her and bit her. When the teacher confronted him, he defensively retorted, "That's what tigers are supposed to do." The teacher punished him by taking away his stripes and making him sit in time-out for the remainder of the day.

In a sense, the boy was right. If he were really a tiger, then biting the little girl would have been appropriate. But he really wasn't a tiger. He was only wearing the stripes of one. Still, that didn't matter as long as he had convinced himself that he was a tiger.

It's similar with playing the part of a failure. Once you step into the shoes of a failure, you are obliged to walk in them. This is what you *should* be doing as a failure, namely, fail. And like the little boy, you now have a prepared excuse for failing: "That's what failures are supposed to do." The fact that you are not *really* a failure may matter less than the fiction of thinking that you are one. This is because you will still suffer the consequences of failing just as the boy suffered the consequences of having bitten another classmate.

But the little boy was jolted back into reality when the teacher took away his stripes and sat him in time-out. Unfortunately, the lessons of a self-proclaimed failure tend to support continuing to play the role of failure. The more you fail, the more you convince yourself that this is your true self.

So what will it take to help the self-proclaimed failure out of his costume?

The answer to this question depends largely on how *human* nature is to be conceived: What, in the first place, is the philosophical basis of human worth? This question has been pondered by philosophers from antiquity, and their answers have been various. Still, their responses yield useful antidotes to self-damnation.

Antidotes to Self-Damnation

Antidote 1

Accept your self-worth unconditionally, not as a variable that changes with successes, failures, or the approval and disapproval of others. (Kant)

Some philosophers have located the source of human worth in the capacity for rational self-determination (autonomy). For example, the eighteenth-century philosopher Immanuel Kant says that

> rational beings . . . are called persons, because their very nature points them out as ends in themselves, that is as something which must not be used merely as means . . . (and is an object of respect).[19]

According to Kant, because people have the capacity for rational decision making, they have a dignity that should be respected. Since people, unlike mere objects, can rationally determine their own courses of action, they shouldn't be manipulated and used as though they were just things. Kant puts this by saying that human beings, persons, are not "mere means," that is, mere instruments for the satisfaction of our desires. For example, this is precisely what made slavery so abominable. It degraded human beings by treating them like mere objects to be used and manipulated to satisfy the selfish desires of their "masters."

In contrast to mere objects, the rational nature of persons does not depend on how useful they are or on how well they satisfy someone's desires or purposes. For example, when your car gets old and run down, you might trade it in for a newer model. But people are not like cars. There is something wrong with "trading in" your spouse for a newer model when he or she gets older or less virile. This is because the value of a person is a *constant*, not something that can be diminished (or increased) with its usefulness.

Kant sums up his antidote against the degradation of human worth in the form of an *unconditional command of self- and other-acceptance*, which goes like this:

> So act as to treat humanity, whether in your own person or in that of any other, in every case as an end in itself, never as means only.[20]

Notice that Kant is saying that you should not only treat other people as ends in themselves but also extend the same respect to *yourself*. But, obviously, in damning yourself, what you are doing is violating this command to unconditionally respect yourself. You are denying what is yours by virtue of your rational nature. You are denying your self-worth as though your worth as a person could be subtracted from you like some object.[21]

You are telling yourself that if you screw up, then you are worthless. You are telling yourself that your worth does not extend beyond the immediate purpose you failed to fulfill; so, like a malfunctioning gadget, you put yourself out with the trash. Even malfunctioning cars are often repaired and put back on the road. In damning yourself, you are saying that you're not even worthy of repair.

A very common form of self-damnation is *achievement damnation*.[22] This amounts to telling yourself that you must achieve your mark in order to have worth as a person. For example, athletes not uncommonly tie their self-worth to winning. So if they fall short of their mark, they damn themselves. As a result, even when they are on a winning streak, they suffer a good deal of anxiety, for they know that they can be flying high today and shot down tomorrow. And when the stakes are conceived in terms of your self-worth, the fear of failing becomes ominous.

Let me illustrate further with a former student of mine who was taking a philosophy course I was teaching. This particular student had a propensity to cheat on exams. Catching him red-handedly in the act of copying off his neighbor's exam, I brought him to my office to speak. After a while, he began to open up about his reasons for cheating. He also informed me that he had cheated on the other two exams he had taken in the course. He went on to explain how he had been cheating his way through all his other classes as well. When I asked him why he resorted to cheating instead of simply studying, he told me that, if he cheated and failed, then it was alright, but if he studied and failed, then that would mean that he *really* was a failure. So he preferred to cheat rather than to risk failing on his own.

What did I do about this intriguing case? I spent some time helping him to see the self-damning rule that undergirded his fear of failing, and I worked with him on its refutation. Then I gave him an appropriate behavioral assignment. I asked him to study for the final exam, and when the day came to take the exam, I seated him in the front row, where he couldn't cheat without being discovered. Glorious day—he ended up with the highest grade in the class on the exam.

Kant's antidote? Accept your self-worth unconditionally, as an unconditional command. Regardless of whether you win or lose or succeed or fail, you are still a person with dignity—come hell or high water.

Antidote 2

Be true to your sentient nature; increase your lasting pleasure through unconditional self-acceptance. (Epicurus, Bentham, Mill)

Some philosophers have rejected Kant's idea that reason is the source of human worth. For example, so-called hedonist[23] philosophers like Epicurus, Jeremy Bentham, and John Stuart Mill thought that it is the *sentient* nature of people that gives them worth, that is, their ability to experience pain and pleasure. For these philosophers, what makes our lives valuable is pleasure, and what diminishes this value is pain. Since we are sentient beings, it is wrong to cause us pain and right to promote our pleasure. We should therefore act to increase the pleasure in our own lives and in the lives of others and to diminish the pain. Pleasure, Epicurus says, "is the beginning and the end of the blessed life."[24]

This means that you must not degrade and belittle yourself because this is needless infliction of pain and suffering. Self-damnation is the opposite of what you as a sentient being should be doing: increasing your pleasure and diminishing your pain.

This doesn't mean that you should always do what's pleasant. Some things that are pleasant in the short term may produce long-term suffering, such as taking a dangerous, addictive drug like crack. On the other hand, some things that are painful in the short term can lead to more enduring pleasure in the long run, such as undergoing painful surgery to stop the progress of a life-threatening or debilitating disease. But self-damnation is senseless infliction of pain. It typically has no redeeming value in the long run. In fact, it promotes further suffering by leading you to avoid taking constructive actions in the future. If you think yourself worthless, you will tend to act the part and pay the price in pain and suffering and missed future opportunities.

On the other hand, *unconditional self-acceptance*, that is, accepting yourself even when you screw up or don't get the approval of significant others, is typically the best way to avoid self-inflicted pain. As Albert Ellis says, "All people strongly wish to perform well and to win significant others' approving. If they unconditionally accept themselves as 'good' humans even when they are performing badly and relating poorly, they can minimize their anxietizing and depressing."[25] For the hedonistic philosophers, this is a winning philosophy of life, and I would agree.

I would add, though, that being a hedonist doesn't mean you can't also accept Kant's unconditional command to treat yourself as well as others as an end in itself and not as a mere means. In fact, both of these philosophies support accepting yourself unconditionally. Kant thinks this human worth is based on the rational nature of human beings, while hedonists think it is based on their sentient nature. But human beings are actually both rational and sentient. This is in fact what old Aristotle meant when he defined us as "rational animals." For Aristotle, we have worth and dignity deriving from our rational nature, but insofar as we are also animals, we must tend to our sentient nature in the practical affairs of life.

Antidote 3
Love yourself as your own best friend; assess your accomplishments rationally and wish yourself well. (Aristotle)

While Aristotle did not regard pleasure as the primary thing that made life desirable, he still recognized its importance. For this philosopher, the most rational and rewarding form of self-assessment avoided two extremes: vanity and mock modesty. The vain person claims greater achievements than he has actually attained. The mock-modest person disclaims his achievements or belittles them. But the virtuous person avoids both extremes by "owning to what he has and neither more nor less."[26]

Self-damnation is an extreme form of mock modesty. It is a false, over-generalized, unrealistic *under*assessment of self-worth. The person who unconditionally accepts herself does not confuse her personal self-worth with attaining the approval of significant others or with achievements. As a result, she is able to realistically assess her accomplishments. She does not take failing at something as a mark of worthlessness. Instead, she strives to do better in the future.

In fact, Aristotle says that a person should love himself as his own best friend:

> For men say that one ought to love best one's best friend, and a man's best friend is one who wishes well to the object of his wish for his sake, even if no one is to know of it; and these attributes are found most of all in a man's attitude towards himself, and so are all the other attributes by which a friend is defined. . . . All the proverbs too agree with this, e.g., "a single soul," and "what friends have is common property," and "friendship is equality," and "charity begins at home"; for all these marks will be found most in a man's relation to himself; he is his own best friend and ought to love himself best.[27]

According to Aristotle, your true self is your *rational* self. Self-love therefore involves a commitment to living rationally. Obviously, this would include a commitment to rational self-assessment. A person who truly loved himself would not berate and degrade himself since this is to fly in the face of reason. Be your own best friend. Whatever you do, wish yourself well.

Antidote 4

Stop treating yourself like mindless, inert garbage. You're a thinking, conscious, self-aware being capable of conceiving and fashioning your own, unique future. Act like it. (Descartes, Sartre)

In case you still doubt your worth, you might do some comparative shopping. Consider for a moment a state-of-the-art computer. It can certainly process a lot more data and a lot faster than a human mind. It is really a very impressive machine. But there is something you can do with your mind that the computer can't: think.

The computer does not have a conscious existence. It manipulates strings of symbols extraordinarily well, but it is not aware of what it's doing. It's a grand machine. You, on the other hand, have a conscious life. You can think.[28]

For some philosophers, your conscious existence is what makes you a person. Descartes shares his thoughts:

> I find here that thought is an attribute that belongs to me; it alone cannot be separated from me. I am, I exist, that is certain. But how often? Just when I think; for it might possibly be the case if I ceased entirely to think, that I should likewise cease altogether to exist . . . . [T]o speak accurately I am not more than a thing which thinks, that is to say a mind or a soul, or an understanding, or a reason. . . . What is a thing which thinks? It is a thing which doubts, understands, affirms, denies, wills, refuses, which also imagines and feels.[29]

You are essentially a thinking thing, says Descartes. That is what is essential to you. Take away your legs, and you can't walk, but you still can imagine yourself existing—albeit without legs. But take away your mind, and you're a goner! This is why we lament when a loved one falls into a persistent vegetative state. The body of the person may live on, but in some very real sense the person we once knew and loved is gone.[30]

It is easy enough for us to overlook the magnificence of the human mind when we are wrapped up in some mundane problem. We do not ordinarily say to ourselves, "Well at least I still have my mind, and what an awesome thing this is!" Instead, we damn ourselves for messing up or for losing something not nearly as precious. It is usually only when we see others lose their cognitive abilities (for example, when someone is stricken with Alzheimer's disease) that we are reminded of how lucky we really are. But why wait? Affirm your value today and keep reminding yourself through thick and thin. Remember what Descartes said. You wouldn't exist without your conscious mind. Celebrate your mind.

Jean-Paul Sartre drives home Descartes' point from an existential perspective. "Man," says Sartre,

> has a greater dignity than a stone or table . . . man first of all is the being who hurls himself toward a future and who is conscious of imagining himself as being in the future. Man is at the start a plan which is aware of itself, rather than a patch of moss, a piece of garbage, or a cauliflower.[31]

For Sartre, your life starts with your conscious awareness of yourself continuing through time, as a work in progress, and it ends when this self-consciousness ceases. Your life is a series of undertakings fashioned from your conscious choices. You are what you will yourself to be according to your conscious plan. What gives you dignity is this freedom to choose stemming from your conscious awareness. A patch of moss, a piece of garbage, or a cauliflower doesn't have a subjective life through which it projects a plan out into the future. It has no such dignity because it has no ability to plot its own course. But you are a special sort of being because you have such an ability stemming from your conscious self-awareness.

In damning yourself, you surrender this dignity; you cop out on your responsibility to forge ahead into the future. Easier to be a piece of garbage since garbage doesn't have to make any choices. It is put out for trash and hauled off. But you are not a piece of garbage. You have a dignity that transcends such a dead, insensible, inert existence.

In damning yourself, you act in *bad faith*. This means that you lie to yourself about your self-worth. You cannot assert your total worthlessness without denying that you are a conscious, self-aware work in process since this is precisely what gives you your worth and dignity in the first place. But the more you deny or doubt this, the more evident it becomes that you are indeed such a conscious, self-aware being since doubting and denying are themselves self-conscious activities. Only in bad faith, therefore, can you relegate yourself to the status of a piece of garbage. Only by lying to yourself can you escape your freedom and responsibility to forge ahead, affirming your worth and dignity with each successive, conscious, self-aware decision.

Antidote 5

Instead of withdrawing from life for fear of failing, live and learn from your past mistakes. (Hume, Ellis)

But what if you act and fail, falling flat on your face? Does that not lessen your self-worth, if not destroy it?

No. Failing is an essential part of trying. And if you don't try, you damn well won't succeed. Unless you get off your rump and try, you will, in Sartre's immortal words, end up defining yourself negatively "as a disappointed dream, as miscarried hopes, as vain expectations."[32]

Not only that; failing can be a useful learning experience. Knowing what doesn't work can often be a useful prelude to finding out what doesn't work. In his famous discussion of reasoning about factual matters, Hume bluntly stated the point:

> It is certain that the most ignorant and stupid peasants—nay infants, nay even brute beasts—improve by experience, and learn the qualities of natural objects, by observing the effects which result from them. When a child has felt the sensation of pain from touching the flame of a candle, he will be careful not to put his hand near any candle; but will expect a similar effect from a cause which is similar in its sensible qualities and appearance.[33]

And hear too these immortal words of Hume's predecessor, John Locke:

> Let us suppose the mind to be, as we say, white paper, void of all characters, without any ideas; how comes it to be furnished? Whence comes it by that vast store, which the busy and boundless fancy of man has painted on it with an almost endless variety? Whence has it all the materials of reason and knowledge? To this I answer, in one word, from EXPERIENCE; in that all our knowledge is founded and from that it ultimately derives itself.[34]

According to Locke, without experience, you would have nothing to think about. You would literally know nothing. For Hume, you could not make any judgments about any matters of fact without first having had experience of them. You could not tell that touching the flame of the candle would cause you pain before having put your hand on the flame, unless of course someone else were to tell you. But anyone else who had this knowledge would have learned it either through her own experience or else eventually through someone else's. In the end, experience—living and learning—provides your basis for making practical decisions.

This experience includes not just pleasant ones but also ones that are unpleasant. Getting burned every so often by putting your hand in the proverbial fires of life can be a great teacher. You perform poorly on a job interview and use your experience to correct your mistakes on the next interview; you drop out of school, have a difficult time finding a desirable job, and decide to return to school and devote yourself to academic excellence; or you get in trouble with the law and decide to go straight. The list of lessons you can learn through the trials of life is infinite. Whether you heed these lessons is largely up to you. If you take failure as signifying lack of self-worth, then you'll learn nothing. On the other hand, if you look on it as an unavoidable, useful component of learning and growing in life, then you can be the greater gainer in the long run.

This doesn't mean that you should deliberately sabotage yourself, set yourself up for failure, or do something that causes you serious hardship when you know better. If you know better, then do better. But if you mess up, you can still gain from the mess you have made. Human beings are imperfect by nature; we are born to screw up. Screw up gracefully. Accept yourself and learn from your mistakes.

The insights of Locke and Hume underlie the core concepts of learning theory and in particular of contemporary cognitive-behavior therapy. This type of therapy (including the logic-based type discussed in this book) assumes that people's psychological problems are sustained largely through self-defeating behavioral responses to situations. It therefore helps folks to expose these problematic responses and to learn alternative, more adaptive ones.

One common form of cognitive-behavioral technique is that of *homework assignments* in which clients are asked to *do* certain things in addressing cognitive-behavioral issues. For example, I once had a client who suffered from extreme anxiety stemming from approval damnation. A psychiatric nurse, he feared doing something "wrong" that would meet with disapproval from his supervisor. He mentioned to me how much he liked picturesque ties with tropical scenes painted on them, but he was deterred from buying and wearing such a tie to work for fear that his supervisor might disapprove. So, his homework assignment was to buy and wear one to work. Eventually, the client bought the tie, wore it to work, and unexpectedly received compliments on it from his supervisor.

As part of my own training and certification in rational-emotive behavior therapy, I was asked to perform a "shame attacking" exercise, that is, to do something that I was ashamed of in order to refute the idea that I must have the approval of others in order to retain my self-worth. During my lunch break, I went to a restaurant in downtown Orlando (where my training program was being held) and struck up a one-way conversation with a waiter. I spoke to her in great detail about experiences and intimate encounters we had together. The poor woman stared at me as though I were completely insane. In reality, I didn't know her, and she didn't know me. But it really didn't matter anyway what she thought of me.

"Live and learn" is not a trite advisement. Much of what causes people's headaches is due to inexperience. My client didn't expect that he could do something "outlandish" like wearing a loud tie and still get the approval of his supervisor, but even *if* he didn't garner that approval, what difference would it have made anyway?

Nor did it really matter whether a complete stranger thought that I was crazy. Yet if I lived my life, as so many of us do, worrying about what insignificant people might think of me, then I would never have done many of the most rewarding things I have done in my life—including becoming a philosopher.

It is, of course, preferable to have the approval of others—maybe even of complete strangers—and, while failure enlightens, it would be nice if we could always learn from others without experiencing it firsthand for ourselves. But to demand these things in this imperfect world is unrealistic. You can choose to retreat from this world and to define yourself negatively through inactivity; or you can choose to venture out into the sea of life, knowing full well that you will sometimes falter. But a seasoned captain will learn from his exploits and will use his knowledge to become a better seaman. The venture is much more exciting than staying on shore where nothing is gained. When you falter, welcome the experience as a guide to future growth and prosperity, not as an opportunity to sink your own ship by condemning it.

Antidote 6

Instead of condemning yourself to burn in hell, accept your divinely conferred self-worth and use it to do good works. (Aquinas)

If you also want a religious justification for accepting yourself, you don't have to look very far. Religious thinkers from antiquity have stressed the sanctity of human life. Insofar as God creates only good things, human beings have worth as creatures of God. In addition, human beings naturally possess reason, which, as St. Thomas says, "is nothing else than an imprint on us of the Divine light."[35]

This is not to say that human reason is perfect. It is senseless for beings imperfect by nature to demand perfection. At the same time, it's equally senseless to berate yourself as worthless. As a creature of God infused with the Divine light of reason, you are blessed. Thank the Lord for His special gift: accept yourself unconditionally.

This too is the first step toward "atonement for your sins." You can't even begin to work toward constructive change if you don't acknowledge your inalienable, God-given ability to do good works. In damning yourself, you have already condemned yourself to burn in hell. There's no salvation for the damned. Don't be damned; be self-accepting.

Unconditional self-acceptance should not be mistaken for vanity, and there is no sin in it. As St. Thomas said, "The desire for glory does not, of itself, denote a sin: but the desire for empty or vain glory denotes a sin: for it is sinful to desire anything vain."[36] As mentioned, the vain person has an overinflated idea of his accomplishments. To accept yourself unconditionally rather means that you have a realistic idea of your accomplishments and you do not confuse these with your self-worth. As Kant emphasized, your self-worth is a constant; it's not a function of your accomplishments. Vain people usually do not accept themselves unconditionally. That's why they try to build themselves up by inflating their accomplishments.

DAMNING OTHERS

Antidotes to Damnation of Others

Antidote 1
Stick to rating other people's behavior rather than their persons. Adopt a moral theory of your choice to affirm the worth and dignity of other persons. (Kant, Sartre, Locke, Aquinas, Aristotle, Plato)

The philosophical perspectives I have already discussed, which justify self-worth, can also be harnessed against the tendency to damn *others*. Kant's point that people are ends in themselves and not mere means should give you pause against objectifying another human being. Did you ever notice that people often call other human beings dehumanizing names before they act aggressively toward them. "Why, you no good piece of shit!" or some equivalent dehumanizing phrase is often spoken by an aggressor just before he "flushes it." The rule "Anyone who treats me unjustly is a piece of shit" joined with the report "He treated me unfairly" yields "He's a piece of shit." Just add the behavioral rule "Shit must be flushed," and voila. You have a violent assault perpetrated on another human being.

Kant's antidote to the rescue. Treat people as ends in themselves, not as mere objects. Therefore, don't flush human beings. They are rational, autonomous beings, not inert chunks of disposable matter.

This does not mean that you shouldn't condemn the deed. "What you did was really very shitty" is not equivalent to "*You* are shitty." The first leaves the dignity of the deed-doer intact; the second confuses the dirty deed with the doer. The first, unlike the second, is consistent with a respectful resolution of a grievance within a community of "ends in themselves."

This is why moral philosophers from antiquity have attempted to develop rational standards, so-called moral theories, for making moral judgments. These theories have carefully distinguished between damnation of others and correct moral appraisal. For example, Kant stressed acting according to the right motive, which he defined in terms of intrinsic respect for persons, for example, helping others because it's the right thing to do and not because you might be rewarded in some way for it. In contrast, hedonist philosophers have stressed promoting pleasure and minimizing pain among affected parties. Existentialists like Sartre have stressed human, conscious self-awareness. Other philosophers, such as John Locke, have taken a "natural law" perspective, recognizing certain inalienable human rights such as life, liberty, and property. Others have stressed the importance of emotions such as caring and empathic understanding in satisfying human desires and needs.[37] Still others, notably St. Thomas, have based morality on God's "Eternal Law." Still others, such as Plato and Aristotle, have focused on the rational capacities of human beings.

But none of these theories condones total devaluation of another human being. To the contrary, all of them have recognized the inherent worth and dignity of humanity, and they have accordingly attempted to provide rational standards for deriving respectful resolution of interpersonal problems. From among these varying perspectives, you may choose to regard your compatriots as the following:

- Ends in themselves
- Bearers of inalienable rights
- Sentient beings

- Conscious, self-aware beings
- Foci of needs and desires
- Imprints of the Divine
- Rational beings

Now, regardless of which of these views floats your boat,[38] their point is to affirm and protect the inherent value and dignity of human life, not to demoralize and damn it. In fact, the core basis of having moral standards and making moral criticisms is to guide human behavior toward a satisfactory life in common, in a manner that respects this inherent human dignity. When you call the guy who stole your car a worthless shit, in what way are you guiding anyone's behavior? Do you want to punish him for being a worthless shit or for stealing your car? Obviously, it is for stealing the car. In damning the *entire* person instead of the theft, you miss the point of moral assessment in such a context.

In domestic quarrels, the failure to aim condemnatory remarks at the deed rather than the doer not infrequently leads to self-defeating results. Verbal assaults lead to physical assaults and terminate in criminal convictions and divorce proceedings. In the workplace, there is little recourse to charges of insubordination for calling your boss a worthless shit. On the other hand, denouncing his discriminatory promotion practices can be successfully argued in a court of law. On the highway, damnation of other motorists can spawn road rage and turn deadly.

Antidote 2

For the sake of your own peace and happiness, stop damning others; treat them instead with the same dignity and respect with which you would want to be treated. (Hobbes)

So, given its self-destructive character, why do people so often damn others? It is, after all, hard to deny the human tendency to do this.

Perhaps this tendency toward damnation is a preprogrammed human response to environmental danger. By making a sweeping condemnation of someone perceived to be a threat in some way, you are able to protect yourself from this person—either by attacking this person or by avoiding him. Along these lines, the sixteenth-century philosopher Thomas Hobbes maintained that human beings were motivated primarily by a self-protective, survival instinct. In fact, Hobbes went so far as to say that, in a state of nature, where there was no central government to keep the peace, this instinct would lead to a dog-eat-dog state of "war of all against all" in which human lives would be "solitary, poor, nasty, brutish, and short."[39]

The human tendency to damn others appears to fit Hobbes's characterization of humans as self-protective creatures who perceive others largely as threats to their survival. But Hobbes also emphasized the need of people to live peacefully and respectfully with one another. As long as you are at war with your neighbor, said Hobbes, the outlook for your own survival is bleak. Hobbes's solution was to have a strong central government that would maintain law and order.

As long as you go about damning others when you perceive them to be in some way a threat to your survival or personal welfare, then, for that long you will not live peacefully and happily. To exit this precarious state of nature will require rigorous self-governance over your irrational tendency to damn your compatriots. Whether on the highway, at work, at home, or in social gatherings, you should exercise strong central control over your tendency to damn others. Someone who insults you may have spoken indiscreetly, but that doesn't make her a "no good, rotten bitch"; the motorist tailgating you is violating traffic safety laws but is still a person, not a stinky pile of garbage; and the person who stood you up last night is not a slithering snake in the grass.

Hobbes sums up his antidote in one familiar formulation: "Do not that to another, which you would not have done to thyself."[40] Otherwise, your own peace and happiness will be breached. If you go about damning others, you can well expect them to do the same back. Since denouncing another as worthless inevitably leads to aggressive and disrespectful treatment of them, you defeat your own self-protective instinct by going about damning your compatriot.

Antidote 3

View people's moral character in terms of habits that can be changed instead of as fixed, inborn properties. (Aristotle)

Still, aren't there some people who are evil just as there are others who are good?

First, notice that calling someone *evil* means that the person is *morally* deficient, not that the person is deficient in *every* respect. For example, if anyone was evil, surely Adolf Hitler was, but he also had some positive, nonmoral attributes, such as his artistic ability. Further, it's not strictly true that anyone can be *totally* evil. This would imply that the person *never* acted morally or had kind thoughts, which is usually an unjustified assumption. So what does it mean to say that someone is evil?

You need look no further than Aristotle's analysis of moral virtue and vice to find a useful answer. According to Aristotle,

> By doing the acts that we do in our transactions with other men, we become just or unjust, and by doing the acts that we do in the presence of danger, and being habituated to feel fear or confidence, we become brave or cowardly. The same is true of appetites and feelings of anger; some men become temperate and good-tempered, others self-indulgent and irascible, by behaving in one way or the other in the appropriate circumstances.[41]

Aristotle is saying that people are not born good or bad; they get into good habits or bad ones depending on what kinds of acts they perform. For example, you are not a liar because you have occasionally told a lie. On the other hand, you become a liar by getting into the habit of lying. To be a liar means that, as a result of repeatedly saying false things with the intent to deceive, you have developed a habit or disposition to perform this deceitful behavior.[42] The extent to which a person is good or bad is therefore the extent to which the person has formed good or bad habits. This means that calling someone good or bad is always a generalization about the quality of a person's behavioral habits. So why not cut to the chase and address these good or bad habits?

In the first place, the main point of calling someone good or bad is that of guiding human behavior. For example, as philosopher P. H. Nowell-Smith explains,

> The point of telling you that Jones is a good or a bad man is that you should imitate or not imitate Jones, that you should or should not give Jones the job or do whatever else might be in question.[43]

But, in giving moral advice to others (or to yourself), it is surely better to be specific about what personal habits you should or should not imitate or otherwise choose to support. If you are having a spat with your spouse and in the process tell him that he's evil, what have you accomplished besides insulting him? On the other hand, in telling him that he has a habit of losing his temper or of being dishonest with you (remember that habits are not just occasional incidents), you can focus the discussion on changing the objectionable behavior without launching a global attack on him.

An important feature of Aristotle's analysis of moral virtue and vice in terms of habits is that these can be changed. A person can work cognitively and behaviorally to attain greater control over emotions like anger and fear, speak more truthfully, and become more empathic, friendly, just, and so forth. These are not innate and carved in stone. For example, on this view, the charge that "He's Latin, so he has a bad temper" is a myth. According to Aristotle, "Neither by nature nor contrary to nature do the virtues [and vices] arise in us; rather we are adapted by nature to receive them and are made perfect by habit."[44] This means that it is by repeatedly failing to control your temper that you become intemperate and by repeatedly succeeding in controlling your temper that you become temperate. So, it's "nurture," not "nature," that is the deciding factor as to what habits you ultimately cultivate.

Never mind if you think that some people have genetic predispositions toward certain types of behavior. The important point is that habits are formed by repeating the same behavior. Since human beings have the ability to change and redirect their behavior, they can still, with varying effort, control the habits they get into and out of. It is therefore important to keep an open mind about the possibility of change. Giving up on others, no less than on yourself, is a bad-news philosophy. If you give up on them, they are likely to give up on themselves too. This is especially true of children, who are in the formative stages of cultivating habits. Redirecting and encouraging constructive behavior is a helpful strategy for building virtuous habits. Making condemnatory, self-fulfilling prophecies is just the opposite.

Calling someone evil usually implies their inability to change. Most people who globally denounce others as evil or immoral do so with the assumption that they are irremediably bad. This usually brings constructive and respectful discourse about meaningful change to an end.

NOTES

1. René Descartes, *Meditations*, in *Descartes: Philosophical Essays*, trans. Laurence J. LaFleur (Indianapolis: Bobbs-Merrill, 1976), "Second Meditation," 85.

2. David Hume, *A Treatise of Human Nature*, pt. 4, sec. 5, "Of Personal Identity," in *Hume Selections*, ed. Charles W. Hendel Jr. (New York: Charles Scribner Sons, 1955), 85.

3. Jean-Paul Sartre, "Existentialism," in *Philosophers at Work: Issues and Practice of Philosophy*, ed. Elliot D. Cohen (Fort Worth, Tex.: Harcourt, 2000), 447.

4. William James, *Psychology* (Cleveland: World Publishing Company, 1948), chap. 12.

5. Gottfried Leibniz, cited in Samuel Enoch Stumpf, *Philosophy: History and Problems* (New York: McGraw-Hill, 1994), 257.

6. St. Augustine offered a similar argument: "If the beauty of this order fails to delight us, it is because we ourselves, by reason of our mortality, are so enmeshed in this corner of the cosmos that we fail to perceive the beauty of a total pattern in which the particular parts, which seem ugly to us, blend in so harmonious and beautiful a way." *City of God*, chap. 4.

7. Gottfried Leibniz, *Theodicy*, in *The Individual and the Universe: An Introduction to Philosophy*, ed. Oliver Johnson (New York: Holt, Rinehart and Winston, 1981), 355.

8. Richard Rorty, "The Pragmatist's Approach to Truth," in *Philosophers at Work: Issues and Practice of Philosophy*, 1st ed., ed. Elliot D. Cohen (New York: Holt, Rinehart and Winston, 1989).

9. Jacques Derrida, "Signature, Event, Context," in *From Plato to Derrida*, 4th ed., ed. Forrest E. Baird and Walter Kaufmann (Upper Saddle River, N.J.: Prentice Hall, 2003), 1198–217.

10. Indeed, there are *many* different interpretations; however, I am not claiming that there are *no* rational limits to interpreting reality. That is another absolute you should avoid. As discussed in chapter 11, there are rational standards in filing reports about the world. Further, as discussed in chapter 9, there are also rational limits to tolerance of alternative perspectives. For example, I am not saying that the worldview of an Adolf Hitler is on the same reality footing as that of a Mother Teresa. In the end, some worldviews will help to promote your happiness better than others, and some will seriously undermine it. As I have stressed, while human beings are different, there are also common human interests that unite us. Some worldviews (like that of Hitler's) aren't even fit for human consumption.

11. Buddha, "The Sermon at Benares," in *The Teachings of the Compassionate Buddha*, ed. E. A. Burtt (New York: Penguin Books, 1991), 30.

12. Buddha, "The Parable of the Mustard Seed," in Burtt, *The Teachings of the Compassionate Buddha*, 45.

13. See chapter 1 in this book.

14. James, *Psychology*, 188–89.

15. James, *Psychology*, 189.

16. Martin Buber, "I and Thou," in Cohen, *Philosophers at Work*, 533–37.

17. As discussed in Neil Gillman, "Evil and the Limits of God: Jewish Perspectives," in Cohen, *Philosophers at Work*, 546–62.

18. As cited in Allen I. Freehling, "The Philosopher as Rabbi: Confronting Evil in the Face of the HIV/AIDS Pandemic," in Cohen, *Philosophers at Work*, 573.

19. Immanuel Kant, *Groundwork of the Metaphysics of Morals*, trans. H. J. Paton (New York: Harper & Row, 1964), 96.

20. Kant, *Groundwork of the Metaphysics of Morals*, 96.

21. Albert Ellis speaks explicitly of "unconditional self-acceptance," which he claims to have taken from several existential philosophers, especially Paul Tillich. See Ellis, *Overcoming Destructive Beliefs, Feelings, and Behaviors* (Amherst, N.Y.: Prometheus Books, 2001), 23.

22. Elliot D. Cohen, *What Would Aristotle Do? Self-Control through the Power of Reason* (Amherst, N.Y.: Prometheus Books, 2003).

23. From the Greek, *hedone*, meaning "pleasure."

24. Epicurus, *Letter to Menoeceus*, in Baird and Kaufmann, *From Plato to Derrida*, 251.

25. Ellis, *Overcoming Destructive Beliefs, Feelings, and Behaviors*, p. 28.

26. Aristotle, *Ethics*, bk. 4, chap. 6. These extremes of self-assessment are discussed more fully in chapter 8 in this book.

27. Aristotle, *Ethics*, bk. 9, chap. 7, 1086.

28. I am using "think" here to imply self-awareness in the sense of being conscious of oneself. Computers are not conscious of themselves, at least at the current stage of technology.

29. Descartes, *Meditations*, Second Meditation, 85.

30. I am assuming that in a persistent vegetative state, the person no longer has a conscious life.

31. Sartre, "Existentialism," in Cohen, *Philosophers at Work*, 445.

32. Sartre, "Existentialism," in Cohen, *Philosophers at Work*, 447.

33. David Hume, *Enquiry concerning Human Understanding*, in Baird and Kaufmann, *From Plato to Derrida*, sec. 4, pt. 2, 731.

34. John Locke, *An Essay concerning Human Understanding*, in Baird and Kaufmann, *From Plato to Derrida*, bk. 2, chap. 1, 560.

35. St. Thomas Aquinas, *Summa Theologica*, in *Introduction to St. Thomas Aquinas*, ed. Anton C. Pegis (New York: Random House, 1965), "Treatise on Law," question 91, art. 2.

36. Aquinas, *Summa Theologica*, in Pegis, *Introduction to St. Thomas Aquinas*, "Of Vainglory," question 132.

37. This theory, known as care ethics, has grown out of the feminist movement beginning in the 1960s. Its most prominent defender is the Harvard psychologist Carol Gilligan. See her book *In a Different Voice: Psychological Theory and Women's Development* (Cambridge, Mass.: Harvard University Press, 1993).

38. This is not intended as an exhaustive treatment of all ethical theories from which to choose.

39. Thomas Hobbes, *Leviathan*, in *The English Philosophers from Bacon to Mill*, ed. Edwin A. Burtt (New York: Random House, 1939), 161.

40. Hobbes, *Leviathan*, in Burtt, *The English Philosophers from Bacon to Mill*, 172.

41. Aristotle, *Ethics*, bk. 2, chap. 1, 953.

42. Notice that lying involves more than just saying false things. It also involves acting with a certain *motive*. More generally, for Aristotle, actions can be evaluated

as virtuous or not, depending on whether they are performed "at the right times, with reference to the right objects, toward the right people, with the right motive, and in the right way." *Ethics*, bk. 2, chap. 6, 1106b15–24.

43. P. H. Nowell-Smith, *Ethics* (New York: Penguin Books, 1964), 12.

44. Aristotle, *Ethics*, bk. 2, chap. 1, 952.

4

BEING YOUR OWN PERSON

$\mathbf{A}$re you easily led along by others who set the trends that you follow? Could you easily be seduced into a cultist lifestyle? Have you already been largely brainwashed by social and political trendsetters?

Whether you tend to think of yourself as a leader or follower, to one extent or another, the likely reality is that you are a conformist of a magnitude that transcends even your own awareness. This is because you, like the rest of us, have been raised in a society with surrounding cultures and subcultures and socialized into accepting certain moral standards, etiquette, laws, taboos, gender roles, prejudices, religious doctrines, standards of physical attractiveness and unattractiveness, concepts of cool and nerdy, economic ideologies (capitalism is good, socialism and communism are bad), material values, party politics, traditions, and many other commands, demand, prescriptions, and proscriptions that flesh out the landscape of a rigorous and thoroughgoing socialization.

It is in the context of this social indoctrination that each of us forges a personal identity. It should therefore be evident why a special effort to do your own independent thinking is necessary to becoming your own person. Those who blindly conform to group standards lose the opportunity to develop an essential ingredient of human happiness, namely, individuality.

In his famous treatise on liberty, John Stuart Mill eloquently stated this point:

> The human faculties of perception, judgment, discriminative feeling, mental activity, and even moral preference, are exercised only in making a choice. He who does anything because it is the custom makes no choice. He gains no practice either in discerning or in desiring what is best. The mental and moral, like the muscular powers, are improved

only by being used. The faculties are called into no exercise by doing a thing merely because others do it, no more than by believing a thing only because others believe it. If the grounds of an opinion are not conclusive to the person's own reason, his reason cannot be strengthened, but is likely to be weakened by his adopting it: and if the inducements to an act are not such as are consentaneous to his own feelings and character (where affection, or the rights of others, are not concerned) it is so much done towards rendering his feelings and character inert and torpid, instead of active and energetic. He who lets the world, or his own portion of it, choose his plan of life for him, has no need of any other faculty than the ape-like one of imitation.[1]

Mill is here calling attention to one of the most destructive fallacies endemic to humankind. This fallacy has popularly been called "jumping on the bandwagon." Here's what this rule says:

Jumping on the Bandwagon: If others are *acting* a certain way, then the very fact they *are* acting this way is good reason for you also to act this way.

The "others" in question may range from a small group of friends to a religious group to an entire nation. Mill uses the term "customs," which usually applies to social groups larger than a clique or a group of friends, but the bandwagon rule can also refer to smaller groups.

There is also another version of this fallacy known as "parroting." The difference is that jumping on the bandwagon tells you to *do* stuff, whereas parroting tells you to *believe* stuff. Mill draws this distinction when he states, "The faculties are called into no exercise by *doing* a thing merely because others do it, no more than by *believing* a thing only because others believe it" (emphasis added). Here's how this rule goes:

Parroting: If others believe or say something, then the very fact they *do* believe or say it is good enough reason for you to also believe or say the same thing.

Both rules suffer from the same disease: they tell you to follow others *blindly*. Here are their respective refutations:

Bandwagon
Refutation: The bandwagon rule tells you to discount evidence and instead to do what the pack is doing just because it's doing it. But this is blind obedience, the kind of stuff that, sooner or later, leaves you wishing you had looked before you leaped.

Parroting

Refutation: The parroting rule tells you to believe or say something just because others are. But the mere fact that others believe or say something is not itself evidence that the belief in question is true—unless the others in question happen to be experts on the subject of the belief, such as that all are heart surgeons and the belief is about heart surgery. Failing this, you are likely to end up believing or speaking falsely when you make a parrot of yourself.

In the end, parroting can have the same destructive results as jumping on the bandwagon because false belief generally leads to regrettable action.

JUMPING ON THE BANDWAGON

All of us—and I mean all, unless you happen to be a recluse—are bombarded daily with assorted and sundry bandwagon enticements. Advertising media prey on our tendency to join the pack: "Over two billion sold daily," "America's largest selling cigarette," and "The breakfast of champions." Popular media images of the in-crowd encourage us (especially the young) to drive fast, wear designer clothes, have promiscuous sex, and get high; women are expected to acquiesce in a "custom" of pay inequity in which they receive less money than men for the same work. Motion picture companies insert themselves into their productions. (For example, 20th Century Fox shows the masses listening to its sister news network, Fox News Channel, in the movies it produces.) And politicians ask "all freedom-loving Americans" to vote for them.

So we think nothing of it when we eat burgers dripping with fat, light up a carcinogenic Marlboro, watch "fair and balanced" Fox News, buy a shirt because it has "Polo" sprawled across it, and vote for the candidate who spends the most on manipulative and deceptive campaign ads. Convinced that we are the masters of our own fate, we are none the wiser as we exchange individuality for an automated, standardized archetype of the good life. So, it is not surprising that so many of us find ourselves losing our very selves and feeling so damned unfulfilled and unhappy in the process.

Antidotes to Jumping on the Bandwagon

Antidote 1
Instead of getting lost in the "they," confront your existential angst. (Heidegger)

Philosophers have had important things to say about this surrender of authenticity and personal freedom to blind conformity. Speaking of how we permit our freedom and individuality to be lost in conformity to a nameless, faceless "they" (that is, the crowd), philosopher Martin Heidegger admonishes us:

> "They" even hide the process by which "they" have quietly relieved us of the "burden" of making choices for ourselves. It remains a complete mystery who has really done the choosing. We are carried along by the "nobody," without making any real choices, becoming ever more deeply ensnared in inauthenticity. This process can be reversed only if we explicitly bring ourselves back from our lostness in the "they." But this bringing-back must have that kind of being by the neglect of which we have lost ourselves in inauthenticity.[2]

Heidegger's antidote to our "lostness" is first of all to become aware that we are lost. The illusion of freedom needs to be exposed before real freedom can replace it. For Heidegger, getting lost in your socialization insulates you from your own finitude. Lost in the "they," you can escape the angst of being a "being-toward-death." Cosmetic surgery and hair dye hide the telltale signs of aging and the inevitability of your death. As the "man of the house," you must toe the line and bring home the bacon; as the homemaker, you must tidy up and do the work of nurturing and caregiving. At each turn, there is a rule to define your next move. At no point are you alone with your angst to write your own script. The script is already written *for you*, and you simply play the role as written.

True, you can decide the details for yourself such as whom to marry, but society imposes marriage itself. It determines the basic rules, such as whether it can be heterosexual or homosexual, monogamist or polygamist. A woman must jump on the bandwagon of matrimony if she is to avoid the ridicule of becoming an "old maid"; she must produce offspring to remain true to her God-given purpose. A man must do his part in the natural order by taking a bride and providing the "seed."

Once you tear back the layers of socialization insulating you from your existential being, you can begin the process of digging yourself out of inauthentic existence. Since you don't have an eternity, you should "get real" about what you want to do with your life. Your angst about dying isn't a bad thing. It's the virtual wake-up call to get cracking. Unfortunately, in getting lost in the "they," you will sleep through it. Bandwagon jumping won't define *your* happiness. This only you can do.

Antidote 2

Don't act like a paper cutter: define your own essence. (Sartre)

Sartre expressed this point by saying that "existence precedes essence."[3] What he means is that you are not like some manufactured object that has a preestablished purpose (essence). When you come on the scene (exist), you are nothing until you define yourself as something. Unlike a paper cutter, which is designed in advance for the purpose of cutting paper, you are not born with a preordained purpose. Your nature is that you are without a nature except that which you yourself fashion. If you want to renounce the institution of marriage and spend your life as a bachelor, if you never want to have children but want to spend your time and money elsewhere, that is your choice. There is no preordained human nature that *demands* one thing or the other. Social institutions are human artifacts, not commandments from on high.

Of course, the religious person will interject, but isn't it God who defines human nature just like an engineer designs the paper cutter's nature? Ah yes, Sartre would say, but only if you accept God as your creator in the first place, and that is still your choice. You are free to do so, but this is your personal decision, and you are still responsible for it. It is only when you say, "I *must* marry or live this way or that way," that you will live an inauthentic existence. You are not obligated to believe that there is a God who demands that you fulfill such purposes.

Nor does God create you in his image, claims Sartre; rather, it is you who creates God in yours. Sound like blasphemy? No problem. You can still believe in God and recognize your freedom to choose your lifestyle. The religious view would not deny that you have free will. It's your call. Whether you want to attain greater control over your life is up to you.

Several years ago, I worked with a group of displaced homemakers in a university women's program. All these women were either recently widowed or divorced in their middle age. All had adult children, and the thought of doing anything other than being a wife and mother gave all of them extreme anxiety. Each of these women held a similar worldview. Each perceived the natural, God-decreed purpose of a woman to be a wife and mother. This gender role was so deeply embedded in their psyches that, in the course of their lives, they had never even once questioned it. For them, it was axiomatic. There was no more need to question it than that two plus two equals four. But this was exactly what these women had to do if they were to take control of their lives.

In the end, many of these women came to see that the role they had assumed was a choice that was made for them by society. Now they had an opportunity to redecide the direction of their lives. In the words of Heidegger, the women now had the opportunity to "bring themselves back from their lostness in the 'they.'" The women had to confront their angst head-on. Their mortality stared them in the face. This was a new phase in a process of life that was moving inevitably toward death. This was also their opportunity to make an authentic decision. The choice was one that affected *them*. It was *their* choice, not one of some nameless, faceless crowd, and it was a choice the women were making in the light of their angst about their own personal mortality.

In Sartre's words, these women had to redefine their "essences" through authentic decisions about their own concrete, individual existences. For them, their existences preceded their essences, not the other away around. They had to muster the willpower to make this change against the inertia of lifelong adherence to a rule prescribing conformity to a tradition they were socialized to accept from childhood.

You too have the ability to examine and change the rules you were socialized to accept. You too can authenticate yourself. Instead of riding on a bandwagon that takes you nowhere or, worse, down the tubes, you can decide whether you are up for the rest of the ride. You may want to get off the bandwagon and step into the driver's seat yourself. Are you frustrated about something but not quite sure of the source? Do you feel like you have little control over your own life? Do things seem routine, uninteresting, unexciting? Do you find yourself trying to please others until there is no time left for you? Do you find yourself doing things (on the job or in social groups) that are at odds with your sense of propriety? Do you find yourself being intimidated into doing things? Are you often embarrassed or uncomfortable about saying what you really think or feel? These are signs that you may be up for an "essence" realignment. This need not be a major overhaul, but you may be riding on some bandwagon, imperceptibly cogging along just because it is what that obscure, abstract "they" do. But it may not be what concrete little old *you* really wants to do. Do some soul-searching. Seek, and you shall find.

Antidote 3
Instead of passively taking your place among prisoners in a humdrum cave of conformity, break these shackles of oppression (and depression), venture out into the sunlight, and explore your creative potential. (Plato)

It takes courage (guts, nerve, you name it) to be authentic in a world that tends toward uniformity and conformity. It's easier to retreat, get lost in the crowd, sell out your values, or turn chameleon and go with the flow than against it.

The tendency of human beings to conform and to fear change is well illustrated in Plato's famous Allegory of the Cave.[4] On the surface, this is a tale of people who have been imprisoned in a cave from childhood, chained by their legs and necks so that they cannot move and can see only what is in front of them. Behind them is a fire burning, and between the fire and these prisoners is a track with a parapet built along it resembling the screen of a puppet show, hiding the puppeteers as they show their puppets above the top. Hidden behind the parapet are puppeteers carrying stone and wooden objects, including figures of men and animals. Unable to turn their heads, the prisoners see only the shadows of these objects cast on the cave wall in front of them; consequently, they recognize as reality only these passing shadows. Conversant only about these shadows, the prisoners pass their days playing games about which shadow will come next.

Plato asks you to imagine what would happen if one of the prisoners was set free and forced to turn around and see the objects that were casting the shadows, look directly at the fire, and, ultimately, behold the world outside the cave. At first, says Plato, the prisoner would stubbornly attempt to hang on to his former view of reality, but after some time of getting used to the light, he would finally come to see that what he previously thought was reality was but an illusion and would rather be a vagabond than to return to his former way of life.

As Plato recounts, if this liberated prisoner went back into the cave to inform the others of about the outside world, they would ridicule him, think him insane, and even try to kill him if they could get their hands on him.

According to Plato, these prisoners depict the human race: afraid of change and stubbornly resistant to giving up old ways in favor of new ones. Great innovators have, indeed, seldom been appreciated in their lifetimes. Instead, they have often been ostracized, persecuted, and even killed. Plato clearly has the execution of his own teacher, Socrates, in mind, but subsequent history is rich with examples of how human beings have rejected those who have attempted to liberate us from our own "caves of ignorance."

This attitude of resilience to change is a universal one, not merely a problem for some of us but not others. We are, all of us, residents of some cave or other. Even philosophers can be stubborn. Let me give you an example.

Much of my formal training was in what has come to be called "pure philosophy." Roughly speaking, this is philosophy that answers the question "What should I think?" rather than "What should I do?" For example, the popular philosophical questions "What is knowledge?" "Do human beings have free will?" and "What is the relationship between the mind and the body?" are primarily questions about what we should think. On the other hand, applied philosophy is interested in the bearing of such theories and concepts on solving practical human problems. How can David Hume's analysis of causality in terms of habit or custom provide an antidote to stubbornly damning yourself for your mistakes instead of learning from them? How can believing in free will help you take control of your life and do better and feel better? What difference will it make in your life to believe that you are the same as your body or that you have an independent mind or soul? These are questions that aim primarily at what to do rather than at what to think.

Quite obviously, the "What should I think?" question is related to the "What should I do?" question since theories that answer the first question can be applied in answering the second. This book is a testament to the fact that the philosophers of antiquity have provided an abundant garden of practical guidance for us if only we are willing to harvest its fruits. Unfortunately, the rise of applied philosophy has been thwarted by philosophers who were contented to ask the questions of pure philosophy without also looking at them with an eye toward practice. In my early days, these philosophers were quick to charge that philosophers interested in practical questions were not doing "real" philosophy and were in fact not "real philosophers." Only those philosophers who remained at the level of pure abstract thinking qualified for the status of real philosophers, according to this perspective.

I am pleased to say that this archaic view has become less popular at the time of this writing, but it still does have its devout followers. I know exactly how these philosophers think since I received the same indoctrination as they did in my graduate days at Brown University. I had written my doctoral dissertation on a pure question of value theory, namely, what does it mean to say that some property of a thing makes it valuable (or disvaluable)? For example, what does it mean to say that the fact that something is painful *makes* it bad? Here I was interested mostly in what the "makes" meant rather than with the nature of human pain and the ways to reduce it. I produced an elaborate set of definitions that carefully defined the relationship, and I defended this intricate network with great ease, received kudos from my committee, and the rest is history—except for one comment that my dear, sweet wife, Gale Spieler Cohen, made to me when I was in the process of finalizing my thesis.

She said, "That's really very nice, but what are you going to do with it?" Stumbling on my words, I really didn't have an answer, just some very vague idea that it would somehow advance human knowledge and welfare. That question has provided the guiding light of my subsequent work. It woke me from my dogmatic complacency in a pragmatically bankrupt philosophical outlook.

This also inspired me to look into areas of philosophy that were glossed over in my formal education, such as feminist philosophy and existentialism. The tradition of Anglo-American philosophy in which I was reared didn't look carefully into these; however, the practical as well as theoretical merit of these perspectives is now abundantly clear to me.

Determined to help put applied philosophy on the map, in 1981, I founded a professional journal called the *International Journal of Applied Philosophy*. This was the first comprehensive journal of applied philosophy ever to be published. As a young editor, treading in an area that challenged the status quo of philosophy, I was a maverick. My credibility as a philosopher was repeatedly challenged, and many of my contemporaries didn't take me seriously.

In the mid-1980s, I began work in applied value theory.[5] My wife, who at the time was studying to be a therapist, saw a resemblance between this early work of mine and that of psychologist Albert Ellis, whom she had studied in her course work. This introduction set the stage for my development of logic-based philosophical therapy, a philosophically robust variant of Ellis's Rational-Emotive Behavior Therapy.

In 1990, after about five years of clinical research at my own institute, I cofounded the American Society for Philosophy, Counseling, and Psychotherapy (ASPCP). My primary goal was to advance research and development of philosophical practice by increasing cooperation between philosophers and psychological practitioners. These two professional groups had typically worked independently and, as a result, tended to reinvent the wheel. I am pleased to say that the ASPCP's mission is steadily advancing in the States and abroad.

Here's the upshot. Take it from me. Don't be afraid to break out of the conventional mold. I owe my most important contributions and the most exciting aspects of my professional career to my willingness to resist the tendency to conform to the status quo simply because it *was* the status quo. Remaining in Plato's cave and counting shadows on the wall can get very boring, and it's very uninspiring. It is a good way to keep yourself in a perpetual state of low-grade depression.[6] As John Stuart Mill rightly noted, progress is not made when people live on a bandwagon. Get out of your cave and live creatively. As Plato pointed out, you are likely to get ridiculed by the cave people if you venture out into the sunlight, but in the long run it is well worth it.

Antidote 4

Let the standard of utility be your guide. Try out some experiments of living and speak out against attempts by government to restrict your personal freedoms and those of your countrymen. (Mill)

On the other hand, when your life is ruled by blind adherence to custom, you can end up wearing a mask that hides who you really are underneath. For example, in a homophobic nation such as ours, this has been a serious problem for many gay and lesbian people who try to live the straight life. I once had a client who went through two marriages trying to be straight. As a result of a strong religious indoctrination forbidding homosexuality and a desire to fit in, he jumped on a heterosexual bandwagon and lived a lie that had untoward consequences for all concerned. Unfortunately, the last I heard, this poor fellow was still aboard the same bandwagon destined to suffer and to cause others to suffer more anguish and frustration.

It takes courage for gay folks to be open about their gayness. But, in so doing, they remain true to themselves in spite of the tremendous pressure to sexually conform. A heterosexual client of mine who learned that her husband was gay expressed a desire to try to convert him to heterosexuality. I asked her to imagine what it would be like living as a heterosexual in a predominantly homosexual culture and then being asked to try to "convert." This is not like changing your clothes, your name, or even your faith. You cannot wake up one morning and decide to change your sexual orientation, nor is there a credible clinical procedure to make the transition. The only credible option here is to come clean and be the person you really are inside and out.

The humanistic psychologist Carl Rogers has argued that *being congruent* is an important condition of constructive change. According to Rogers, to be congruent means that your inside matches your outside. It is to be transparent: what you really think and feel is just as you say. It means you are not a phony; you put on no mask or social facade. For Rogers, this is a necessary condition of forward-moving, psychological growth, in short, of human happiness.[7]

In his essay *On Liberty*, John Stuart Mill recommended "experiments in living" as an antidote to the blind adherence to customs and traditions:

> As it is useful that while mankind are imperfect there should be different opinions, so it is that there should be different experiments of living; that free scope should be given to varieties of character, short of injury to others; and that the worth of different modes of life should be proved practically, when anyone thinks fit to try them. It is desirable, in short, that in things which do not primarily concern others, individuality should assert itself. Where not the person's own character, but the traditions or customs of other people are the rule of conduct, there is wanting one of the principal ingredients of human happiness and quite the chief ingredient of individual and social progress.[8]

Mill believed you should consider the "utility" of an action in order to determine whether it is right or wrong. If an alternative lifestyle maximizes human happiness (defined as pleasure and the absence of pain), then it is right to pursue it, wrong if it does not.[9] According to Mill, people who jump on social bandwagons instead of pursuing their own lights tend to act wrongly on this "utilitarian" standard.

So, instead of simply *assuming* that society knows best, you should try out some alternatives and see if they work to better promote your happiness. This isn't to say that you should scrap things simply because they are customary. If it's not broken, then you shouldn't try to fix it. But often, rules of conduct that are supported by custom or tradition do not satisfy Mill's utilitarian standard. Often, these rules are rigid and stifle human happiness.

Not only are individuals stifled, but so too is society when we aren't given the opportunity to explore alternative ways of life. When people think and act in conformity with little variation, progress is not likely to occur. The United States is a multicultural, multiethnic nation with great cultural diversity. This is what makes this nation a great place. Political leaders who would thwart this diversity by requiring uniformity in social policies threaten this nation's democratic foundations. For example, a constitutional amendment that would define marriage as necessarily between a man and a woman would contradict the Declaration of Independence, which enjoins "life, liberty, and the pursuit of happiness." For the sake of happiness, you should oppose any such attempt to violate personal freedom of expression. Even if it is not your own self-expression that is on the chopping block, what goes around often comes around.

The pursuit of happiness comes in many different varieties. As Mill says, as long as you are not hurting anyone else through your endeavor, you should be allowed to pursue it. You should not be dissuaded by bandwagon thinking from following your creative lights—different strokes for different folks. What makes you happy may not work for someone else, so don't try to make one size fit all. You know what it's like to buy a garment that's made to fit everyone. It fits everyone and no one. You are an individual with a right to life, liberty, and the pursuit of happiness. Walking lockstep with others simply to conform is not likely to maximize your happiness in the long run. If a custom or tradition does meet this standard, then keep it, but if it is a source of your unhappiness, then toss it and try something else.

Antidote 5
Instead of looking to others for approval, think of yourself as an independent, autonomous, creator of values. (Nietzsche)

In walking lockstep to the beat of what others say, you assume that the values of others are somehow better than your own. But in making this assumption, you subvert your own creative capacity to *make your own values.* This subjectivist stance on value was articulated by existentialist philosophers, notably Friedrich Nietzsche. "The noble kind of man," said Nietzsche, "experiences himself as a person who determines value and does not need to have other people's approval. . . . He understands himself as something which in general first confers honour on things, as someone who creates values."[10]

Nietzsche's antidote to mindlessly jumping on the bandwagon is therefore to elevate yourself above the perceived necessity of needing the approval of others and instead to experience yourself as the incontestable author of your own creative values. Instead of simply following the values that others lay down for you—this is what Nietzsche appropriately called the "herd morality"—you can ennoble yourself by accepting your own creative powers to make values and then to act on them.

I am not suggesting that you should subvert law and order merely to exercise your creative juices. But even here, there is room for courageously challenging those laws and government policies to which you perceive good reason to object. The voice of a healthy democracy is one composed of many people with diverse, creative perspectives who are not intimidated to speak their minds.

PARROTING

Antidotes to Parroting

Antidote 1
Learn from history: Don't believe things just because they are "official." (Santayana, Mill)

The First Amendment of the U.S. Constitution grants you freedom of speech. As long as you are not using your speech to harm others, such as yelling "Fire!" in a crowded auditorium, you have a right to speak your mind and your conscience. Unfortunately, there are—and doubtless will always be—political, legal, and social pressures to accept the views of the establishment.

But what is lost when pressures to conform destroy your freedom of speech? According to Mill, the human race always loses something valuable when people are prevented from expressing themselves freely, for if a suppressed opinion is true, others are prevented from being enlightened, and if it is false, others miss the chance to strengthen their conviction by seeing it in collision with error. Either way, true or false, we lose when free speech is trumped by pressures to accept the prevailing view.[11]

Since even true opinions are rarely completely true, they can usually be improved by rational discussion. And, unless we allow the pros and cons of a purported truth to be freely and openly probed, the reasons for accepting it will escape us, and we will end up holding it as a dogma or sacred cow instead of a reasoned conviction. Says Mill, "Both teachers and learners go to sleep at their posts as soon as there is no enemy in the field."[12] Nor should any traditional view be so obvious as to put it beyond doubt. "The fatal tendency of mankind to leave off thinking about a thing when it is no longer doubtful, is the cause of half their errors."[13]

When you simply accept the views of the establishment or of officialdom, without probing into their veracity, not only do you increase the odds of believing falsely, you also fortify an unthinking and rigid habit of conformity that makes you liable to the deceitful manipulation by the powers that be. Allow me to illustrate.

In the 1960s, when the Vietnam War was waged, it was popular to believe that this war was necessary to prevent communism from "coming here." So, to defend our freedom, all "patriotic" Americans were expected to support the war. Those who opposed it were labeled "hippies" and "draft dodgers."

Those who lost their lives, their limbs, or their mental health while defending our nation in the jungles of Vietnam were well meaning and trusted the establishment not to deceive them. In retrospect, however, history has shown that the threat of communism invading our shores was a crock and that the war was waged for economic and political gain. While the military–industrial complex made out like bandits, faithful young soldiers were being mangled and destroyed.

The lesson to be learned here is one that is at least as urgent now as it was then. Do your own independent thinking. Don't believe something just because someone tells you it's true. Instead, require evidence before you believe it. The fact that someone says something is not itself evidence. As Watergate clearly demonstrated, not even the president of the United States is above the law and beyond question.

Unfortunately, these hard-won insights are destined to be in vain unless we keep them in the forefront as we confront our futures. As philosopher George Santayana stated, "Those who cannot learn from history are doomed to repeat it."

Prior to the U.S. invasion of Iraq, the government claimed that there were weapons of mass destruction (WMD) in Iraq and that its leader, Saddam Hussein was an "evil man" who would use these weapons on us as he did on his own people. But the claim that Saddam harbored such weapons was based largely on the assumption that because he had such weapons in the 1980s, he must also have them now. Moreover, after twenty years of laboring under the belief that he had these weapons (in fact, the United States had helped Saddam obtain them to use against the Iranians), it was bewildering why the need to stop him suddenly became so urgent as to warrant a preemptive war with all its risks and sacrifices. After the attacks of September 11, 2001, the government attempted to find such a rationale by trying to link the attacks to Saddam.

Despite the fact that there was shoddy evidence for WMD in Iraq and for a connection between September 11 and Saddam, the media parroted the official line instead of doing its own careful investigative reporting. Unfortunately, many Americans swallowed it hook, line, and sinker. When the conjecture that these weapons still existed was disproved along with the myth that Saddam somehow had something to do with September 11, the official line became tempered. Now the rationale for preemptive war was to stop Saddam from brutalizing his own people. Yet the brutality of this dictator was nothing new and had been ignored for two prior decades.

So, while companies like Haliburton got no-bid contracts in Iraq for exorbitant amounts of money and media giants like General Electric's

NBC, Time Warner's CNN, Viacom's CBS, Disney's ABC, and News Corp's Fox cooperated with the federal government in order to maximize their bottom lines, we Americans were fed the official line and were expected to swallow it.[14]

For those of us who have lived through the Vietnam era, this course of events is neither surprising nor new. It is the same old bullshit of waging bloody war for economic interests, cloaked in an atmosphere of officialdom and concern for humanity. It is, just as Santayana said, a failure to pay attention and learn from past history. It is, as Mill admonished, failure to exercise our reason and instead to believe things just because someone in an official position said them. The end product of this parrotfest is mass destruction of innocent lives.

In case you ever wondered how the people in Nazi Germany were able to follow Adolf Hitler, look no further. These people were no different than any other people. They were not especially ruthless and callous. They believed what they were told. It was the same old falling for the official line, believing because the words were spoken and not because they were proven. This is the deadly truth about parroting.

Antidote 2
Be a true patriot, not parrot; support democracy, not parrotdom. (Dewey)

A useful antidote to this disease is to become an ardent supporter of democracy, and I mean *real* democracy, not in name only. The point of living in a democracy is to live creatively by your own lights consistent with others doing the same. John Dewey has made plain the importance of education to this mission. He eloquently stated,

> The devotion of democracy to education is a familiar fact. The superficial explanation is that a government resting upon popular suffrage cannot be successful unless those who elect and who obey their governors are educated. . . . But there is a deeper explanation. A democracy is more than a form of government; it is primarily a mode of associated living, of conjoint communicated experience. The extension in space of the number of individuals who participate in an interest so that each has to refer his own action to that of others, and to consider the action of others to give point and direction to his own, is equivalent to the breaking down of those barriers of class, race, and national territory which kept men from perceiving the full import of their activity. These more numerous and more varied points of contact denote a greater diversity of stimuli to which an individual has to respond. . . . They

secure a liberation of powers which remain suppressed as long as the in-
citations to action are partial, as they must be in a group which in its ex-
clusiveness shuts out many interests.[15]

Groupthink, mindless parroting of the established view, is oppressive
because it excludes interests that lie outside the status quo. This is the antithesis of democracy, which is supposed to bust its gut to accommodate a
diversity of interests, not shut them out.

For Dewey, the educated person is someone who has developed active,
flexible, adaptive habits, that is, ways of creatively and intelligently managing the environment. This is the opposite of rigid habits of conformity that
stifle creativity and in which

> what is distinctively individual . . . is brushed aside, or regarded as a
> source of mischief or anarchy. Conformity is made equivalent to uni-
> formity. Consequently, there are induced lack of interest in the novel,
> aversion to progress, and dread of the uncertain and the unknown.[16]

The mark of an educated person is a tendency toward creative diver-
gence, not blind conformity. Fascist states welcome the latter and spend
their energies subduing individuality and instilling unthinking habits of
conformity. Democracy is just the opposite. It is defined by its tolerance
for diversity of viewpoints. Be patriotic. Support democracy. Don't be a
parrot.

Antidote 3
Before you believe something, check out its "cash value." (James)

What you *think*, just as what you do, has consequences. To use an example of William James, if you are lost in a forest, having a true belief at
your disposal that tells you how to get out can save your life. If your belief
is false, you may well perish in that forest. "'The true,'" James said, "is only
the expedient in the way of our thinking, just as 'the right' is only the expedient in the way of our behaving." A true belief, he said, has "cash
value";[17] it leads or tends to lead to satisfying results if acted on, at least in
the long run. No wonder we try to fill our memories with truths and not
falsehoods. When the occasion arises, we take the truth out of cold storage
and put it to work in the world to solve practical problems.

Now parroting doesn't have "cash value." To the contrary, it tends to
lead you on a mindless path of regrettable actions. This doesn't mean that

there can't be instances where blind belief works for you. Some random person tells you to invest in a certain stock, and you listen and make millions. It could happen, right? But the operative word is "could." It probably won't.

Of course, it's different if your stockbroker tells you to invest in a certain stock and you take his advice. The stock market is admittedly a crapshoot, but if your broker tends to be well informed and has had a good track record of helping others, then it is not irrational to take his advice seriously. But even here, before you act, it is good form to ask questions so that you have satisfied any reasonable concerns you might have.

This can be even more important in seeking medical advice. According to the old-fashioned model of medical paternalism, doctors were presumed by patients "to know best," and prospective patients were socialized to accept whatever the doctor said without further inquiry. Fortunately, today there has been significant movement toward a model of health care that emphasizes patients' rights, especially patient autonomy and informed consent. Nevertheless, there are still people who take the old-school approach and think the doctor should rarely if ever be questioned. Of course, if the medical problem is a relatively innocuous one, say something no more life-threatening than an ingrown toenail, then this may not cause much trouble. However, it is a fixed and rigid habit of indiscriminate belief that can get you into trouble. If the medical problem is a serious one, such as a heart problem, then you should do your level best to take an interest in your medical condition, ask relevant questions, inform yourself about your illness, and seek medical opinions from other qualified physicians. Unfortunately, those who are habituated according to the old model of medical paternalism simply believe because the doctor said so and thereby take greater risks with their health than they need to.

In fact, competent physicians generally welcome patient involvement rather than discourage it. Those who have "God complexes" and expect you to blindly follow them have vanity problems, which also raises questions about their competence.

So parroting, even when you are listening to competent advisers, generally lacks "cash value." Better to be in a habit of exercising rational, autonomous judgment than to be in a habit of mindless parroting. If you are presently reading this book, then you are up for the challenge. As James would say, it's the "cash value" of a belief that makes it "true"—its ability to satisfy, not the mere fact that someone said it. Go for the gold.

NOTES

1. John Stuart Mill, *On Liberty*, in *John Stuart Mill*, ed., Mary Warnock (New York: Meridian Books, 1968), chap. 3, 187.

2. Martin Heidegger, *Being and Time*, retrieved January 14, 2006, from http://www.tc.umn.edu/~parkx032/XP226.html.

3. Sartre, "Existentialism," in *Philosophers at Work: Issues and Practice of Philosophy*, ed. Elliot D. Cohen (Fort Worth, Tex.: Harcourt, 2000), 444.

4. Plato, *The Republic*, in *From Plato to Derrida*, 4th ed., ed. Forrest E. Baird and Walter Kaufmann (Upper Saddle River, N.J.: Prentice Hall, 2003), bk. 7, 137–142.

5. This work led to publication of my book, *Making Value Judgements: Principles of Sound Reasoning* (Malabar, Fla.: Krieger, 1985).

6. The clinical term for such low-grade depression is dysthymia. See American Psychiatric Association, *Diagnostic and Statistical Manual of Mental Disorders* (Washington, DC: American Psychiatric Association, 2000).

7. Carl Rogers, *On Becoming a Person* (Boston: Houghton Mifflin, 1961).

8. John Stuart Mill, *On Liberty*, chap. 3, 185

9. John Stuart Mill, *Utilitarianism*, in *John Stuart Mill*, ed. Warnock, chap. 2.

10. Friedrich Nietzsche, *Beyond Good and Evil*, trans. Helen Zimmern, in *The Philosophy of Nietzsche* (New York: Random House, 1954), chap. 9, sec. 260, 579.

11. Mill, *On Liberty*, chap. 2.

12. Mill, *On Liberty*, chap. 2, 170.

13. Mill, *On Liberty*, chap. 2, 170.

14. See Elliot D. Cohen, *News Incorporated: Corporate Media Ownership and Its Threat to Democracy* (Amherst, N.Y.: Prometheus Books, 2005).

15. John Dewey, *Democracy and Education*, chap. 7, retrieved January 14, 2006, from http://www.ilt.columbia.edu/publications/Projects/digitexts/dewey/d_e/chapter07.html.

16. Dewey, *Democracy and Education*, chap. 4, retrieved online on January 14, 2006, from http://www.worldwideschool.org/library/books/socl/education/DemocracyandEducation/toc.html.

17. William James, "Pragmatism's Conception of Truth," in *William James: Pragmatism*, ed. Ralph Barton Perry (New York: New American Library, 1955), 145.

5

CONTROLLING YOURSELF

Frequent use of the words "I can't" or other words implying them can be a sign that you are *can't*stipated and unwilling to take a laxative (antidote) to regulate yourself (attain self-control). What does it mean to be *can't*stipated? It means that you keep yourself from being happy by telling yourself that you can't. You hold in the "can't" and refuse to poop it out.

There are three ways to *can't*stipate yourself:

1. Emotionally (emotional *can't*stipation)
2. Behaviorally (behavioral *can't*stipation)
3. Volitionally[1] (volitional *can't*stipation)

The first way is to accept this rule:

> Emotional *Can't*stipation: If you feel upset, someone or something else *caused* you to feel this way, and, therefore, you cannot and should not even try to control the way you feel.

This rule tells you to blame your depression, guilt, anxiety, anger, and other negative emotions on external events, objects, and other persons rather than to accept personal responsibility for your emotions. Here are some common examples of externalized blame supported by this rule:

- You really piss me off.
- That aggravates me.
- You depress me.
- It makes me feel like dying.
- She's driving me crazy.

111

- He makes me feel guilty.
- I have a bad temper because I'm Latin.

Each of these (and countless versions of them) implies that some other person or thing *caused* you to feel the way you do and therefore that you're not responsible for your own emotions. In such cases, you *can't*stipate your emotions by assuming that you *can't* control them; you suppose that they are no more in your power to control than a bolt of lightning striking you from out of the sky and therefore that you shouldn't even bother trying to control them. By failing to excrete this "can't" by taking an appropriate laxative, you persist in the same self-destructive emotional state.

When you say that somebody *pissed you off*, you blame the pissing on this other person, not on yourself. In so blaming, you excuse yourself from even having to try to control the way you feel. Instead, you leave it up to the other guy to change his ways. You turn your personal feelings into the passive playthings of others and accordingly reduce yourself to a kind of object manipulated.

The implications of *can't*stipating your emotions in this way are far reaching indeed. If people were fully determined by external conditions, then it would make no sense, either legally or morally, to disclaim human emotions. It wouldn't make sense to tell people that they shouldn't get angry or feel depressed, anxious, or guilty over things since, as Kant perceived, "ought" implies "can." That is, there is no point in telling people how they *ought*—or *oughtn't*—to feel if they can't even control the way they feel in the first place. By the same logic, it would be meaningless to hold people legally or morally responsible for their emotional responses, such as flying into a deadly rage, if their emotions were completely determined by external conditions and therefore beyond their control. But certainly we do sensibly hold people legally and morally responsible for their emotional responses, and we do sensibly advise people about how they should or shouldn't feel, all of which would be meaningless if the emotional *can't*stipation rule were really valid.

In contrast, logic-based therapy (LBT), the approach developed in this book, maintains that you are largely responsible for your own emotions because you *deduce* them from premises in your reasoning. Accordingly, your emotions are not the effects of causes (like a flame is an effect of a struck match) but are instead human *decisions* or *choices*. And the antidotes you construct and use against irrational rules in your reasoning can, with the exercise of willpower, give you considerable power over many self-destructive emotions. LBT therefore squares with our ordinary intuitions about holding people responsible for their emotional responses and about giving people advice about how they should or shouldn't feel.

This view, that human emotions are largely under our control, is not an *all-or-nothing* thesis, however. It is plainly false that *all* self-destructive, human emotions can *always* be overcome. In some cases of major depression, bipolar disorder, obsessive-compulsive disorder, and other mood disorders, there may be biochemical imbalances that make it difficult or impossible for a person to effectively construct and apply antidotes in overcoming irrational rules. Such cases may require drug therapy to restore homeostasis before logic-based interventions can be useful. But in the vast number of cases, where people are their worst enemies by virtue of the types of irrational rules they accept and apply, the methods of LBT can be extremely useful in overcoming irrational emotions.[2] In *can'tstipating* your feelings by "holding in" the "I can't," you give up the opportunity to exert considerable control over your emotional life.

So, in sum, here's a refutation of the emotional *can'tstipation* rule:

> If you couldn't exert any control over your own emotions, then you would be a biological machine that responds to external stimuli automatically. There would be no point in telling people how they should feel since "ought" implies "can," and it would not make sense to hold people legally or morally responsible for criminal acts that stem from irrational emotions. It would *always* be a waste of time to even try to overcome your irrational emotions by finding antidotes to them and exerting your willpower because your emotions would always be beyond your control anyway. But, as the logic-based approach has repeatedly, empirically shown, this is plainly false to fact because many people do, indeed, succeed in overcoming their irrational emotions by applying rational antidotes. This means that people *can* follow advice about how to feel and can therefore be accountable for their emotional responses.

The second type of *can'tstipation* is when you tell yourself that you can't control your own *behavior*. Here you *can'tstipate* your behavior by tenaciously thinking you *can't* do otherwise, thereby permitting yourself to repeat the same self-destructive behavior. Here are some examples:

- I can't ever be happy.
- I can't get along with others.
- I can't get close to others.
- I can't stop thinking about it.
- I can't do anything daring or adventurous.

- I can't give up my nasty habits.
- I can't speak up in class or at work.
- I can't make friends.
- I can't improve my skills or learn new ones.
- I can't forgive and go on with my life.

The "can't" here prevents progress and more adaptive behavior. Instead of meaningful change, you lock yourself into the "same old, same old." The rule of behavioral *can't*stipation says this:

> Behavioral *Can't*stipation: If you have a behavioral problem, you can't really do anything about it anyway, and so you shouldn't even try.

In *can't*stipating your behavior, you disable and cripple your own capacity to make rational choices about constructive change. Instead, you turn yourself into a biological mechanism that drones out the same old self-defeating, programmed responses.

The refutation of behavioral *can't*stipation is accordingly similar to that of emotional *can't*stipation:

> If you couldn't exert any control over your own behavior, you would be a biological machine that responds to external stimuli automatically. Directives about what you should—and shouldn't—*do* would be pointless, and it would not make sense to hold anyone legally or morally responsible for their behavior any more than it would make sense to put a programmed computer in prison for committing a felony. But this is false to fact since many people succeed in changing their behavior, and, as the logic-based approach has repeatedly shown, people can change their irrational behavior by applying rational antidotes. Consequently, people, unlike programmed computers, can reasonably be held accountable for their behavior.

Having been in the philosophy business for so many years, I don't have to draw a breath before I can imagine some critical philosopher decrying this refutation by claiming that even computers could be programmed to change their behavior. But never mind this. If computers get to be as advanced as us humans in consciously and intentionally working to overcome their irrational behavior by applying rational antidotes, then they may equally be proper subjects of the rights and responsibilities (and privileges and burdens) of full-fledged persons living in a democratic society. But, until then, I will rest my case on what is—at least for now—a valid distinction between human beings, who *can* change their behavior and be held both legally and morally accountable, and computers, which don't have a clue.

Now if we could only produce a cyborg that had more patience than many of us. Unfortunately, volitional *can't*stipation (*can't*stipation of the will) is endemic to the human population and is a common way in which folks undermine their personal and interpersonal happiness and prosperity. This is when you exaggerate your inability to tolerate frustration by telling yourself you can't stand something when it becomes difficult or challenging. It is tolerance for frustration short-circuited and diminished by what Albert Ellis called "I-can't-stand-it-itis," that is, telling yourself you can't stand something when it requires tolerating frustration. Here are some examples:

- I couldn't take it if they promoted that new guy instead of me.
- I can't stand waiting to afford a new car.
- I can't take being mocked out.
- I couldn't survive if my husband left me.
- I can't handle that algebra class.
- I couldn't stand to live if I lost my money.
- I can't put up with stupid people.
- I couldn't take getting locked in an elevator.
- I can't deal with not getting what I want.
- I can't take it when a creeping car gets in front of me in the fast lane.
- I can't stand to eat alone in a restaurant.
- I can't stand to make mistakes.
- I couldn't cope with going bald.

You get the idea. Examples of volitional *can't*stipation can be produced ad nauseum. The rule goes like this:

Volitional *Can't*stipation: If you find something difficult or challenging to cope with, then it must be beyond your capacity to tolerate, and you *cannot* and must not ever hope to succeed at it.

The refutation for this rule is glaring. If only we could keep it in the front of our minds throughout our encounters with frustration:

Refutation: If people never tried to overcome difficult or challenging things and instead retreated from them by telling themselves that they couldn't stand them, then there would be few human accomplishments worthy of pride since all or most human accomplishments worthy of pride are made in the face of adversity.

EMOTIONAL *CAN'T*STIPATION

Antidotes to Emotional Can't*stipation*

Antidote 1
When you are disturbed, don't blame others; blame instead your own irrational inferences. (Epictetus)

It is easy to allow yourself to become distraught as long as you can blame someone or something else for your feelings. Since you are the only one who can ultimately save you from your distress, you are destined to suffer until you finally come to your senses and get on with your life. Now, it's an ancient Stoic insight that it's not the events in the external world that disturb us but rather how we ourselves regard these things. Thus spoke Epictetus:

> It is not the things themselves that disturb men but their judgements about these things. For example, death is nothing dreadful, or else Socrates too would have thought so, but the judgement that death is dreadful, *this* is the dreadful thing. When, therefore, we are hindered, or disturbed, or grieved, let us never blame anyone but ourselves, that means, our own judgements.[3]

LBT agrees with Epictetus. More exactly, it holds that what upsets people are their irrational *inferences*. When you accept an irrational rule like awfulizing, you can wind up deducing a judgment like it's awful that people die. Such a judgment in turn sustains your emotion, for example, anxiety over the inevitability of death. In other words, if you stop inferring that death is awful, you can stop feeling anxious about it.

Epictetus' antidote to emotional *can't*stipation is to remind yourself of your ability to control the inferences that you make. Once you give up the idea that your feelings are caused by external things and see instead that they are conclusions *you* infer from premises in your reasoning, you are ready to take control. For example, suppose you have inferred that the motorist in front of you is a miserable shit because he's creeping along and making you late to an important appointment. You can address your anger by saying to yourself, "I'm in charge of my own emotions, no one else. I'm the one who's inferring that this guy's a miserable shit because he's going too slow.

Nobody else is making this inference but me, so I'm the one *making myself* angry."

Once you concede this to yourself, you can then decide *against* continuing to make the inference and instead pursue a more rational line of reasoning: "Going too slow doesn't make him a miserable shit. After all, he's still a person, a being with intrinsic worth and dignity, a creature of God, a conscious, self-aware center of value."

You've got the power. You can choose to keep yourself in a tailspin or to straighten yourself out. You can choose to go with the flow of your self-destructive tendencies to apply irrational rules, or you can take a rational stand against them. You can do it. Yes you *can*. Excrete that disempowering *can't* by telling yourself *you can*. Empower yourself.

Antidote 2

Avoid language that denies responsibility for your emotion, such as "you made me angry," "you upset me," "you pissed me off," and "you aggravated me." Use instead the language of responsibility, such as "I made myself angry," "I upset myself," "I pissed myself off," and "I aggravated myself." (Epictetus, Wittgenstein, James)

The language you use to describe your emotions can have implications for whether you are empowered against irrational emotions. When you speak of your emotions in the passive voice ("I was angered," "It made me angry," "They pissed me off" . . .), you take the responsibility for your emotions away from yourself and place it on some external person or thing. You thereby deny any role in your emotionality as though you were suddenly abducted by some powerful assailant, shoved into a car, and taken for a wild ride.

On the other hand, you can speak about your emotions in an active voice that takes responsibility rather than deflects it onto others. "I made myself angry" and "I pissed myself off" are expressions of responsibility. Speaking in these ways empowers you against irrational emotions rather than enslaves you to them.

Epictetus himself would have favored this active voice when referring to emotions because he believed that, while events in the external world were fully determined, you nevertheless could exercise control over what went on internally, inside your own mind. But you don't have to get too deep in the murky metaphysical waters of free will versus determinism to find ways to justify speaking in the active rather than the passive voice about your emotions. Philosopher Ludwig Wittgenstein said that "language is an instrument. Its concepts are instruments"; and, he added, "concepts lead us to make investigations; are the expressions of our interest, and direct our interest."[4] The interests we have can therefore be crucial to what concepts we apply. As William James pointed out, reality is not simply handed to us without our own input into it. "We add, both to the subject and to the predicate part of reality. The world stands really malleable, waiting to receive its final touches at our hands."[5]

In the end, what language we use may depend more on what value we reap than on any intrinsic features of reality. The language of passive submission to our emotions is not serviceable for purposes of attaining happiness. Its "cash value," as James would say, is poor. On the other hand, the language that implies responsibility for our emotions is in harmony with attaining happiness. In fact, it is crucial. As Epictetus admonishes, unless you acknowledge responsibility for your emotions, your search for happiness is bound to fail.

Antidote 3
Prove that you are more than just some preprogrammed biological mechanism. Put yourself to the empirical test. (Hume, Ayer)

Proof is in the doing. The hypothesis that you have considerable control over your emotions is not only a valuable one. It has the backing of one of the most philosophically significant theories of knowledge in the history of philosophy. The theory in question is known as *empiricism*. This is the view that factual statements (statements that expand our knowledge about things existing in the world) are meaningful or true only if they can be verified by experience.[6] David Hume put this view into sharp focus when he raised skeptical doubts about the validity of religious or metaphysical doctrines not verifiable through experience. He queried,

> Does it contain any abstract reasoning concerning quantity or number? No. Does it contain any experimental reasoning concerning matters of fact or existence? No. Commit it to the flames: For it can contain nothing but sophistry and illusion.[7]

In this same venerable tradition, British philosopher Alfred Jules Ayer proposed his "criterion of verifiability," according to which a statement is

> factually significant to any given person if only if he knows how to verify the proposition which it purports to express—that is, if he knows what observations would lead him, under certain conditions, to accept the proposition as being true, or reject it as being false.[8]

Are there any observations that would verify that you *can*, indeed, control your emotions, or should we commit this doctrine to the flames?

Suppose that, in the midst of a strong tendency to have a cow, you stopped yourself by finding and applying a rational antidote. Would you not then be satisfied that you have this power? I would venture to say so. In the process of overcoming your emotional *can'ts*tipation, you would have to excrete your *can't*stipating *I can't* and replace it with an empowering *Yes I can*. If after doing so you avoided feeling the anger you were accustomed to feel under similar circumstances, would you not have proven to yourself that you can indeed control your emotions? Yes.

By pushing yourself to verify your own power of emotional control, you can join many others who have used the tools of LBT to control their emotions. The ability to overcome your emotional *can'ts*tipation by practicing LBT techniques is not some metaphysical mumbo-jumbo grist for the flames. It is a factually significant proposition that has the backing of observation. If you are blocked by the *can't*, then it behooves you for the sake of happiness to try your hand at un-*can't*stipating yourself. Prove it. Do it.

Antidote 4
Put on a happy face and send your blues packing. (Ryle)

There is an intimate connection between doing and feeling. Emotions engender behavior. If you feel miserable, you will typically act like it. In fact, some philosophers have attempted to define emotions entirely in terms of behavior. In his classic book *The Concept of Mind*, philosopher Gilbert Ryle claims that the discovery of emotions—your "inclinations" and "moods"—is no different than any other perceptual knowledge:

> I hear and understand your conversational avowals, your interjections and your tone of voice; I see and understand your gestures and your facial expressions. . . . My discovery of my own motives and moods is not different in kind, although I am ill placed to see my own grimaces and gestures, or to hear my own tones of voice.[9]

As for discovering your emotions by tending to your own inner states of consciousness, he bluntly states that emotions "are not 'experiences' any more than habits or maladies are 'experiences,'"[10] thus Woody Allen's quip about what one behaviorist says to another when they meet: "Your fine. How am I?"

The jest underscores the absurdity of trying to define emotions *purely* in terms of behavior without acknowledging the existence of other mental components—cognitions and bodily sensations—to which only the person having an emotion has access. Nonetheless, your emotions are still largely—although not entirely—a behavioral affair. By changing your behavior, you *can* change the way you feel, even on the inside.

Did you ever feel down for one reason or another and not really in any mood to see anyone? However, because you have some obligation to be somewhere—work, school, or some other social gathering—you pull yourself out of bed, force yourself to get washed up and dressed, and listlessly dump yourself into your car. On arrival, you put on an act, trying your best to hide your lousy mood. With a self-conscious effort, you fashion your lips into a smile, speak in a pleasant tone, and generally feign a pleasant disposition. After a while, what happens? You guessed it. If you are like most of us, you will discover yourself actually *feeling* better, not just outwardly but also on the inside.

Antidote 5
When you are in an emotional tizzy, change the focus of your consciousness to a different, less contentious object. (Husserl)

Not only can you approach emotional *can't*stipation from the *outside in*—changing what's going on inside by changing your outward behavior—you can also approach it from the *inside out*—changing your outward behavior by changing what's going on inside. You can do this by intentionally changing your object of consciousness. By "object of consciousness" I mean that which you are conscious *of*.

According to one philosophical current known as phenomenology, all states of consciousness, including emotions, refer outwardly to some object such as a person, an event, a problem, or a thing. As Edmund Husserl, a leading exponent of phenomenology, states, "The essence of consciousness, in which I live as my own self, is the so called intentionality. Consciousness is always conscious of something."[11] For example, when you are angry, you are angry *about* something, such as the guy cutting you off on the highway, a nasty comment, a political decision, or being stood up. Your anger has an *intention*, which means that it is directed or focused on some object.

LBT holds that the report you file under a rule when you have an emotion is actually the filling out of the intentional object of your emotion.[12] For example, when you are angry about being cut off on the highway, the premises of your reasoning might look like this:

Rule: If someone does something shitty to me, then he's a worthless shit.

Report: This guy has cut me off on the highway [which is a shitty thing to have done to me].

Emotion: Anger about this guy's cutting me off on the highway.

See how the object of your anger is really the report you have filed? Then it should be clear to you that your emotion could not persist without the filing of this report. As soon as you are distracted from filing it, the emotion begins to fall apart. You can think of the object of your emotion as being much like the eye of a hurricane. When it is tightly wound (focused), the hurricane is strong. But when the eye begins to get less clearly defined, the hurricane begins to break up. The same is true with emotions and their objects. The object holds the focus of the emotion and keeps it tightly wound. When it is no longer "intended," the emotion breaks up. For example, you can break up your anger if you stop tending to the guy who just cut you off and instead intentionally direct your focus elsewhere on the highway. For example, I find it useful to travel in a less congested area of the highway (if possible) rather than to drive amongst a cluster of cars. If you've ever noticed, cars tend to travel in packs, so you could find a clearing and make it your goal to get there. After a bit, when your bodily juices have settled, the anger will be history.

Want to break up your anger, depression, guilt, anxiety, or other gnawing emotion? Take your focus off its object and direct your consciousness to a different, less contentious object. After a while, the storm will subside, and you can move on with your life.

Antidote 6

Don't make excuses for succumbing to an irrational passion. Change can't *to* won't. *(Sartre)*

From an existential perspective, human existence is without excuses. You are responsible not only for what you do but also for how you *feel*. Sartre is very blunt about this:

> The existentialist does not believe in the power of passion. He will never agree that a sweeping passion is a ravaging torrent which fatally leads a man to certain acts and is therefore an excuse. He thinks that man is responsible for his passion.[13]

Being responsible for your passion means excreting *can't* and replacing it with *won't*. It also means, as mentioned earlier, speaking as though you're responsible. It is not someone or something else that's upsetting you. *You* are the one who's doing it by the inferences you are making. *You* have the power to stop inferring horseshit. You *can* do it.

If you are indeed able to control your emotions, then it is a bald-faced lie (to yourself) that you can't stop upsetting yourself. It is plainly bad faith, and the antidote is to fess up to it by saying *won't* rather than *can't*. You said, "I *can't* stop feeling down about messing up so badly today at work." Correction: You *won't* stop inferring horseshit. But *won't* is consistent with *can*. You *can*, but you *won't*. The next step is to change your *won't* to *will* and do what you can to stop disturbing yourself. For example, you can intentionally change your object of consciousness, as discussed.

Antidote 7
Be passionate about overcoming your irrational emotions. (Nietzsche)

Your will to overcome an irrational emotion is not itself without emotional import. According to LBT, people can and should be motivated by rational emotions, that is, emotions that are deduced from rational premises. For example, suppose you are *can't*stipating your interpersonal happiness with the bullshit that you can't ever get close to anyone. Suppose also that you rationally come to see that this really is bullshit and that, if you keep it up, you will end up living a desolate, lonely existence of your own choosing. Under these conditions, it is likely that you will also deduce fear of sticking to your irrational rule of life. This rational emotion could then motivate you to overcome your irrational fear of commitment. As Nietzsche said,

> The will to overcome an emotion, is ultimately only the will of another, or of several other, emotions.[14]

Whoever said that a rational will could not have the backing of your emotions? On the contrary, I would urge you to be passionate about defeating your irrational emotions. There is nothing irrational about being moved by an emotion to overcome another (irrational) emotion, just as long as this motivation is itself rational.[15] In fact, seeing the destructiveness of your irrational emotions, I hope you will be emotionally aroused to do something about it.

BEHAVIORAL *CAN'T*STIPATION

Antidotes to Behavioral Can'tstipation

Antidote 1

Don't confuse what goes on under your skin for what you, as a person, can and can't do. (Melden)

When you say that you can't stop thinking about something or that you can't speak up, get along with others, or change your bad habits, what exactly does the *can't* mean? Is it physical constraint? Surely you can't lift ten thousand pounds merely with your naked arms. This *can't* follows from the laws of physical science. But when you say things like you can't get along with others, you are not into physical laws. There is no physical law that clearly exempts you from getting along with others. So maybe it is some psychological impossibility. But again, I will eat my psychological hat if you can produce a law of psychology that makes it impossible—and I mean impossible, not just difficult or challenging—for you to get along with others.

Maybe there are some events going on in the depths of your body, especially your central nervous system, that render you a helpless victim of your biology. After all, this is what some philosophers have meant in denying the existence of "free will." According to this view, we are all basically very complex biological robots whose actions can be predicted just by knowing enough about the biochemical processes going on in our bodies in interaction with our physical environments. According to this view, the fact that we are not very adept at making such predictions only underscores the fact that we know so little about the sort of physical events that determine human behavior.

But let's get real. When you say that *you* are helpless or that *you* can't change your behavior, you are talking about what you, *the person*, can't do. This does not mean the same as that there is some brain event determining your behavior. Brain events are not helpless; people are. Brain events are not capable or incapable of human actions; people are. People think and make decisions; brain events don't. So you can't, logically, reduce talk about what you can and cannot do to talk about bodily events.

Philosopher A. I. Melden expressed this point succinctly:

The alleged conclusion that each of us is a helpless victim of the events transpiring in the central nervous system is simply a logical howler [a fallacy]. "Could have done" and "could not have done," "helpless,"

etc.—these are expressions employed not with respect to events occurring in the mechanism of the body, nor to mental events . . . but to *persons.*[16]

Regardless of what's going on in the depths of your body, it won't do
to say you *can't* change your behavior because of these inner bodily states.
Surely, you don't even know what's happening inside your nervous system,
so you are not justified in saying that this is what prevents you from changing your behavior. From the outside, you are a person who thinks, decides,
acts, and many other things that don't even make sense at a deeper level of
bodily functions. As a person, you are confronted with what to do about
your life, and what's happening below your skin does not, at this personal
level, foreclose your existential role in making a choice. As Sartre once expressed, "You are condemned to be free."[17] Saying that you can't is just a
dodge of your personal responsibility. No sophistical flimflamming will get
you out of this responsibility.

Antidote 2
*Ask yourself if what you did was due to external compulsion or ignorance. If not, ex-
crete the* can't *and accept responsibility. (Aristotle)*

Aristotle thought that actions for which you could be held responsible
must be ones that you do voluntarily. For example, you don't act voluntarily if what you do is done under external compulsion. Actions, says Aristotle, are so done "when the cause is in the external circumstances and the
agent contributes nothing."[18] Suppose that somebody rear-ends your car,
setting it in motion, causing it to rear-end the car in front of you. You are
not really responsible for your action (of rear-ending the car in front of you)
because it was done involuntarily. But this is certainly different from rear-
ending the car in front of you, say, because he "flicked you off." Surely, it
won't work to deny responsibility for your action by claiming that it was involuntary. For, as Aristotle says, voluntary acts are ones where "the moving
principle is in the agent himself"; "the acts whose moving principles are in
us must themselves also be in our power and voluntary."[19] Now, surely, the
moving principle is *in us* when we perform such intentional acts.

Aristotle also says that some involuntary acts are ones done by reason
of ignorance of particular circumstances. For example, suppose you tell
someone something not knowing that it was supposed to be a secret. Aristotle would say your act was involuntary, provided that you regretted what

you had done and were not responsible for your ignorance (you could not have reasonably foreseen it was a secret). But clearly you don't act by reason of ignorance in this sense when you intentionally ram the car in front of you because the driver did something you disliked, even if you regret what you have done afterward.

Aristotle also distinguishes between acts done *by reason of* ignorance and actions that are simply done *in* ignorance. If you drive drunk and run someone down or fly into a rage and strike someone, you act *in* ignorance, "for the man who is drunk or in a rage is thought to act as a result not of ignorance but of one of the causes mentioned, yet not knowingly but in ignorance."[20] Such actions, the philosopher says, are voluntary, and you are responsible for them, "for the moving principle is in the man himself, since he had the power of not getting drunk and his getting drunk was the cause of his ignorance."[21] And the same thing can be said of other actions resulting from irrational states of emotion.[22]

So, with the exception of external compulsion and certain actions done by reason of ignorance, your actions are voluntary, and you are responsible for them. No excuses or bullshitting allowed. Don't say, "The devil made me do it" or "That guy pissed me off." If anyone does the pissing, it's you. Remember, "the moving principle is in you." You are your own driver. Emancipate yourself; un*can't*stipate yourself.

Antidote 3

Give yourself some behavioral assignments, including going in the opposite direction to which you are inclined. (Aristotle)

Aristotle would also remind you that you become the sort of person you are by repeatedly doing the same things. You create your own irrational inclinations by continually acting irrationally. If you make a habit out of overeating, your stomach will accommodate more food, and you will find it easy enough to pig out and increasingly more difficult to eat in moderation. If you repeatedly retreat from social contexts, you will make yourself reclusive, and it will become increasingly more difficult to control yourself.

Behavioral therapy takes its cue from Aristotle by realizing that a constructive way to change bad habits is to change your behavior. So instead of pigging out, you can put less food on your plate and avoid the all-you-can-eat buffets. And, instead of shying away from social contact, you can deliberatively put yourself in a social situation, such as going to a party or talking to a stranger in line at the supermarket.

If you have a behavioral problem, for example, asserting yourself in a social context—speaking up in class, asking someone out on a date, requesting a well-deserved raise, making a public speech, and sundry other social inhibitions—then you are merely reinforcing your problem by repeating the same old avoidance behavior. To break the old self-defeating habits, you can and should change your behavior. Speak up, ask for a date, request the raise, and deliver a public speech. Only by doing these things can you break the inertia built up from repeatedly engaging in avoidance behavior. Only by doing such things, grabbing the bull by the horn, can you make yourself do and *feel* better.

Aristotle had a very useful suggestion for "straightening ourselves out":

> We must consider the things towards which we ourselves also are easily carried away; for some of us tend to one thing, some to another; and this will be recognizable from the pleasure and the pain we feel. We must drag ourselves away to the contrary extreme; for we shall get into the intermediate state by drawing well away from error, as people do in straightening sticks that are bent.[23]

For Aristotle, going to extremes is always irrational. Being a coward is an extreme of controlling your fears. Being a fool is the other extreme. But being courageous is the mean between these extremes. It is the "golden mean" between these two extremes, where you are afraid only when it is rational to be afraid and not afraid when it is irrational to be afraid. But if you have a tendency to be cowardly, then you can try going to the extreme of being fearless. Since you tend in the opposite direction, you will not really end up being fearless but rather will get closer to being reasonable about what to fear. Just like you can pull a stick that is bent in one direction in the opposite direction so that it snaps back and gets closer to the middle, you too can you straighten yourself out by attempting to go to the other extreme.

So take some advice from old Aristotle. If you tend to be self-deprecating, try to be a braggart. If you are introverted, try acting like an extrovert. If you tend to be melancholic, try being a clown. If you have anxieties about socializing, try being a party animal. If you tend to be a stick in the mud, try being a rolling stone. If you tend to be a worrywart, try being a rock. If you are a workaholic, try to be bum. In doing so, you are not likely to become a braggart, extrovert, clown, party animal, rolling stone, rock, or bum. But you are more likely to level off somewhere closer to the middle.

VOLITIONAL *CAN'T*STIPATION

Antidotes to Volitional Can'tstipation

Antidote 1

When desire inclines you toward what you know is wrong or away from what you know is right, don't say you can't do otherwise. Say you can and make the effort to overcome your inclination. (Aristotle, Campbell, Santas)

In nature, things tend to take the path of least resistance. As water tends to take the path least obstructed, so too do humans in their commerce with life. In many cases, this presents no problem and is rational and beneficial. This confirmable, human tendency is probably part of a process of natural selection whereby human beings, like other creatures, cope with their environment in order to survive. You become sleepy, and it's easier for you to fall asleep than to remain awake, and in doing so, you get the sleep your body requires to continue operating. But a problem occurs when you fall asleep at the post you were entrusted to guard.

Not uncommonly, you can be the greater gainer by working against the current of your body. In fact, currents change when you create new paths of least resistance, as when you fight the craving for sweets and eat healthy, eventually getting used to a different diet and finding it easier to avoid sweets. But people often yield to temptation. Even though they know something isn't good for them, they do it anyway.

Aristotle was the first to systematically examine this problem of *weakness of the will.* Suppose that you are on a low-carb diet and have recently adopted a new rule, "I *shouldn't* eat sweets," whereas your rule, since early childhood, had always been, "I *should* eat sweets." Now let's say that you are at a social and that, there before you, is a sumptuously sweet brownie.

According to Aristotle, you have, in this situation, a conflict between two lines of reasoning: one bidding you to eat the brownie and other forbidding it. One says, "I should eat sweets" and "this is sweet." The other says, "I shouldn't eat sweets" and "this is sweet." Since you also have a bodily drive or "appetite" for what is pleasant and since you know that sweet things like brownies are pleasant to eat, you will have a tendency to eat the brownie. This is the path of least resistance. You are physically (biochemically) disposed toward eating it.

LBT accepts Aristotle's view of how we come to follow an irrational rule even though we may know that it is irrational. It holds that human beings have the power to defeat irrational rules by opposing them with rational ones. For example, in Aristotle's example, the rule forbidding eating sweets can be viewed as a rational antidote to the rule bidding you to eat sweets.

Unfortunately, many of us suffer from weakness of the will. We do not muster up the strength to overcome the bodily tendencies, appetites, and cravings that move us toward following irrational rules, even when we know that they are irrational.[24] Instead, we *can'ts*tipate ourselves by saying we can't.

The *can't* short-circuits even trying. So you tell yourself you just *can't resist* that sumptuous brownie. Then, taking this declaration as your proverbial green light, you reach for it.

Did you ever start eating your favorite crunchy and then try to stop in the middle? There you are, your hand moving back and forth between your mouth and a newly opened bag of Doritos nacho chips. Back and forth you go, funneling chip after chip into your mouth. Okay, now stop cold. Don't put a single additional chip into your mouth.

Can you *feel* the current of your body moving you to reach for another chip? Indeed, it is easier to tell yourself you can't resist this current as you reach for another, and another, and still another, until there is not even a fragment left in the bag.

It is in situations like this where there is temptation that it makes sense to speak of an *effort* of will. As C. A. Campbell expressed it, "We are conscious of making an effort of will only when we choose a course that is contrary to the course towards which we feel that our desiring nature most strongly inclines us."[25]

In resisting your urge to take another chip, you can perceive your effort of will. This perceived power is what I mean by *willpower*. If you make an effort to overcome your "desiring nature" to reach for another chip, you can be said to have *exercised* your willpower.

In an important article, philosopher Aristotelis Santas defines *will-power* as

(a) the power or ability to refrain from doing something (either before you do it, or while in the midst of doing it) even though you are strongly inclined to do it; or (b) the power or ability to continue doing something even though we are strongly inclined not to.[26]

Santas emphasizes the significance of willpower for our practical freedom.[27] Without it, you would be little more than a biological machine responding automatically to your environment. Your ability to consciously and deliberatively stop a mechanical progression of bodily motions makes you different than a mere machine, which simply follows its internal circuitry and programming. The importance of this power should not be understated. It's what makes you a *free* agent.

*Can't*stipation of the will renders you *unfree*. In telling yourself that you can't stand things as soon as they get difficult or challenging, you automatically set yourself up for failure. Even if you know right from wrong, rational from irrational, it won't much matter if you simply take the path of least resistance and give up.

The obvious first step in un*can't*stipating your will is to excrete the *can't*, which keeps you from making an effort to control yourself. Saying *can* instead of *can't* and *will* instead of *won't*, you can free yourself to make an effort.

Antidote 2
To increase your willpower muscle, start small and build yourself up gradually. (Epictetus, Santas)

Obviously, making an effort is one thing, and actually succeeding in overcoming a deeply ingrained habit is another. As Santas stresses, some people may have more willpower than others and to that extent are freer. This disparity in willpower may well be partly due to individual biological differences between us. Nevertheless, all of us—yes all of us—have to varying degrees the ability to endure short-term frustration in order to reap long-term satisfaction.

More good news. Willpower can be strengthened through practice. Santas usefully compares willpower to a muscle that can be increased by exercising it. Just as a bodybuilder starts with lifting small amounts of weight and works up to larger quantities, so too can you increase your willpower.[28]

What counts as starting small is to some degree relative to particular persons. For example, you might find it easier to control yourself in relating to strangers, while I might have a harder time with friends and family. If you have an anger management problem, it will probably be harder to stop yourself from flying into a rage than to keep from eating an additional chip, but the "muscle" you exercise in both cases is one and the same. By starting small, you can build up to the more difficult tasks.

Suppose you have a tendency to damn others when they do things you don't like. It may be easier to stop yourself from damning someone who clumsily steps on your toe in the supermarket than to stop yourself from damning your significant other when he or she forgets your birthday. Yet by exercising your willpower in the easier cases, you can increase your prowess to handle the more difficult ones.

In the course of a day, there are typically lots of mundane things that you can disturb yourself over if you let yourself. Here lies an excellent training ground for strengthening your will. As Epictetus reminds us,

> Begin, therefore, with the little things. Your paltry oil gets spilled, your miserable wine stolen; say to yourself, "This is the price paid for a calm spirit, this the price for peace of mind." Nothing is got without a price.[29]

Good habits, like bad ones, tend to generate the same and crowd out their opposition. If you can get through a single day without disturbing yourself, then you have made an important start, which can begin to gain its own momentum as you incrementally increase your range of self-control.

Backsliding is inevitable. As an imperfect human, you will mess up and blow your cool, but the important point is to build up your tendency to stay cool. It is not any single episode that will determine such a tendency but rather many episodes collectively.

Keep a *mental notebook* on your progress. How far have you come in a week, a month, or a year? Are you losing it less and less? Are you generally attaining greater peace of mind? Remember, building willpower and overcoming irrational thinking is a life pursuit; it's not something you attain at any given time so that you can sit back and not concern yourself with it. As an imperfect human, there will *always* be room for improvement. As soon as you say to yourself, "I don't need to work on my thinking any more," you'll find yourself backsliding.

I recommend adopting a *rational recovery model* similar to a drug and alcohol addictions recovery model. According to this approach, you are never completely *recovered*; instead, you are always *recovering*. This means that you will always run the risk of lapsing back to your old irrational habits if you get sloppy and stop practicing your LBT and will-strengthening exercises.

Antidote 3
Reframe challenging situations as opportunities to strengthen your willpower muscle. (Nietzsche)

What other things can you do to strengthen your willpower muscle? Again, since exercising willpower is a conscious effort that you can use in applying antidotes to overcome irrational thinking, you can gain lots of practice by consciously working through and practicing the steps of LBT in your everyday life,[30] especially in any practical context in which you use *can't* to *can't*stipate your will. These cases present direct challenges to your willpower because as soon as you say, "I can't stand it," you have directly disavowed yourself of the willpower to succeed. By making the effort, you can prove to yourself that you have the power.

Nietzsche, a firm advocate of the will to power, which was, for him, the will to live, eloquently stated the point:

> "Man" has grown most powerfully to a height . . . that for that to happen the danger of his situation first had to grow enormously, his power of invention and pretense (his "spirit") had to develop under lengthy pressure and compulsion into something refined and audacious, his will for living had to intensify all the way into an unconditional will for power.[31]

In adversity and under great pressure, you may have your greatest opportunities to prove your own willpower to yourself and to grow stronger.

Suppose, for example, you're telling yourself that you couldn't stand to visit your in-laws on Sunday. "What a miserable waste of my day off," you think as memories of your in-laws' condescending banter fill your mind. You can now take a more constructive approach: "What a great opportunity to strengthen my willpower muscle," you say. "Instead of going to the gym to work out, I can visit my in-laws to work on my flabby will. With the way they go at me, I could be Hercules by the time I'm finished visiting!"

Antidote 4
Strengthen your will by practicing shame-attacking exercises. (Ellis)

Shame-attacking exercises are an excellent way to put some muscle on your will. As discussed earlier, this means pushing yourself to do things that you are especially ashamed of doing. Don't get me wrong. I'm not referring to immoral or illegal things. I'm talking about things that are relatively benign but that you feel embarrassed to do.

I once bought a pink sport jacket at my wife's bidding. She also tried to convince me to buy the pants, but unfortunately I refused. The same day, I was in a grocery store wearing my new jacket when I saw another man wearing the exact same garment but also carrying a matching pocketbook. He approached me and complimented me on my fine taste in jackets. I vowed not to wear it again, but when I told my students about it, they entreated me to wear it to class. I wore it, and my students respected me for it. It was an excellent shame-attacking exercise for me since it helped me overcome my *can't*stipated socialization about how a "real" man should look. (Too bad I didn't also buy the pants!) You too can find something you can use to *un*shame yourself. Go for it. Excrete your *can't* and add some muscle to your will.

Antidote 3
Be courageous: don't let your irrational passions enslave you and turn your life upside down. (Plato)

In strengthening your will, you will make yourself brave. In fact, according to Plato, the will is not functioning properly unless you have cultivated the willpower to act rationally in spite of your irrational tendencies.

Here's a bit of Platonic psychoanalysis. Your soul consists of three parts: reason, appetites (the passions), and spirit (the will). Each of these parts must be doing its proper job in order for you to be well adjusted. So what are the proper functions of each part of your soul? Plato speaks:

> It will be the business of reason to rule with wisdom and forethought on behalf of the entire soul; while the spirited element ought to act as its subordinate and ally. . . . When both have been thus nurtured and trained to know their own true functions, they must be set in command over the appetites, which form the greater part of each man's soul and are by nature insatiably covetous. . . . And so we call an individual brave in virtue of this spirited part of his nature, when in spite of pain or pleasure, it holds fast to the injunctions of reason about what he ought or ought not to be afraid of.[32]

That is, you are functional when your reason calls the shots and you have the willpower and therefore courage to act rationally despite your strong, irrational, bodily drives for pleasure and avoidance of pain.

Let's suppose you perceive someone to have done something wrong to you, such as having lied to you. You say, "That SOB deserves hell and damnation," and you have a strong irrational desire to trash him. But, in spite of your intense passion, you use a rational antidote to calm yourself down and to respond in a more constructive way. This would be to act bravely since reason would triumph over irrational inclinations to act in a self-defeating manner. And this is, for Plato, as it is for LBT, a mark of the well-adjusted person. In such a person, reason works in cooperation with the will to overcome the irrational rule-driven passions, which, unless constrained by reason, will almost invariably lead to destructive results.

For Plato, the real enemy of your soul is therefore not the external events and contingencies of life about which you disturb yourself but rather the unbridled, human tendency to deal irrationally with these events, a tendency that has, by its nature, the capacity to "enslave the others [reason and will] and to usurp a dominion to which it has no right, thus turning the whole of life upside down."[33] On the other hand, as discussed earlier, when your emotions are themselves directed by reason (deduced from rational premises), they are functioning appropriately and can be helpful in overcoming other, irrational emotions.

For Plato, it is therefore your *irrational* emotions that challenge your strength of will. The person who fearlessly flies off the handle in the face of danger demonstrates both weakness and cowardliness. For the sake of happiness, be strong and brave: flex that willpower muscle.

Antidote 4
Apply the hedonic calculus toward your long-term happiness. (Bentham)

*Can'ts*tipation of your will signifies low frustration tolerance. As a result, you trade long-term satisfaction for immediate relief of frustration. It is easier to give up than to persevere, so you do just that. As a result, you end up missing out on what you might have achieved had you hung in there.

The distinction between short-term satisfaction and long-term satisfaction is one enshrined in the annals of philosophy. In particular, it is carefully addressed by Jeremy Bentham in his famous "hedonic calculus."

Bentham, as earlier noted, was a hedonist philosopher, which means that he thought the value of anything depended on how much pleasure it could yield. Some things, such as money, are *instrumentally* valuable, which means they can be used to produce pleasure, such as when you purchase a movie ticket and enjoy the show. In contrast, some things may be *intrinsically* valuable, that is, valuable *for their own sake*, such as the pleasant sensation of a cool drink on a steamy day when you are parched. Some things can be *dis*valuable intrinsically yet valuable instrumentally, such as a visit to the dentist. Indeed, unless you are a masochist, there is nothing pleasing about the feel of a dentist's drill on the nerve of your tooth. Nevertheless, removing the decay from a tooth by drilling it out may be necessary if you are to enjoy good dental hygiene in the future. So, in such a case, you endure the short-term intrinsic displeasure for the sake of the long-term pleasures of good dental health.

Now Bentham's practical contribution has been to provide standards for assessing both the intrinsic and the instrumental value of a pleasure.[34] To assess the intrinsic value of a pleasure, he says to consider these circumstances:

1. Its *intensity*
2. Its *duration*
3. Its *certainty* or *uncertainty*
4. Its *propinquity* or *remoteness*[35]

The idea here is to try to have pleasures that are intensely pleasurable, long lasting, likely to be had, and as immediate as possible. Take a sexual pleasure, for example. Although it may be brief, it might be very intense, probable, and immediate (for example, a pickup at a nightclub). But in going in for such a pleasure, you may be blindsided by your desire for immediate gratification without considering the potential for dangerous "side effects." So Bentham adds these standards:

5. Its *fecundity*, or the chance it has of being followed by sensations of the *same* kind, that is, pleasures, if it be a pleasure; pains, if it be a pain
6. Its *purity*, or the chance it has of not being followed by sensations of the *opposite* kind, that is, pains, if it be a pleasure; pleasures, if it be a pain

For example, you would also need to consider whether going in for this sexual pleasure would lead to further pleasures. That's what he means by "fecundity." And you would need to consider whether it would lead to other pains. That's the "purity" standard. If this is a one-night stand, then the only pleasure you're going to get out of this is the pleasure of the moment: no further pleasures and a low fecundity rating. But that's not the end. If the person with whom you've had sex is infected with venereal diseases, HIV, or hepatitis C, then you may be in for a *very* low purity rating. In such a case, the immediate intrinsic gratification you get out of a roll in the hay may be far outweighed by the negative instrumental impact on the rest of your life.

Here's Bentham's advice, straight up, for managing a *can't*stipated will: Before you act, do the math. If you are risking your future happiness for the sake of fleeting jollies in the short term, you had better put your willpower muscle to work, even if it's very strenuous. All buoyed up, it may be hard to put on those mental breaks or to persevere in spite of your frustration. But, as Plato would say, reason needs to take the reigns of your soul and commandeer the will. This means applying *all* six of Bentham's standards to direct your will instead of slavishly nodding to a shortsighted, self-defeating *can't*.

NOTES

1. "Volitional" refers to *can't*stipating your *will*.

2. Even in cases where drug therapy is indicated, these drugs do not themselves do the thinking *for* the person with the biochemical imbalance. The medication restores homeostasis and thereby makes it easier for the person to use logic-based methods, which can then become very helpful for the person in question.

3. Epictetus, *Encheiridion* (Manual), in Baird and Kaufmann, *From Plato to Derrida*, 260.

4. Ludwig Wittgenstein, *Philosophical Investigations*, trans. G. E. M. Anscombe (New York: Macmillan, 1968), 569, 570.

5. William James, "Pragmatism and Humanism," in *William James: Pragmatism*, ed. Ralph Barton Perry (New York: New American Library, 1955), 167.

6. This tradition distinguishes between statements that can be known through experience (statements known a posteriori) and ones that can be known independent of experience (a priori). According to the standard interpretation of this tradition, the latter class of statements contains only definitional truths that don't really expand our knowledge of the world, for example, "All triangles have three sides." The truths of mathematics and logic are also said to be included in the latter class.

7. David Hume, *Enquiry concerning Human Understanding*, in *From Plato to Derrida*, 4th ed., ed. Forrest E. Baird and Walter Kaufmann (Upper Saddle River, N.J.: Prentice Hall, 2003), sec. 12, pt. 3, 790.

8. Alfred Jules Ayer, "Sense-Experience as the Standard of Truth," in *Philosophers at Work: Issues and Practice of Philosophy*, ed. Elliot D. Cohen (Fort Worth, Tex.: Harcourt, 2000), 334.

9. Gilbert Ryle, *The Concept of Mind* (New York: Harper & Row, 1980), 115.

10. Ryle, *The Concept of Mind*, 115.

11. Cited in Albert B. Hakim, *Historical Introduction to Philosophy*, 4th ed. (Upper Saddle River, N.J.: Prentice Hall, 2001), 562.

12. Elliot D. Cohen, *What Would Aristotle Do? Self-Control through the Power of Reason* (Amherst, N.Y.: Prometheus Books, 2003), 123.

13. Jean-Paul Sartre, "Existentialism," in Cohen, *Philosophers at Work*, 446.

14. Friedrich Nietzsche, *Beyond Good and Evil*, trans. Helen Zimmern, in the *Philosophy of Nietzsche* (New York: Random House, 1954), pt. 4, sec. 117, 460. The idea of overcoming an emotion with another emotion is all that I attribute to Nietzsche here. The idea that we should overcome irrational emotions using *rational* ones would probably have been more at home with Aristotle than it would have been with Nietzsche.

15. I am not assuming the view that the will itself is reducible to such other emotions or that the will must always be propelled by other emotions. Nor am I excluding this possibility. Generally, a good philosopher does not bite off more than he has to.

16. A. I. Melden, "Free Action," in *Free Will and Determinism*, ed. Bernard Berofsky (New York: Harper & Row, 1966), 219.

17. Sartre, "Existentialism," in Cohen, *Philosophers at Work*, 446.

18. Aristotle, *Ethics*, bk. 3, chap. 1, 965.

19. Aristotle, *Ethics*, bk. 3, chap. 5, 972.

20. Aristotle, *Ethics*, bk. 3, chap. 1, 966.

21. Aristotle, *Ethics*, bk. 3, chap. 5, 972.

22. "Of involuntary acts some are excusable, others not. For the mistakes which men make not only in ignorance but also from ignorance are excusable, while those which men do not from ignorance but (though they do them in ignorance) owing to a passion which is neither natural nor such as man is liable to [that is, which are irrational and destructive], are not excusable." Aristotle, *Ethics*, bk. 5, chap. 8, 1016.

23. Aristotle, *Ethics*, bk. 2, chap. 9, 963.

24. As discussed in chapter 1, this is what is called *cognitive dissonance*, that is, when your actions are out of gear with what you know to be rational.

25. C. A. Campbell, "The Psychology of Effort of Will," in Berofsky, *Free Will and Determinism*, (New York: Harper & Row, 1966), 346.

26. Aristotelis Santas, "Willpower," *International Journal of Applied Philosophy* 4, no. 2 (fall 1988): 9.

27. Santas contrasts practical freedom with metaphysical freedom, where the latter implies a state of not being determined by underlying causes such as biology and environment. On the other hand, practical freedom simply means the ability to overcome an otherwise automatic activity and to reflectively choose an alternative activity.

28. Santas, "Willpower."

29. Epictetus, *Encheiridion* (Manual), in Baird and Kaufmann, *From Plato to Derrida*, 261.

30. (1) Find your irrational premises, (2) refute them, (3) find antidotes for your refuted premises, and (4) exercise your willpower to implement your antidotes.

31. Nietzsche, *Beyond Good and Evil*, pt. 2, "The Free Spirit," sec. 44, 429.

32. Plato, *The Republic*, in Baird and Kaufmann, *From Plato to Derrida*, bk. 4, 105–6.

33. Plato, *The Republic*, Baird and Kaufmann, *From Plato to Derrida*, bk. 4, 106

34. Jeremy Bentham, *An Introduction to the Principles of Morals and Legislation*, in *The English Philosophers from Bacon to Mill*, ed. Edwin A. Burtt (New York: Random House, 1939), chap. 4, 803.

35. By "propinquity," he means the amount of time you have wait to have the pleasure.

6

BECOMING MORALLY CREATIVE

Do you perceive yourself to have a moral duty to upset yourself when something you deem important goes wrong? A telltale sign that you subscribe to such an "Eleventh Commandment" is that you require that others, for whom you also think it a problem, follow your lead and likewise upset themselves. "How," you ask, "can you be so calm and undisturbed at a time like this? Don't you even care?" And so others too must dutifully lower their heads and furrow their brows and beat themselves over the head with the problem until it gets resolved or something "more urgent" takes it place.

The rule in question says that you *have* to be disturbed, that there is a sacred moral duty, and that it is blasphemy for you or others relevantly situated to do anything pleasurable, relaxing, or otherwise productive that has nothing significant to do with the problem at hand. No, you must instead suffer on the altar of the almighty problem, giving yourself up to it, and exploring every nook and cranny of it, over and over again, until you see some light at the end of the dark tunnel. And even then, you must persevere until the problem is *definitely* eradicated and you can rest—although not for very long, as the next dark tunnel is predictably not far in the offing. This self-defeating rule says this:

> Thou Shalt Upset Yourself: If you encounter a problem in your life that you deem important, then you have a *moral duty* to ruminate over it, never stop thinking about it, make yourself miserable and upset over it, and demand that others, for whom you also deem it a problem, do the same until you have certainty—or near certainty—about a solution.

Notice that this rule prescribes a *moral duty*, that is, a *moral must*. It doesn't simply say you must because you *can't* as a psychological fact do otherwise.

This is essentially what the *can'tstipation* rule says. So the thou-shalt-upset-yourself rule is not the same thing as the *can'tstipation* rule, although many people who have perceived a duty to upset themselves have, when they have tried to renounce it, fallen back on the *can'tstipation* rule. I often admonish my clients and students that fallacies travel in herds. It's a good idea to keep this in mind as you work on overcoming the thou-shalt-upset-yourself rule. As you tear away this layer of irrationality, you may well find, underneath it, another layer of *can'tstipation*.

Now, what about a moral duty, an ethical command, to upset yourself? That's a crock if I've ever heard one. Not that this rule isn't popular among us messed-up humans. In fact, it's one of the most popular ways people drive themselves up a tree. But here I'm speaking as a professional ethicist. Having, for many years, studied ethics (meaning the *philosophical* study of morality), I've yet to come across an ethical thinker who, on philosophical or theological grounds, would defend a duty to make oneself miserable when one has a problem. Even "fire and brimstone" preachers like Jonathan Edwards did not entertain such a duty.

Edwards does seem to have come very close when, in speaking of sinfulness, he said,

> There are some sins especially, of which they have been guilty, which are ever before them, so that they cannot get them out of their minds. Sometimes when men are under conviction, their sins follow them, and haunt them like a specter.[1]

But here Edwards was referring to those who have committed serious sins. He never said that people should torment themselves when they are faced with problems of living. This would have been twisted and misplaced even for the likes of Edwards.[2]

Nor is a duty to upset yourself over your personal problems documented in the annals of classical ethical theory. An ethical theory is a perspective on how to determine right from wrong, good from bad. Far from recognizing such a duty, all these different perspectives would consistently regard such conduct as morally objectionable.

In the philosophical study of morality, a distinction is commonly made between consequence-based ethics and *non*–consequence-based ethics. The former includes views that determine right action by the tendency of an act to have good consequences. While these theories disagree about what a good consequence is, none of them could justify a duty for you to upset yourself over your problems of living.

You have already been exposed to one such theory—hedonism—according to which the good is defined as pleasure and the bad as pain. But there is simply no evidence that, by stressing yourself out when confronted with a problem, you will attain long-term satisfaction. In fact, there is good reason to think that such stress has adverse physiological effects on cognition and memory that make it *more difficult* for you to think effectively and therefore to attain a satisfactory resolution of your problems. So, from a hedonist perspective, you are defeating your purposes by wearing yourself out ruminating over your problems.

The most famous non-consequence-based theory is Immanuel Kant's. His theory emphasizes motive and discounts consequences altogether. According to Kant's theory, your motive is acceptable when everyone could consistently act on it. For example, it would be inconsistent and therefore unacceptable for you to refuse to rescue a drowning person since you yourself would want to be rescued if you were in the same situation.

As discussed in chapter 4, Kant also had another ethical standard, namely, to treat yourself as well as others as "ends in themselves" and not "mere means." This means to treat people as valuable *for their own sake* and not simply because you can use them to attain some desired goal. So, by refusing to save the drowning person, you deem him or her to have no value for his or her own sake and therefore violate this Kantian standard of respect for persons.

Here's a bit of Kantian logic: Would you want others to intrude on your personal autonomy by commanding you to upset yourself every time *they* perceived a problem? If you wouldn't want to be treated like this by others, how could you consistently justify treating others this way? Further, if you really had a duty to upset yourself every time you perceived a problem, then *all* human beings would also have such a duty. But would you even want to live in a world in which everybody always went around preoccupied with their personal problems to the exclusion of all other concerns, even your own? If you are rational, you wouldn't want to live in such a world. So, by Kant's logic, upsetting yourself over personal problems and dragging others along is unacceptable because it is not something everyone could consistently do. So *you* shouldn't do it.

And by Kant's alternative standard, the same thing would hold true. According to this standard, you shouldn't treat human beings, including yourself, as though their only value was to attain a certain goal. But in trashing your own happiness and that of others for the sole purpose of solving a problem, that's exactly what you are doing. As you have already seen, according to Kant, your value is a constant that does not wax and wane with the rising and falling tides of life.

Nor will you find any other theory of ethics that justifies a duty to upset yourself. Aquinas used "natural law" to determine right from wrong. He said that people should follow their natural inclinations since these were imprints on us of God's will. But while Aquinas talked about a natural disposition to seek survival, to educate one's young, and to avoid harming others, he never mentioned a natural inclination to make yourself miserable when you perceive a personal problem. So, obsessive worriers won't find an ally in Aquinas either.

John Locke, the famous seventeenth-century British philosopher and statesman, talked of the rights to life, liberty, and property, which is reflected in the Fifth Amendment of the U.S. Constitution. The Declaration of Independence also mirrored this language, replacing "property" with "pursuit of happiness." While a duty to upset yourself doesn't fall under "the pursuit of happiness," it still could be included under one of your personal liberties. After all, if you want to tear your hair out, that's your right. But while you may have a right to worry and aggravate *yourself* to death—regardless of whether this is a rational thing to do—that still doesn't make it a *duty*. A *right* means you have permission—it doesn't mean you are required. Moreover, it hardly seems permissible for you to impose on others' personal liberty by insisting that they enlist in your ruminations.

Nor would Aristotle recognize such a duty. Aristotle said to avoid the extremes, and certainly the duty to ruminate and upset yourself over problems until you find a solution is clearly excessive. On Aristotle's reading, far from being a virtue, this alleged duty would actually be a vice.

So there are solid ethical reasons for turning thumbs down on the thou-shalt-upset-yourself rule. Here's the refutation in summary:

> A moral duty to make yourself and/or others miserable and upset whenever you encounter what you perceive to be a significant life problem is morally bankrupt. It cannot be derived from the promotion of human happiness, pleasure, alleviation of pain and suffering, reason, obedience to God, nature, or any other philosophical standard that has been used to justify human duties. In fact, such a demand is inconsistent with and contrary to these ethical standards. It is also unrealistic to demand perfect certainty in resolving your practical problems before you can stop thinking about them. This is true because the reports you file in practical reasoning are always tentative and at most only probable.

Giving up your irrational idea of a duty to upset yourself sets you free to become *morally creative*. This means taking constructive actions instead of procrastinating until you lose the opportunity to act. It means not being afraid to frame and try out different, novel approaches to living; it means realizing that fulfillment in life includes positive, life-affirming values and experiences, not just preoccupation with a series of self-stultifying, negative problems terminating in death; it means realizing your inherent freedom to apply rational moral standards toward enhancing the lives of self and others.

ANTIDOTES TO THE
THOU-SHALT-UPSET-YOURSELF FALLACY

Antidote 1
Emancipate yourself from your own, self-inflicted tyranny. Announce your own declaration of independence asserting your rights to life, liberty, and the pursuit of happiness. (Jefferson and others)

I mentioned that you have a right to tear your hair out if you want. But you also have a right to be happy. If you are of a different mind, then it may be useful to recall the immortal words of the Declaration of Independence:

> We hold these truths to be self-evident, that all men are created equal, that they are endowed by their Creator with certain unalienable Rights, that among these are Life, Liberty and the pursuit of Happiness.—That to secure these rights, Governments are instituted among Men, deriving their just powers from the consent of the governed,—That whenever any Form of Government becomes destructive of these ends, it is the Right of the People to alter or to abolish it, and to institute new Government, laying its foundation on such principles and organizing its powers in such form, as to them shall seem most likely to effect their Safety and Happiness.[3]

In telling yourself that you have a *duty* to sweat bullets when you perceive a personal problem, you are in fact telling yourself that you don't have a right to pursue your own happiness. This is because a duty is a requirement, while a right is a permission. If you are required to make yourself *un*happy, then it is not permissible for you to be happy. But surely it *is* permissible for you to be happy.

When the Founding Fathers of our nation encountered a tyrannical government, they declared their independence and freedom and the right to do so for the sake of their happiness and prosperity. If you are living under the oppressive regime of the thou-shalt-upset-yourself rule, you also have the right to divest yourself of this oppression, to throw off your chains, and to declare your freedom. Now repeat after me: "I have a right to life, liberty, and the pursuit of happiness. I don't have to live under any oppressor, even if this oppressor is *me*. I can 'alter or abolish' this oppressive government and institute a new one—one that is mindful of my right to be happy." After all, the Founding Fathers formed a new nation to ensure the collective happiness of its citizens. Now why would you want to squander such hard-won freedom when you can write your own declaration of independence?

Here then is an antidote to thou shalt upset yourself straight from the Founding Fathers to you. Give yourself permission and, indeed, affirm your moral right to be happy and to not suffer even if something seems wrong or doesn't go your way.

Antidote 2
Content yourself with probability, not certainty, in resolving your problems of living and in framing your expectations. (Plato, Sartre)

The thou-shalt-upset-yourself rule tells you to keep yourself in an emotional tizzy until you have certain or near certain resolution of your problem. In principle, this means that you will almost never give up since attaining certainty or near certainty about life issues is not ordinarily possible. Remember what Plato said about this physical world of ours. It's imperfect. According to Plato, your judgments about this world are always fallible and never fully verifiable. Are you sure the scale is accurate that says you are five pounds heavier than you thought you were? You could, of course, keep checking your weight on different scales, but there's still a chance, even if slight, that the other scales are also broken. If you demand absolute certainty, there will always be room for checking—and checking and checking and checking.

One of my clients would spend hours and hours looking up disease symptoms on the Internet to find out what was wrong with her or her significant others. Of course, some articles confirmed some of her fears (usually her worst ones), while others confirmed other explanations. Since the amount of links she could search was voluminous, she could never seem to satisfy her obsession. So she kept herself in a state of suspended frustration until by sheer exhaustion she let the worry go, typically only to replace it with another obsession in a matter of days or hours.

The rational approach to problem solving is therefore not to require certainty or even near certainty since such a demand will only fuel an obsessive tendency for you to make yourself miserable.

Sartre has driven this point home:

> When we want something, we always have to reckon with probabilities. I may be counting on the arrival of a friend. The friend is coming by rail or street-car; this supposes that the train will arrive on schedule, or that the street-car will not jump the track. I am left in the realm of possibility; but possibilities are to be reckoned with only to the point where my action comports with the ensemble of these possibilities, and no further. The moment the possibilities I am considering are not rigorously involved by my action, I ought to disengage myself from them, because no God, no scheme, can adapt the world and its possibilities to my will.[4]

Sartre is telling you to live according to probabilities. Regardless of what you want, you can never attain certainty. The most you can do is act on the basis of what seems likely and hope for the best. By abandoning your reliance on probabilities and instead expecting the world to conform to your expectations, you will remain a very unhappy camper.

On the other hand, by living according to probabilities rather than will-of-the-wisp certainty, you will live creatively and constructively. You will act instead of becoming paralyzed by doubt; you will take rational risks, play the odds, and confidently hope for the best. But if you sometimes falter (as you will), you will see that this was the unavoidable consequence of an imperfect universe in which there can be no absolute guarantees and no human omniscient powers. So you will pick yourself up and get back into the race, playing once again the probabilities and looking forward to the probable outcomes.

Antidote 3
Avoid casting life in terms of problems in the first place. In particular, avoid thinking of it in terms of unsolvable dilemmas. (Kierkegaard, Buddha)

If you no longer expect what is *unlikely*, it won't remain a problem, or at least not so much of one. Søren Kierkegaard said that, "Life is not a problem to be solved but an experience to be lived."[5] Here is a way of reframing your perspective on life that offers more hope for your future happiness. If you stop turning things into a problem in the first place and concentrate on *living* instead, you will avoid a bumpy life journey on a road fraught with anguish. So how can you stop being problematic and start living instead?

If you demand that nothing shitty happens before you give yourself permission to be happy, then you will remain unhappy. Nor is it necessary to lie to yourself about what you can and cannot control. The first of the Four Noble Truths of Buddhism has sometimes been interpreted as "Pain is inevitable. Suffering is optional." Suffering, on this view, arises because you *demand* of the universe something you just can't have.[6] You can't stop the aging process, disease, death, and other natural forms of deterioration. But that doesn't mean you have to ruminate over them and torment yourself. This really *is* optional.

If you want to avoid such suffering, then you should take heed of *dilemma thinking*. This is when you interpret reality in terms of a rock and a hard place. Yes, death is inevitable, but that doesn't mean you should say to yourself, "Well, either I can go through life and end up dying anyway, or I can end it all now and cheat myself out of living. Either way, I'm dead!" This is what is known as *dilemma thinking*. It is when you give yourself two shitty-sounding alternatives and then ruminate about how deep in shit you are no matter what you do. Virtually any situation can be interpreted in terms of a dilemma. As a result, you can, if you so choose, turn life into a series of problems to be suffered ad nauseum.

You can instead interpret things without formatting them as dilemmas. So you can say, instead, "Yep, I'm gonna die, but that doesn't mean I can't live a productive, happy life. Anyway, death doesn't have to be something dreadful. It can be a useful reminder to get off my butt and do something with myself!" Here you affirm the same fact—that you are going to die—but absent is a suspended state of savoring the unsavory horns of a dilemma. Absent is the suffering. For the sake of happiness, try your best to interpret reality without turning things into a dilemma in the first place.

Do you have a tendency to *automatically* shape the facts into an unsavory dilemma? Does this sound like you? Then try to *reframe* (reinterpret) reality more optimistically, without the dilemma.

This isn't to say that it's always irrational to perceive a dilemma. Philosophers have long distinguished between true dilemmas and false ones. A false dilemma is one that has at least one false premise. For example, the premise that death makes life futile is a false one since many people have managed to lead happy, productive lives notwithstanding their mortality. On the other hand, a true dilemma is one that does not have easily refutable premises. A woman with a life-threatening pregnancy is faced with carrying the pregnancy to term or saving herself. Given the medical probabilities, she must risk something lousy no matter which way she chooses.

Regardless of whether your situation is truly a dilemma, the possibility of reinterpreting it in a manner that saves you considerable suffering is almost invariably open to you. The woman who decides to carry to term can see her sacrifice as fulfillment of God's will, or she can perceive the birth of her fetus as something that simply "was not meant to be."

Antidote 4

Take responsibility for your interpretations of life signs and omens. Instead of ascribing self-destructive, negative meanings to the events in your life, invent life-affirming, constructive ones. (Sartre)

Sartre has given a stark example of the unavoidability of interpreting reality and the difficulty inherent in trying to apply hard-and-fast ethical standards.[7] He speaks of one of his students who came to see him during the Nazi occupation of France. The boy was caught between joining the free French forces to avenge the death of his older brother and staying at home to care for his grieving mother. He knew that his mother lived only for him and that she would plunge herself into morbid despair if he left her and possibly died in battle. On the other hand, in staying behind to care for his mother, he would miss the opportunity to avenge his brother's death and to help his countrymen in defeating the Nazis. The one act was concrete and probable but would help only one person, his mother. The other was more abstract and iffy (he could join up and get stuck at a desk job), but it still had the potential to help many people.

As Sartre relates, no ethical theory could help this perplexed lad solve his dilemma.[8] Consequence-based ethics couldn't help him choose between a probable act that could help just one person and an iffy act that could potentially help many. Nor could Kantian ethics be of much use since in remaining at home, he would be treating all others who risked their lives in battle as mere means, whereas in going off to war, he would be treating his mother as a mere means. Nor could any other ethical standard be of much help. Christian doctrine says to love your neighbor, but who was his "neighbor" in this case, his mother or his fellow countrymen?

In the end, this is what Sartre advised the boy: "You're free, choose, that is, invent." According to Sartre,

> No general ethics can show you what is to be done; there are no omens in the world. The Catholics will reply. "But there are." Granted—but, in any case, I myself choose the meaning they have.[9]

The idea that you have freedom to choose, indeed to "invent," the ultimate meaning and import of life events is one I would entreat you not to let go. This doesn't mean there are no "objective" facts or conditions of living to take into account in making your choices. As Sartre himself would tell you, we are all born into "the human condition." For example, as a matter of fact, you are mortal and will someday die. Maybe you were born into poverty, maybe with certain physical anomalies—such as being congenitally blind or paralyzed.

Nor do you have to take moral relativism to extremes to accept this idea of freedom to choose your own life meanings. True, ethical theories won't by themselves tell you what to do since, as Sartre says, you must inevitably choose the meaning and import of these theories. But this doesn't mean there are no reasonable limits to these interpretations. There are some things that won't pass muster no matter how hard you try to make them fit. In particular, a perceived duty to torment yourself *needlessly* inflicts suffering on you and your significant others. It hinders and harms rather than helps, and it treats people—yourself and others—as "mere means."

This still leaves open a vast palette of life-affirming, constructive meanings out of which to paint life. Sartre illustrates this point in describing the life of another young man who ended up becoming a Jesuit priest. As Sartre relates, this young man had several bad breaks. When a child, he was left in poverty when his father died. Made to feel like a charity case at a religious school he attended on scholarship, he never received the honors of his peers, and later on, when he was eighteen, he "bungled" a love affair. Then, at twenty-two, he confronted his "last straw" when he failed military training. Sartre explains,

> This young fellow might well have felt that he had botched everything. It was a sign of something, but of what? He might have taken refuge in bitterness or despair. But he very wisely looked upon all this as a sign that he was not made for secular triumphs, and that only the triumphs of religion, holiness, and faith were open to him. He saw the hand of God in all this, and so he entered the order. Who can help seeing that he alone decided what the sign meant?[10]

As Sartre perceived, the young man might have drawn other interpretations from his negative life encounters. He might have, for example, become a carpenter or a revolutionary. He might also have plunged himself into deep despair, become an alcoholic, or otherwise trashed himself. Instead he used his freedom to choose wisely.

But why was his choice a wise one?

It was wise because he interpreted his series of misfortunes not as a set of insurmountable problems about which to despair but instead as an *affirmative* sign to live a more productive, alternative life. Again, as Kierkegaard would say, he perceived that "life is not a problem to be solved but an experience to be lived."

If you are a chronic worrier, then you have made a poor choice about how to interpret the events of your life. It's far wiser to affirm life than to stifle it with a relentless duty to disturb yourself. Nowhere is such a duty written, not in the mind of God, not in nature, not in the theories of great philosophers. As Sartre would say, only you alone are responsible for such a dismal fate. And if you are in disagreement with this, then it is your choice to disagree. But then you bear the weight of your own suffering.

Antidote 5

Replace your pseudoduty to upset yourself with a practical, action-oriented, human duty to seek the truth. (James)

It is not enough to interpret reality; you also have to act on it. As Sartre says, "There is no reality except in action." You don't solve your practical problems just by talking about them. Typically, you will need to do something about them. The boy faced with the decision whether to join the free French forces or to stay at home with his mother could make the choice only by acting on it. The young man who interpreted his life misfortunes as a sign to pursue the challenges of religion, holiness, and faith did not make his decision until he took steps toward entering the Jesuit order. When you are faced with a practical problem, the solution is typically more than talk.[11]

Decision by indecision is often the product of not acting on your attempt to resolve a problem. Time and circumstances change as you procrastinate about the "right thing to do," and your decision is made for you. You are not sure about your vacation plans, and when you finally call for a flight, there are no fares left. You are not sure whether to take that job offer, only to find out that the position has been filled. You are thinking about signing up for courses toward your degree, but when you finally inquire, registration is over. You are not sure about whether you want to go out again with that person, and when you finally start to think you might accept, you run into the person on an intimate date with someone else. Decisions are not made until they are trans*acted*. A plan of action to resolve a practical problem is completed only by the action the plan prescribes.

"Man's destiny is within him . . . action is the only thing that enables a man to live."[12]

Tormenting and making yourself suffer does nothing to confirm the right thing to do. Only action can yield truth. Your beliefs are verified only by acting on them. The American pragmatist William James has built his philosophy around this point. As mentioned earlier, James thinks that the truth of a belief lies in its "cash value," that is, its ability to lead to satisfaction when acted on. If you are lost in the woods and starved, said James, the true belief is the one that enables you to escape. Its practical value is that when acted on, it can save your life. In the proverbial woods of life, it is not useful to spin your wheels ruminating and upsetting yourself over what to do. There is no truth in such antics, only *de*structive desperation. In contrast, truth is *con*structive.

In fact, James tells you that you have a "primary human duty" to seek the truth:

> We live in a world of realities that can be infinitely useful or infinitely harmful. Ideas that tell us which of them to expect count as the true ideas in all this primary sphere of verification, and the pursuit of such ideas is a primary human duty.[13]

For James, this is a duty that leads to satisfaction, not to misery. It is a *get-off-your-rump-and-verify-your-belief-by-acting-on-it* duty, not a *sit-around-and-ruminate-and-torment-yourself* pseudoduty. Nor is this a duty to wait until your are absolutely sure before putting your belief to the test. Indeed, this would be self-defeating since you do not verify a belief until you act on it. You can't be sure of anything before acting on it, and even then, circumstances change, and what worked now may not work later. "We have to live today by what truth we can get today," says James, "and be ready tomorrow to call it falsehood."[14]

As a truth seeker, you are hereby barred from ruminating yourself and others to death. In the name of truth, stop ruminating because this prevents you from verifying your ideas. And stop tormenting yourself since this leads to the opposite of satisfaction, which is what seeking the truth is all about— making lives happier. Give up the demand for certainty since true ideas are not absolutely, unconditionally true but true for now and only after you have verified them, that is, acted on them.

This doesn't mean you should act on a whim or not weigh in on the side of reason before acting. As mentioned earlier in this chapter, you should live by probability but not by certainty. Extremes, as Aristotle would admonish, usually lead you astray. Acting on a whim and waiting to be sure are both extremes. Avoid them both.

You are accordingly relieved of your pseudoduty to sit around and aggravate yourself to death before you can rest contentedly. You are a human being, not God. You are imperfect, and your understanding of the universe will always be imperfect. Within this human sphere, make it your duty to seek after truth, but don't confuse this with a pseudocommandment to look for problems over which to ruminate and make yourself miserable.

NOTES

1. Jonathan Edwards, "God Makes Men Sensible of Their Misery before He Reveals His Mercy and Love," retrieved September 6, 2005, from http://www.biblebb.com/files/edwards/misery.htm.

2. Edwards used guilt and fear tactics to bring "sinners" to their knees. I will discuss the inherent danger of this sort of manipulation in the next chapter.

3. Declaration of Independence, retrieved January 14, 2006, from http://www.ushistory.org/declaration/document.

4. Jean-Paul Sartre, *Existentialism and Human Emotions* (New York: Philosophical Library, 1985), 29.

5. Søren Kierkegaard, *Journals*, retrieved September 8, 2005, from http://zaadz.com/quotes/topics/problems/?page=6.

6. E. A. Burtt, ed., *The Teachings of the Compassionate Buddha* (New York: Penguin, 1991), 28.

7. Sartre, *Existentialism and Human Emotions*.

8. I don't mean to say that such theories are never useful in helping you solve your problems, just that the extent of their usefulness depends on the circumstances and that they *alone* won't typically solve your problem *for you*.

9. Sartre, *Existentialism and Human Emotions*, 28.

10. Sartre, *Existentialism and Human Emotions*, 28–29.

11. I distinguish here between practical problems and theoretical ones. The latter may be talk, but a practical problem is typically a problem about what to do. This is where the rubber meets the road. You can have a plan of action, but what worth has it except in its use?

12. Sartre, *Existentialism and Human Emotions*, 36.

13. William James, "The Pragmatist's Approach to Truth," in *Philosophers at Work: Issues and Practice of Philosophy*, ed. Elliot D. Cohen (Fort Worth, Tex.: Harcourt, 2000), 340.

14. James, "The Pragmatist's Approach to Truth," 343.

7

EMPOWERING OTHERS

D o you try to get what you want by using intimidation, threats, deceit, or other manipulative tactics? If you do, then you are not alone. It is usually a matter of how often and how much we rely on such styles of manipulation than whether we do so at all. However, if you are in the habit of getting what you want by manipulating others, then your interpersonal relations are bound to suffer.

There are several rules of manipulation that will sooner or later stifle your interpersonal relations. Among the most popular varieties are *bullying*, *poisoning the well*, and *bullshitting*. Sometimes the manipulation deduced from these rules is as subtle as an elephant in a china shop ("If you won't have sex with me, I'm breaking up with you"). Other times it is more subtle ("I'm sure you wouldn't want to look stupid.").

Here are versions of these three rules of manipulation:

> Bullying: If you want something from someone, then you should try to get it by using or threatening to use force, blackmail, or other manner of coercion.
>
> Poisoning the Well: If you don't want others to act or think in certain ways, you should persuade them with strong, negative language or other manner of intimidation.
>
> Bullshitting: If you want to gain others' respect, approval, trust, or cooperation, you should make up lies, omit facts, exaggerate the truth, or otherwise deceive them.

It's not hard to see the logical Achilles' heel of each of these rules: all of them, at least in the long run, are self-defeating. They lead to the opposite results of the ones you desire in applying them. In trying to gain cooperation from others by threatening them into compliance, it characteristically creates resistance and resentment instead. So you thwart your interpersonal happiness rather than advance it.

Trying to intimidate others into compliance by using strong negative language also tends to be self-defeating. "Why are you going out with that bum?" is a good question for parents to ask their teenage daughter if they want her to become self-defensive and more adamant about continuing dating "that bum." This isn't to say that poisoning the well never works. For example, telling prospective customers that your business competitor is a "charlatan" or a "crook" can create misgivings about him even if the allegations are groundless. But there are diminishing returns to such tactics when it comes to interpersonal relations. Like other forms of manipulation, it is also likely to backfire, especially when habitually practiced. Telling your spouse that she looks like a "cheap tramp" in her new red mini might intimidate her against wearing it—at least around you—but she is also likely to resent your less-than-subtle insult. There are ways to *argue rationally* for your viewpoint without resorting to intimidation. ("That dress might not be appropriate for work. I can see your cheeks!")

The essence of bullshitting as here understood is deceptiveness. When you bullshit others, you make yourself untrustworthy. In seeking the trust and confidence of others by making yourself untrustworthy, you set yourself up as precisely someone who *should not* be taken seriously. True, you can fool *some* of the people some of the time, but need I say more? Most people who bullshit inevitably gain a reputation for it and thereby defeat the very ends they seek to achieve.[1]

In manipulating others, you treat them like objects and therefore fail to respect their personhood. The refutation of all forms of manipulation is accordingly clear:

> In manipulating others, you insult the humanity of your fellow human beings by treating them as though they were objects to be used for your own self-interested purposes. Whether you try to threaten people into compliance; intimidate them with strong, negative language; or try to gain their trust through deceptive speech, you disrespect and degrade them as persons by denying that they are rational beings capable of deciding for themselves on rational grounds. Because healthy interpersonal relations thrive on mutual respect, you undermine your own happiness as well as those whom you attempt to manipulate. In the end, the very purposes for which you seek to manipulate others are defeated.

The primary goal of philosophical antidotes to manipulation is to cultivate mutual trust and respect through empowering others. This means treating them as rational, self-determining agents. Power plays, intimidation, and deceit destroy the conditions in which mutual trust and respect can flourish. Yet such a relation among coworkers and colleagues as well as among intimates and friends is essential for personal happiness. It is also essential on a national and global scale if human beings are to flourish. A nation that is governed by tyrants who use force and fraud to oppress citizens and to rape and plunder the environment in the name of "national security" destroy the conditions of human happiness. A world in which world powers use chicanery and force to subdue other sovereign nations for imperialistic purposes fosters terrorism and other hate-driven threats to world peace and security.

BULLYING

Antidotes to Bullying

Antidote 1
Deal justly with adversaries. Apply first the provisions of just war theory. Use physical force only to protect yourself against physical harm and only to the extent necessary for this purpose. (Aquinas, Hobbes)

The use of force, especially physical force, is never a first resort in the case of conflict between civilized people. When you can use reason to resolve your difficulties, then it is pointless to use force. From individual skirmishes to international wars, the use of force has invariably taken its toll in death, destruction, and deep-seated hostility and resentment. On the other hand, attaining rational resolutions to conflicts, founded on mutual respect and a willingness to listen to reason, avoids these harmful effects. And, after the use of force, it is still necessary to come to the peace table and to speak rationally to each other if there is to be a resolution of differences.

The history of war is a good example of blood needlessly spilled. The bloodshed alone has never been the basis of lasting peace. The only useful condition that war has provided has been the willingness of those in conflict to discuss, *after the fact*, their differences rationally and to iron out a solution. What a waste of life when the rational discourse could have preempted the war instead of vice versa.

But even the history of war has a tradition that has attempted to use reason to regulate the waging and fighting of wars. This tradition began with

St. Augustine in the fourth century A.D. and was developed in the thirteenth century by St. Thomas Aquinas. According to Aquinas, there are three things that are necessary for a war to be just. First, wars can be authorized not by private citizens but instead by those who have the authority. Private citizens can seek redress for violation of their rights in court. Second, wars must have a just cause, which is to remedy some injustice. Third, there must be a rightful intention to advance the good or to avoid an evil. On the third point, Aquinas quotes Augustine as saying,

> The passion for inflicting harm, the cruel thirst for vengeance, an unpacific and relentless spirit, the fever of revolt, the lust of power, and such like things, all these are rightly condemned in war.[2]

So if you are considering taking action against another, you should carefully consider whether you have justice on your side. As a private citizen, you have no institutional authority to declare war on another. If it is redress you seek for a wrong, then you can take your case to court or seek some other available institutional means for redressing the wrong.

In anger, you can easily lose sight of whether your cause is just or whether your intention is but a "cruel thirst for vengeance" or "the lust for power" or some other inane purpose. So you will need to flex your willpower muscle to keep yourself from perpetrating groundless aggression on others. Keep in mind the conditions of just war as you hold back and let the voice of reason speak to you as you constrain yourself: "I am not authorized to declare war on another private citizen, and my "cruel thirst" to get even or to show who's boss won't cut the mustard." Reason power: flex *that* muscle.

I am not saying that you do not have the right to defend yourself. According to philosopher Thomas Hobbes, your right to defend yourself can never be taken away from you, even by government, since the very purpose of a government is to maintain the safety of its citizens.[3] But self-protection does not equate to using power and aggression for personal gain. It is here that government, according to Hobbes, has a right to restrict your activities for the safety and survival of other citizens.

If someone is attempting to kill or seriously harm you, then even Aquinas would allow the use of force for self-protection. According to Aquinas, you can use force to defend your life against an aggressor as long as your intention is to protect yourself and not directly to harm the assailant and you use no more force than what is necessary to defend yourself.[4]

Antidote 2

Seek internalized cooperation from others by providing them with the rational grounds for your requests. (Hart, Kant)

Now bullying doesn't have to involve the actual use of force. Nor need it involve physical force. A very popular form of bullying is to threaten someone with some unwanted, nonviolent act or omission. For example, a friend of mine who worked as a part-time instructor at a large state university once recounted to me how his boss called him in to ask him to undertake a "special" teaching project. This assignment conflicted with other plans he had already made. Moreover, the extra work would have amounted to a full-time job minus the benefits and commensurate pay. After telling my friend how his participation was "strictly voluntary," he proceeded to mention a new full-time teaching position on the horizon and asked him if he would be interested in applying for it.

No explicit threat was made, but it was easy enough to read between the lines: "If you want to be seriously considered for this new position, then you damn well better take this assignment, like it or not." My friend declined this "generous" invitation, and, although he did later apply for the new position, he was never even called back for an interview. Epilogue: my friend landed a full-time teaching position elsewhere, and, with the support of his new employer, he went on to become a prolific scholar.

Now for the moral. Threatening and blackmailing people is a dead-end philosophy. If you want people to work cooperatively with you, then you will need to respect and treat them as autonomous persons, not like objects used and manipulated. This is the deep practical meaning of Kant's unconditional command to treat human beings, including yourself, as "ends in themselves" rather than as "mere means."

This lesson is enshrined in the philosophy of law. As a vehicle of control, law can be applied coercively and without respect for citizens' rational self-determination. It can be used to threaten people into compliance rather than to provide a rational basis for living a satisfactory life in common. Dictatorial regimes are good examples of such systematic attempts to coerce people into compliance. But, while such systems may sometimes, at least for a while, be effective in frightening people into obedience, they do not promote a stable environment in which citizens can grow and flourish.

To do the latter, legal systems need to be more than externalized means of control, more than just systems of commands backed by threats. They must also be *internalized* means. This requires seeing law as a rational guide to social living.

Did you ever notice how mindful most motorists on a highway are of the speed limit when there is a state trooper traveling in their midst? But what happens when the trooper finally exits off the highway. You guessed it. At least some of these formerly compliant motorists speed off. This is an unfortunate example of how these motorists view speed limits as threats to be reckoned with only because they carry penalties for noncompliance.

The famous Oxford philosopher of law H. L. A. Hart referred to such an attitude toward law as "the external point of view." According to Hart, people who take this attitude to law use such expressions as "I was obliged to do it," "I am likely to suffer for it if . . .," "You will probably suffer for it if . . .," or "They will do that to you if . . ." But these people do not have any need for such other expressions as "I had an obligation" or "You have an obligation" since this is the language of an internal point of view.

For those who take an internal point of view, law is more than simply a prediction about how you will suffer if you don't obey. Rather, from this internal perspective, law is viewed as guides to social living and as the basis for claims, demands, admissions, criticism, punishment, and all other common forms of rule-governed transactions of life.[5]

For Hart, what makes law binding or "obligatory" for people and what accounts for a stable, healthy commitment to it is not the fear of what will happen to you if you don't comply. It is rather that law is internalized as something that *ought* to be obeyed, as providing a *rational basis* for obeying.

Hart's distinction between internal and external points of view sheds light on why the tendency to exact compliance through threats and blackmail is bankrupt. It does not treat people as rational beings who deserve a reason for choosing to comply. When people see authority in terms of something to be feared rather than respected, they may at most go through the motions of complying—if you can scare them enough—but they won't be *self*-motivated to comply. That is, such as view stifles personal autonomy.

In his well-known work *The Prince*, Machiavelli asked whether it is better to be loved than feared or feared than loved. He responded, "It may be answered that one should wish to be both, but, because it is difficult to unite them in one person, is much safer to be feared than loved, when, of the two, either must be dispensed with."[6] But "better" for him simply meant getting people to obey. It did not mean establishing conditions under which people could be happy. You do not achieve the latter by threatening them into compliance.

Antidote 3

In relating to others, strive for mutuality and cooperation through autonomous, democratic participation and partnership, not through tyranny and oppression. (Dewey, Mill, Wilkerson)

This is what is so important about democracy. As John Dewey rightly observed, its core concept is the cultivation of personal autonomy. People work cooperatively to create the rules that govern their lives. It is not unilateral and dictatorial. Democracy is not just a form of political organization to be left at the level of organized states. No, it is also a philosophy of relating on an interpersonal level.

Unfortunately, some believe that someone in a family has to be "the boss." According to the traditional model, this someone is the man who emerges as the familial dictator who may rule by fiat rather than reason. In the extreme, such a relationship is defined by abuse, both mental and physical. The head of such households rules by fear and intimidation. In many cases, the subjected spouse is degraded and told how fortunate she is to be so subjected. Many such victims have already come from such abusive households. Convinced that they are worthless, they seek out spouses who continue the reign of abuse. When children are born into these households, they too become fodder for further abuse, and another generation of victims is conceived.

John Stuart Mill, in his essay *The Subjection of Women*, published in 1869, referred to such abuse victims as "willing slaves." Mill's essay was a powerful indictment of the subjection of women of his day, which he held was based not on men's intellectual superiority to women but rather on their physical advantage. Said Mill:

> The adoption of this inequality [between men and women] never was the result of . . . what conduced to the benefit of humanity. . . . It arose simply from the fact that from the very earliest twilight of society, every woman (owing to the value attached to her by men, combined with her inferiority in muscular strength) was found in a state of bondage to some man. Laws and systems of policy always begin by recognizing the relations they find already existing between individuals. They convert what was a mere physical fact into a legal right, give it the sanction of society, and principally aim at the substitution of public and organized means of asserting and protecting these rights, instead of the irregular and lawless conflict of physical strength.[7]

Here Mill is saying something very disquieting about internalizing laws that never really had any rational basis. Here is where men gave themselves legal permission to abuse women—told themselves it was all right—and then sought to regulate the abuse. For example, in nineteenth-century America, a "rule of thumb" permitted men to beat women only with a stick that was no thicker than their thumb.

While it is no longer legal to take a stick to one's wife in America, the ideology that permitted such abuse in the first place is unfortunately still with us. Given the epidemic of both physical and mental abuse (including sexual abuse) in America today, we cannot afford to hide our heads in the sand. The point is that there is grave need for relinquishing the irrational idea that one human being can attain some quality of life worth striving for by bullying others into compliance.

As Mill pointed out with respect to the subjection of women, no one is the happier for it. Men are saddled with the impossible role of "supreme" head of household in which they are expected to be flawless in their dictatorship, and women are thereby deprived of the advantages of being fully functional autonomous persons.

Men who covet their "male supremacy" are in for a rude awakening—unfortunately, it may come after many years of misery and suffering—their own and those whom they bully. Women who submit to such men will give up ownership rights in their own persons, as in the sale of property, no longer persons in their own right.

Does either of these life scripts even remotely resemble you? A better option is a *partnership* in which both parties are full-fledged autonomous persons, mutually respectful, and entitled to pursue their own happiness without fear of reprisal from the other. It's bad logic to assume that *someone* has to be the boss. In a partnership, there is a democratic, noncoercive sharing of the benefits and burdens of a household. The unequal power structure between men and women is replaced with one in which divisions of labor are autonomously chosen.

Philosopher/social worker Janice Wilkerson sums up such an egalitarian ideal of power:

> Only when we as a society seek to empower each individual member by offering the same opportunities to all will we realize the full splendor, rich strength, and beauty that can be achieved as today's distant possibilities become tomorrow's achievements. Only when we as a society refuse to accept violent assaults on any human life will we be able to stop our worst nightmares about our won inhumanity based on no better rea-

son than a born difference in gender and the subordination of women by men.[8]

Antidote 4

Increase your own authentic power not through violence or threats of violence but through empowerment of others in a democratic forum based on freely given and informed consent. (Arendt)

In contrasting such an ideal of equalitarian power to violence, the German-born American philosopher Hannah Arendt said,

> Power and violence are opposites; where the one rules absolutely, the other is absent. Violence appears where power is in jeopardy, but left to its own course it ends in power's disappearance.[9]

According to Arendt, power involves the free, informed consent of all members of a group to an action, as in a participatory democracy. If you are accustomed to bullying others to get your way, then you are on a collision course with power. Like a weed, your coercive tactics choke the lifeline of power, leaving only its dead, decaying remnants. As Plato would express it, violence, threats of violence, blackmail, and other manipulative strategies are perversions of the ideal of power, and they end with the destruction of power.[10] The only semblance of power in a bully is cooperation of those bullied. By refusing to be bullied, you can eviscerate the bully. In being a bully, you eviscerate yourself and defeat your own purposes by destroying the prospects for building partnerships based on mutual consent.

POISONING THE WELL

Whereas bullying uses coercive tactics on others to try to persuade them, poisoning the well uses strong negative language to intimidate them into compliance with your wishes. As the metaphor suggests, it is at your own peril to drink from a well that has been poisoned. Here are some examples:

- Only an *idiot* would go out with that *loser*.
- Homosexuality is an *abomination*. Are you gay?
- Anyone who criticizes the president is a *traitor*.
- I hate *cheap* people. Can you loan me some money?

- Are you going to sit there like a *wimp* and let him speak to me like that?
- When are you going to show that *bitch* who's in charge?
- Don't be a *chickenshit*. Try some of this acid.

Each of these examples uses negatively charged, evaluative language (the words in italics) to manipulate a response.[11] In their ordinary usage, words like "idiot," "abomination," "cheap," "wimp," "bitch," and "chickenshit" are *evaluative* because they are used primarily to *rate* things rather than report facts. And they are strongly *negative* insofar as they strongly condemn the objects to which they are ascribed.

Antidotes to Poisoning the Well

Antidote 1
Don't free-ride off of human trust. Use evaluative language in a manner consistent with its sincerity requirement. (Nowell-Smith, Kant)

In poisoning the well, you use evaluative language to manipulate people's responses in ways calculated to serve your own personal interests. But this manipulative use of evaluative language is not really its primary function. According to philosopher P. H. Nowell-Smith, the primary function of such language is to give people advice.[12]

Why would you give other people advice? Certainly not to advance *your* interests. The point of giving someone else advice is clearly to help that other person attain something he or she wants, not something *you* want. According to Nowell-Smith, unless evaluative language had first been used in a way that connected what the adviser advised with what the advisee him- or herself wanted, people would never have come to use such language "as levers with which to manipulate the conduct of others."[13]

When you tell someone that he would be a *fool* not to listen to your advice, you imply that your advice is in some way connected with *his* own interests. But if you are using such language for your own gain and not his, you are merely free-riding off of linguistic conventions to get what you want. If your rhetoric succeeds in manipulating the response you desire, it is largely because the person who takes your advice has been duped by your self-serving, misappropriation of linguistic conventions.

As discussed earlier, Kant would tell you to act so that the reasons for your action could be turned into a universal law of nature. For example, he says that deceitful promising (making promises without the intention to keep them) could never become such a law. This is because if no one ever kept their promises, no one would ever trust anyone to keep them. This is why, according to Kant, deceitful promising is morally wrong. It turns the very institution of promising against itself.

In like manner, Kant's point applies to the deceitful use of evaluative language. If everyone always used evaluative language to manipulate others, then the use of such language to give advice would be destroyed. Such a manipulative use turns the very institution of advice giving against itself.

Of course, it is not likely that everyone would, in fact, always use evaluative language in this deceitful fashion. But this is precisely the reason why some of us *can* use it to free-ride off the linguistic rules. It is because people trust one another to be honest. Poisoning the well betrays this fundamental trust. Kant's universal law standard shows how fundamental this trust is for human happiness. People rely on each other for advice. To the extent that the conventional means for advice giving is undermined by poisoning the well, a basic condition of human happiness, your own as well as that of others, is jeopardized.

Antidote 2

Empower others by respecting their rational dignity. Use evaluative language to guide their behavior, not to goad it. (Austin)

In his classic little book *How to Do Things with Words*, J. L. Austin introduced the concept of a *speech act*.[14] According to Austin, when people use language, they do more than simply make certain sounds. They actually perform certain *acts*. If a minister says, "I pronounce you husband and wife," she actually succeeds in marrying two people. If you say to me, "I promise" under certain conditions (for example, we both speak English, I hear what you say, I prefer that you do the thing in question), then you actually *do* something, namely, promise.

Austin distinguishes between two sorts of things you can do with words. Some acts are performed *in* uttering certain words under certain conditions, whereas some acts are performed *by* uttering them.[15] For example, *in* saying "I promise," I promise. *In* saying "I warn you," I warn you. *In* saying "I advise you," I advise you.[16]

In contrast, *by* saying "You would be a horse's ass if you listened to him," I can intimidate you into not listening. Notice I can say "I advise you that," but I can't also meaningful say "I intimidate you that." The latter act (intimidating someone) is done *as a consequence* of what you say, not *in* saying it.

Poisoning the well is something you do *by* (as a consequence of) uttering certain words, not *in* uttering them.[17] You use language to intimidate, goad, or otherwise intimidate others into responding in ways that suit you. You use language like one might use a thumbscrew.[18] Instead of simply *giving* advice, you attempt to *control* the response. This fails to respect others as rational, self-determining persons because you short-circuit their own rational, decision-making powers by goading them into doing something you want them to do.

In advising someone, you leave it open for the person to decide what to do. In advising someone, you *guide* them. By poisoning the well, you *goad* them. Advising depends on rational argument. In advising someone to do something, you imply that you have a rational basis for advising as you do. You imply that there are sound reasons why the advice given would be in the interest of the advised if taken. In attempting to guide a person with rational argument, you affirm the ability of the person to weigh the argument for herself and to make a rational decision. You therefore respect the dignity of the person as a person. In so doing, you set the stage for a relationship based on respect.

In contrast, by poisoning the well, you manipulate and control others for self-serving purposes in the guise of advice. This degrades persons by duping them into compliance and by using them for self-serving ends. This is dishonest, and it makes a mockery of respect. Real advice is empowering, but pseudoadvice based on self-serving manipulation is not. People are much happier when they are empowered.

True, there are some instances in which well-meaning people try to use poisoning the well for other-regarding purposes. For example, a parent, concerned about the welfare of her teenage daughter, might try to dissuade her from dating a particular boy by calling him "a loser." In this case, the underlying motive may not be entirely self-serving since the parent (rightly or wrongly) has the welfare of the child in mind. Nevertheless, this is still manipulative, dishonest, and disempowering. The teen's ability to be convinced by rational argument is discounted in favor of being treated like an object manipulated. For those parents who think modeling such tactics is conducive to their children's happiness, guess again. The teen is more likely to resent the attempt at manipulating her, and the opportunity for respectful, productive dialogue will be lost. Better to respect the teen's dignity as a rational person than to treat her like a thing. Better to guide than to goad.

BULLSHITTING

There are different ways to deceive others. What they all have in common is that they are done intentionally. A bullshitter knows what he is doing. There are no inadvertent cases of bullshitting. If you unintentionally mislead someone, you have not bullshitted. However, bullshitting, unlike poisoning the well, is not a success term. That is, to poison the well, you must *succeed* in intimidating someone.[19] However, you can bullshit someone without succeeding in getting what you want out of that person—their approval, respect, cooperation, and so forth. In fact, it is almost a defining mark of bullshitting that it ordinarily does not succeed. Those prone to bullshitting often have reputations to that effect that precede them.

It's not uncommon for people to talk about the way they successfully bullshitted their way through something—an examination, a meeting, or some other inquiry that assumes a special fund of knowledge. In my undergraduate days, I had a classmate in several of my classes who vigilantly participated in class. Rupert, as I will call him, would speak long-windedly with an impressive vocabulary and in an authoritative tone of voice. Although I often didn't understand what he was saying, I was, at first, taken in. I told myself that it must be me since everybody else seemed to take him seriously, including the instructor. Then I began to listen carefully to what he was saying and discovered that he spoke in irrelevant tangents, which succeeded only in wasting a good deal of class time.

It wasn't long before others in the class began to discover that what he had to say was devoid of content, all nutrients removed, pure bullshit. Rupert was truly a pro, a talented bullshit artist, but even he could not completely pull it off. I don't know where he is today or what he ultimately ended up doing for a living, but it is a forgone conclusion that, unless he stopped his bullshitting and devoted himself to the pursuit of truth, he would continue to waste people's valuable time and to lose credibility among thoughtful people who were willing to listen carefully to what he had to say.

Bullshitting wastes valuable time, and it makes no genuine contribution to humanity. It clogs up interpersonal relationships with fecal contamination and leaves a foul odor. If you want to live a productive life and to cultivate meaningful interpersonal relations, don't be a bullshitter.

Some bullshit, the soft kind, takes the form of exaggeration and half-truth. Here's a sad example of how dangerous even this type of bullshitting can be. After Hurricane Katrina ravaged New Orleans in September 2005, people began to ask why the Federal Emergency Management

Agency (FEMA) was so slow in responding to the needs of countless residents who were left destitute and stranded. At the time, the head of
FEMA was a George W. Bush appointee by the name of Michael Brown.
While Bush praised the job that Brown had done, proclaiming, "Heck of
a job, Brownie," it was evident that he had failed to perform his job com-
petently.

The reason for his incompetence emerged when *Time* magazine exposed serious discrepancies in his résumé. According to Brown's bio
posted on the FEMA website, he was "serving as an assistant city manager
with emergency services oversight." A White House press release from
2001 also said that he was employed by the city of Edmond, Oklahoma,
from 1975 to 1978, "overseeing the emergencies service division." In fact,
it turned out that he was really an "assistant to the city manager," not an
"assistant city manager," which meant that he had absolutely no authority
over other employees.[20] Thus, the reason for his incompetence: he lacked
experience and training in emergency management. Yet the lives of so
many people depended on his doing a competent job. Bullshit can be
lethal.

Here's a half-truth that will live in infamy: "I have never had a sexual
relationship with *that* woman, Ms. Lewinsky." Uttered by President William
Jefferson Clinton in 1998, the statement was true in the biblical sense of not
having had intercourse with her but false in a broader sense that included
oral sex. Unfortunately, Clinton's deception was in failing to mention that
he was using the narrower definition while knowing full well that everyone
else was thinking in terms of the more inclusive definition. So did Clinton
lie? Strictly speaking, his offense was an omission, not a lie. What he said
was ambiguous and misleading but false only if you assume that oral sex
constitutes having had a sexual relationship. Clinton failed to tell the *whole*
truth. This was bullshit.

Clinton was politically skewered for it, and his opponents jumped on
the chance to portray him as morally unfit to be the president of this great
nation of ours. Then it was easy for the Republican Party to shape its platform around restoring moral decency to the White House, and the rest is
history. George W. Bush ran for president largely on this platform.

Whether or not Clinton's opponents would have found something else
to indict him on (for example, his having had an affair with an intern in the
first place) is not possible to say. But this much is clear. The failure to tell
the whole truth landed Clinton in considerable hot water and provided fodder for the Republican Party in their effort to retake the White House.
Need I say more about the dangers of telling half-truths?

In contrast to telling half-truths, lying has an objective dimension: it involves saying something false about the world. Actually, in lying you mislead in three related ways. You misrepresent

1. the state of the *external world* (your statement is false),
2. your *belief* (you say p but really believe not-p), and
3. your *intention* (you intend to *mis*inform rather than to inform).

Some philosophers would say that you still have lied even when the first of these conditions is not satisfied as long as the second two are. For example, suppose you believe that something is false (say that there is really oil in the ground you are trying to sell), but you say it is true anyway with the express intention of deceiving someone. However, suppose it turns out that you are mistaken, and your statement really is true (there really *is* oil in the ground). Whether or not you want to also call this lying—I would prefer to call it an *attempt* at lying—this is still bullshitting. It is bullshitting because you are using deception in order to manipulate someone to get what you want (consummating a land deal).

In any event, all forms of bullshitting misrepresent your intentions. And, by virtue of misrepresenting your intentions, all forms also misrepresent your beliefs. (For example, if my real intention in telling you something is merely to impress you with my knowledge, then I'm also misrepresenting that I really care about *the truth* of what I'm saying.) Finally, some forms of bullshitting, such as lying, also misrepresent the external world.

As such, antidotes to bullshitting are possible that address each of these three forms of misrepresentation.

Antidotes to Bullshitting Involving Deceitful Intentions

Antidote 1
If your bullshit would not be acceptable to you if you were the recipient of it, then don't do it to others. (Kant)

Intentionally deceiving others in order to get something from them, whether it is approval or money, does not usually hold up under moral scrutiny. If you don't give a hoot about morality, then saying this won't mean much. But there is reason why you should, even for narrow, self-interested purposes, care about morality. This is because conduct that does not hold moral water is usually detrimental to your own interpersonal happiness. The poet John Dunn said that "no man is an island," meaning that you will not find it easy to live without the cooperation of others. But by intentionally deceiving others to get what you want, you are likely, sooner or later, to alienate others and foreclose their cooperation.

I am not saying that deceit is always wrong. Even Socrates would have admitted some exceptions. Socrates said,

> Suppose that a friend when in his right mind has deposited arms with me and he asks for them when he is not in his right mind, ought I to give them back to him? No one would say that I ought or that I should be right in doing so, any more than they would say that I ought always to speak the truth to one who is in his condition.[21]

In such a case, if you were to falsely tell your deranged friend that you no longer had the guns in order to prevent him from misusing them, you would arguably still have a moral leg to stand on. Would this still be bullshit? I would say so.[22] Even feces can occasionally have a legitimate use, for example, as a fertilizer.

So, if there can be *exceptional* bullshit that is morally acceptable, the question is, how can you distinguish the acceptable from the unacceptable bullshit?

Recall how Kant emphasized the centrality of human trust for successful interpersonal communication.[23] But what would happen if everyone were to go about bullshitting whenever they wanted to get something from someone? No one would take anything anyone had to say seriously, and all meaningful interpersonal communication would break down. A world in which no one could be trusted to be truthful would be one in which no one would believe anyone else.

Unfortunately, Kant's bullshit alarm goes off even in the case of Socrates' deranged friend who comes to collect his arms. This is true, according to Kant, because it does not matter whether you think you are saving someone's life by deceitfully manipulating another. Deceitful manipulation, were it the rule, would still destroy meaningful interpersonal communication.

Nevertheless, there is another, more realistic way to apply Kant's consistency test. True, you can't have everybody going about bullshitting whenever it suits their fancy. This would surely destroy meaningful interpersonal communication. But what would happen if everyone consistently bullshitted *only* to save a life or to avoid other similarly serious consequences but still remained forthright on all other occasions. I don't think that, in such a world, meaningful interpersonal communication would cease.

In fact, you could ask yourself, would I want to live in a world in which everyone always bullshitted to suit her fancy? The answer is no, right? Because then you would not be able to trust others. So you would be wrong to treat others in this way if you yourself would rationally want to be able to trust others. On the other hand, would you really mind if others occasionally deceived you for such causes as saving a life? I know I would not have a problem with such a world as long as I could generally trust people to be honest with me. So there you go: a modified Kantian bullshit test. The legitimate bullshit is the type that you could reasonably consent to if others did it to you. The unreasonable kind is that garden-variety kind that you yourself could not reasonably accept because it would make trustful interpersonal communication impossible.[24]

Antidote 2

Before you go bullshitting someone, just put yourself behind a "veil of ignorance" and then ask yourself if it would be fair. (Rawls)

Another related test is one made famous by the late Harvard professor John Rawls. Rawls uses what he calls "the original position" as a tool for fairly determining just social arrangements. "The idea of the original position," he says,

> is to set up a fair procedure so that any principles agreed to will be just. . . . Somehow we must nullify the effects of specific contingencies which put men at odds and tempt them to exploit social and natural circumstances to their own advantage. Now in order to do this I assume that the parties are situated behind a veil of ignorance. They do not know how the various alternatives will affect their own particular case and they are obliged to evaluate principles solely on the basis of general considerations.[25]

Now imagine yourself behind a "veil of ignorance," not knowing whether you will be the recipient of bullshit or the purveyor of it. From behind this veil, would you agree to bullshit that sought to keep dangerous weapons out of the hands of seriously disturbed people? Since you don't know whether you will be a victim of such an individual or the perpetrator himself, you can decide fairly from behind the veil of ignorance. Would you not accept such bullshit as fair? I know I would.

But what about bullshitting others for personal gain, say, duping them out of their money? If you didn't know whether you would be the dupe or the duper, it would be too risky to accept such bullshit, right? If so, this bullshit would be unfair, and you shouldn't resort to it.

Got the idea? Just imagine you are setting up a just society without knowing how what you choose will affect you personally. The acceptable deception will be the kind you would accept under such conditions of choosing, and the unacceptable will be that which you would reject. Try it the next time you are thinking of bullshitting someone. Imagine yourself behind a veil of ignorance and then decide.

Antidote 3

If you are contemplating doing something deceptive, put it to the public test first. (Seneca, Bok)

You can also test the level of fecal contamination in your interpersonal relations by subjecting your bullshit to an objective fecal analysis. How so?

One way is to imagine that some other person is looking over your shoulders and judging what you are doing. The Stoic philosopher Seneca had such an approach in mind:

> There is no real doubt that it is good for one to have appointed a guardian over oneself, and to have someone whom you may look up to, someone whom you may regard as a witness of your thoughts. It is, indeed, nobler by far to live as you would live under the eyes of some good person always at your side; but nevertheless I am content if you only act, in whatever you do, as you would act if anyone at all were looking on; because solitude prompts us to all kinds of evil.[26]

The point Seneca is making is that it is easier to deceive others when you think that you are not being watched by someone else who is judging your actions. "Solitude," he said, "prompts us to all kinds of evil." While Seneca thought it would be best for this onlooker to be some "good person always at your side," he thought that even anyone at all would suffice. Of course, this means that you should imagine not some onlooker whom you imagine to be cunning and wily but rather some average person who is not especially prone to vice.

The idea is to somehow make your deceitful intentions public so that you receive objective feedback on them. Yet, as philosopher Sissela Bok points out in her classic book *Lying*,[27] it is often easy for those prone to lying (and presumably other forms of deception) to justify their deception when the only audience is their own conscience or a self-appointed, imaginary onlooker.

While resorting to such an onlooker can be useful and may sometimes be the only publicity test available, Bok suggests two additional levels of public scrutiny that could lend greater objectivity to your decision. A second level is to ask real instead of imaginary people for advice, such as friends, elders, colleagues, and religious and ethical leaders. If you are, say, considering lying to get ahead, you can run it by a close friend first and see what she thinks. Often, by seeking feedback from others, not only can you better come to appreciate the poverty of bullshitting, but you can also gain valuable insight into viable alternatives to being deceitful—ones that are less risky.

For example, suppose you are trying to land a job and are considering bullshitting your experience. Now there is often room for placing your veritable experience in a favorable light without lying or otherwise creating false impressions. For instance, you could focus on your skills—communication, office, and so forth—instead of your prior employment history (assuming the former is stronger than the latter). Since there is usually more than one way to frame reality, you could choose the construction that best suits your interests. As long as you do not misrepresent your qualifications, you can do so without bullshitting. There are, of course, rational limits as to just how far you can go to make something sound impressive before you are guilty of deceptive distortion. But by sharing your ideas with others, you can help to keep yourself from stepping over the line.

As long as the other people you consult are handpicked, this may still not eliminate bias. So, according to Bok, a third level of publicity would be to broaden the sampling to "persons of all allegiances."[28] This sampling would ideally include the perspectives of even those who are prospective dupes.

Bok suggests that this level of publicity could work effectively in the case of deceptive *practices*, such as in government, where those who deceive are in positions of trust. There are some very impressive examples of how publicity has, in recent times, been used effectively (albeit after the fact) to halt improper *government* bullshit. For example, in 2002, when the Bush administration's plan to establish an "Office of Strategic Influence" was leaked to the public, it caved under scrutiny. More appropriately dubbed the "Office of Misinformation," the sole purpose of this office was to spread false information to foreign news organizations in order to use them as pawns. When brought to public light, it gave an air of hypocrisy to a nation whose good reputation was founded on honesty and trustworthiness.

Some more bullshit from the high office: Beginning in 2000, the Bush administration paid public relations agencies heaping sums of taxpayers money to produce an ongoing stream of "prepackaged television news" that seamlessly incorporated government propaganda into the news reports of local affiliates of the major television news networks.[29] These segments, which were not identified as government announcements, were broadcast in some of the nation's largest markets, including New York, Los Angeles, and Chicago, and reached millions of Americans. Presented by public relations and government workers posing as journalists, viewers were deceived into thinking that these segments were produced by the television news networks themselves. For example, in one segment aired after the fall of Baghdad, a joyful Iraqi American quipped, "Thank you Bush. Thank you U.S.A.," attempting to dupe Americans into thinking that this jubilance was the general consensus of the Iraqi people toward the U.S.-led invasion of Iraq.

The *New York Times* broke the story on March 13, 2005, in an article titled "Under Bush, a New Age of Prepackaged TV News." While the mainstream media networks were mum (wouldn't you figure?), the progressive radio stations and the Internet blogs buzzed with discussion. (I confess I did several radio shows trying to get the word out—including a gig in the Big Apple with actress/radio host Jeananne Garofalo.[30]) Congress finally got the message from the public outcry and passed a law requiring that the media make known to viewers the source of such canned "news." In addition, in September 2005, the Government Accounting Office declared illegal such deceitful government attempts to sway public opinion in its favor. Whatever the boys in Washington were thinking when they set out to exploit the public, their scheme didn't survive the test of publicity. Democracy cannot survive in a vacuum. It requires an informed citizenship.

Getting advance feedback from those you are considering duping is usually a good way to put an end to the scheme. "Hey, would you mind if I bullshitted you instead of being forthright?" is not generally a question that would be greeted with affirmation. Yet, in addition to institutional contexts (like government), there are at least some cases in which deception can be usefully discussed in advance with those who would be deceived. For example, it could be useful to query your partner about whether she would prefer to know if she had a terminal illness and only a few months to live. Most people would not want to be deceived about such a diagnosis since they would want the autonomy to decide how to manage their remaining days. On the other hand, for those who might not want to know, it is still inappropriate to deceive them without first discussing such a possibility in advance.

Here's another example. Couples would do well to discuss their views of such deceptive practices as extramarital affairs. For two individuals who have mutually committed to a monogamist relationship, it's not unexpected to find each officially condemning such a deceptive practice. But the reasons why each would condemn it and how each would feel about being so deceived are much more important than the official rejection. It is through such a deeper inquiry that a couple can come to appreciate the values that sustain their relationship.

Unfortunately, many couples sell out their commitments in a moment of sexual indiscretion, only to regret it later when the flames die down. How will the betrayed feel if he or she finds out? How will *you* feel after the fact? What effect will this have on future trust and on others, such as children? At that moment when bodily inclinations to jump into the sack with another are at concert pitch, having such an informed, emotional appreciation of what is at stake can help you rationally overcome these inclinations.

Having a clandestine affair places you in the situation of having to keep up a facade of faithfulness by propagating more and more bullshit:

"Who were you speaking to on the phone, dear?"

"Oh, it was just a wrong number."

"But dear, it sounded like you were whispering."

"I didn't want to wake the kids."

"Don't you remember? The kids are at my mother's."

"Oh, yeah, that's right, I was just . . ."

Bullshit generally breeds more bullshit. Candid, advance discussion by partners about the potential impact of deception on their relationship can be useful preventive medicine.

Antidote to Bullshitting Involving Deceitful Beliefs

Antidote 4

In relating to others, be rationally self-disclosing and congruent. (Rogers, Aristotle, Sartre, Nietzsche, Heidegger)

As mentioned, bullshitting misrepresents *beliefs* as well as intentions. For example, if you are trying to deceive someone into thinking you're patriotic by singing "The Star Spangled Banner," then you must also deceive this person into thinking that *you yourself* believe you're patriotic. So, bullshitting is always *insincere*.

On the other hand, sincerity about what you really believe is an important ingredient of healthy interpersonal relations. It is sometimes more important that you mean what you say than that what you say is true. People tend to be more accepting of people who get things wrong and are honest about it than of those who are insincere about what they really think.

There is always an element of phoniness in bullshitting. Being a phony means misrepresenting *yourself*—what you really think—rather than the external world. It is about saying things not because you really believe them but because you think they will advance your cause. It is about body language—smiles, intonations, gestures, and so forth—that are calculated to achieve an effect, to manipulate rather than to convey what's really going on inside you.

Many of us spend a good deal of our time concocting self-concealing, manipulative means of attaining what we want when we could more readily attain it by being ourselves. I have known many folks—students, clients, and personal acquaintances—who have hidden their real outlooks behind the veneer of pseudoetiquette, pseudointellectuality, macho stereotypes, vanity, and sundry other manners of concealing their true inner persons. You have already seen how existential philosophers like Sartre, Nietzsche, and Heidegger have stressed authenticity; that is, living according to your own lights instead of losing yourself behind such disguises.

The late psychologist Carl Rogers has given empirical credence to this existential insight under what he termed "congruence." According to Rogers, in a therapeutic context, the more congruent—genuine and real—the therapist is, "putting up no professional front or personal façade," the more likely it is that the client will also constructively change and grow.[31] More broadly, in interpersonal relations, such as between parent and child, partners, coworkers, and teachers and students, where pretenses are dropped and there is emphasis on sincere, nonjudgmental interpersonal relating, there is an increased likelihood of constructive change and growth.

In contrast, where people hide who they are behind public facades, these relationships tend to flounder. My own observations, inside and outside the clinic, corroborate Rogers's findings. In over twenty-five years of teaching, I have found students to be abundantly more responsive to my own openness, candor, and self-disclosure than to a more guarded posture. In being "transparent" (Rogers's term) so that my students can see what's going on inside of me, I have consistently noticed how much more self-disclosing, trusting, and willing to learn students become.

On the other hand, I have also known some professors who have hidden behind disingenuous professional facades, revealing very little of themselves. These instructors have tended to be less popular among students, and they have been least likely to be heralded by a majority of students as "great teachers."

Teachers who put on deceitful airs—anything from speaking in excessively technical jargon in effected tones of voice to making well-calculated, condescending gestures and remarks to their students—typically tend to discourage students from participating in class and in getting excited about learning. This is bullshit, and it doesn't take students long to pick up on it.

This doesn't mean that in your interpersonal relations you have to say *whatever* comes to your mind. As Rogers pointed out, being congruent is not an all-or-nothing affair. There are obviously some things that it would be indiscreet to say to others and some things that are plainly irrelevant. As Aristotle would also point out, the right amount of self-disclosure should avoid the extremes, not being overdisclosing and not being underdisclosing. While there is no magic formula for this "golden mean," it is not hard to spot the extremes.

Bullshitting involves more than just underdisclosing. Worse, it's being phony, and phoniness stifles trust. In any relationship that involves trust—and which ones don't?—you are much more likely to succeed by getting real.

Antidotes to Bullshitting Involving Deception about the External World

Antidote 5
Ask yourself what, in the long run, would be the most coherent and expedient way to think. Then speak the truth. (Berkeley, James)

As mentioned, lying involves deliberately making false statements about the external world. Lying is generally bad bullshit because it usually gets you into more trouble in the end than does the truth. In fact, people often waste large amounts of valuable time trying to think up elaborate excuses for their actions when they could simply tell the truth. I have found that, when there is a choice between lying your way out of a jam and telling the truth, the latter not only is easier to defend against when further questions are asked but also tends to get you into the least trouble.

Philosophers have long pondered the nature of truth, and there are fundamental disagreements among them as to how truth should be defined. However, there is considerably little disagreement as to whether truth is to be prized above falsehood. As mentioned earlier, American pragmatist philosophers like William James conceived truth in terms of its "cash value." True belief, he said, would never have been singled out as worth holding if it were not for the fact that it has "cash value"—it give you the results you want when you act on it. Recall James's characterization of the true. It is "only the expedient in the way of our thinking, just as 'the right' is only the expedient in the way of our behaving." True belief gets you where you want to go.

Other philosophers, such as Bishop George Berkeley, have conceived truth in terms of coherence with other beliefs in a system of belief. True ideas, Berkeley said, "are allowed to have more reality in them" than false ones, "that is, to be more strong, orderly, and coherent than the creatures of the mind."[32] On this conception, a belief coheres with a system of beliefs when it supports or is supported by other beliefs in that system. Like a house of cards, each belief in the system holds up other beliefs in that system. For example, my belief that there are presently American troops in Iraq is true because it supports and is supported by everything else I have heard from the media; the Internet; e-mail exchanges; students, local political, community, and spiritual leaders; and a host of other sources. Indeed, to believe that there is *not* such a war being waged at the time of this writing would contradict everything else I now believe and would, given this mutually supportive body of information, be the height of irrationality.

This idea that truths hang together in a coherent fashion is an important reason why truth works better than falsehood. If you believe something that is true, then you can generally expect whatever else you find out to fit in with your belief. This gives true belief greater explanatory and predictive power than false belief.

In contrast, a false claim is a shaky proposition because it will, sooner or later, run up against a system of coherent beliefs that comprise the truth. The person who tells a lie risks being found out in this way, while the person who tells the truth is likely to be born out.

Coherence of truth is the reason why true belief is so useful. Berkeley himself stresses this point:

> This gives us a sort of foresight which enables us to regulate our actions
> for the benefit of life. And without this we should be eternally at a loss;
> we could not know how to act toward anything that might procure us
> the least pleasure, or remove the least pain of sense.[33]

So both pragmatist and coherence approaches agree that truth has practical value because you can count on it in regulating your life.

According to one other popular philosophical approach, truth is not to be confused with coherence or with what works in regulating your life. Instead, it is plain old unadulterated *correspondence to fact*. According to its leading exponent, Aristotle,

> To say of what is that it is not, or of what is not that it is, is false, while to say of what is that it is, and of what is not that it is not, is true.[34]

On this view, true beliefs are, by definition, ones that correspond to the facts, and false beliefs are ones that don't. So if you believe that there are tigers in India and there *are* tigers in India, then your belief is true, whereas if there are *not* tigers in India, your belief is false. But notice that this formal definition of truth still requires you to determine "what is" and "what is not"; that is, you still have to decide what the facts are. How can you do that?

You have to *verify* your belief, which, for the pragmatist, means simply *acting* on it to see if it works. And, for the coherence approach, this means seeing if it fits with other beliefs that are true. So you just can't get around the practical nature of truth no matter what theoretical approach you take.

Truth pays. True belief provides a coherent, reliable framework for navigating *your own* way through life. In telling the truth, you also provide such a reliable framework for *others*—your significant others, friends, coworkers, and so forth. And in telling the truth, you don't have to lie to cover up a lie, and you don't have to risk being exposed when falsehood inevitably collides with truth. Functional relationships run on trust. Lying is usually bad bullshit because it squanders trust.

Antidote 6
Believe according to the evidence, not according to what's more comfortable. (Russell)

Lying to others is not the only sort of lying and sometimes not even the most dangerous sort. There is also lying *to yourself* where you attempt to deceive yourself about the facts in order to make yourself feel better about something, to keep yourself from accepting some unpleasant fact, or to permit yourself to engage in some sort of unjust treatment of others. This is often referred to as *rationalization*.

I'm not saying that rationalizing is *necessarily* a bad thing. You can sometimes benignly make yourself feel better using a little self-deception—"Oh well, I really didn't want him to ask me out anyway." Still, self-deception can be dangerous when it becomes habitual, when it involves doing harm to yourself or others, or when it is used in place of learning an important lesson.

There are abundant examples in the annals of history of how people have oppressed others through self-deception. In fact, most oppressors have been able to maintain their oppressive behavior by lying to themselves. For example, slave owners used to tell themselves that black people weren't really human, domestic abusers that their spouses are fortunate to be in their care, exploiters of the poor that the poor deserve their plight; and so on. Wars have been fought out of conceit, arrogance, and the desire to wield power instead of an honest assessment of the prospects of winning and the real benefits of going to war. Karl Marx is well known for saying that "religion is the opium of the people," meaning that those who get "high" on religion may rationalize and underassess their material needs—food, clothing, and shelter—thereby rendering themselves vulnerable to exploitation by others.[35]

It is a lot easier to mistreat others when, in pursuit of self-serving ends, you deceive yourself about their true welfare. It is also a lot easier to scuttle your own welfare when you deceive yourself about the importance of your own interests in pleasing others. For example, I have seen parents destroy their own happiness in the course of devoting themselves to pleasing ungrateful children, all along trying to convince themselves that their own happiness does not count.

Bertrand Russell has spoken of the great value of *veracity* in overcoming such self-deception. He said,

> Veracity, which I regard as second only to kindly feeling, consists broadly in believing according to evidence and not because a belief is comfortable or a source of pleasure. In the absence of veracity, kindly feeling will often be defeated by self-deception.[36]

In believing on the evidence and not on what makes you feel better, you stand to gain greater happiness for both yourself and those with whom you live and work. Veracity means, in the first place, having the tough-mindedness to ask yourself whether you are being honest with yourself or simply rationalizing. It means pushing yourself to look for the evidence to support your stance before you put it into effect.[37]

The codependent of an alcohol spouse; the conscientious parent who blames herself for a troubled child; the person who belittles and degrades others "for their own good"; the worker who underrates his capacities, staying in a dead-end job instead of trying to advance—these and countless other life instances are fueled by self-deception and a refusal to take a hard, objective look at the evidence.

In this context, "evidence" does not mean "proof" in the sense of absolute certainty. If this perfectionistic demand were what we required before we were satisfied that we were rationalizing, then none of us would ever let go of our self-deceptive ideas. For example, you don't need proof in this absolute sense that you have the capacity to advance, nor does a parent need absolute assurance that she is not responsible for her troubled child. It is a matter of what is *reasonable* to believe, not a matter of what is absolutely certain. The latter demand is what will keep you stuck in your state or self-deception. Liberate yourself and others. Veracity, please.

Antidote 7
In assessing yourself, avoid the extremes of boastfulness and mock modesty and own up, instead, to what you really have. (Aristotle)

In self-assessment, there are two popular extremes to avoid. One is overrating your accomplishments—"boastfulness"—the other underrating them—"mock modesty." According to Aristotle, the boastful person claims

> the things that bring glory, when he has not got them, or to claim more of them than he has, and the mock-modest man on the other hand to disclaim what he has or belittle it, while the man who observes the mean is one who calls a thing by its own name, being truthful both in life and in word, owning to what he has, and neither more nor less.[38]

Both extremes are bullshit insofar as they deceptive, albeit by going to opposite extremes. But, as Aristotle described, there are different types of each, depending on their objects. Boastfulness just for its own sake—delighting in falsehood as such—is, according to Aristotle, wasteful and futile. On the other hand, doing it for honor, reputation, or gain is worse. Boastfulness for the sake of honor or reputation, he said, is, relatively speaking, not as bad as doing it for money or for the things that lead to money. For example, the person who practices medicine without valid credentials risks doing serious harm to others.

Mock modesty that understates obvious qualities—"humbug"—is worse, said Aristotle, than that form that understates things that are less noticeable. For example, a stylish dresser who belittles his dress may even be doing so as way of boasting. The deception involved here is a deliberate attempt to falsely disclaim something in order to achieve the opposite effect.

To the extent that either of these extremes is manipulative and deceptive, it is bullshit and should be avoided. For Aristotle, the proper attitude toward truth is to love it as "noble and worthy of praise" for its own sake—apart from any ulterior object it may serve—and to shun falsehood as "in itself mean and culpable."[39] This perspective on truth is *not* incompatible with the pragmatic conception that values truth for its usefulness. There is, after all, nothing inconsistent with valuing truth for its own sake and *also* for its instrumental value.

NOTES

1. In his little book *On Bullshit*, Harry Frankfurt states that "the essence of bullshit is not that it is false but that it is phony" (47), and he distinguishes between lying and bullshitting. The former involves intentionally saying something false, while the latter is concerned not with the truth or falsity of what is said but rather with an attempt to fake something, for example, to impress someone with your knowledge of a subject or to convince someone that you're patriotic. For Frankfurt, it is the lack of regard for the truth entirely that sets bullshitting apart from lying. Liars are still concerned with truth for purposes of misrepresenting it. See Harry G. Frankfurt, *On Bullshit* (Princeton, N.J.: Princeton University Press, 2005). However, the concept of bullshitting that I discuss in this chapter includes lying as well as the forms of phoniness or fakery that Frankfurt identifies. The core concept of this more inclusive notion is therefore deception.

2. St. Thomas Aquinas, *Summa Theologica*, pt. 2 of pt. 2, Question 40, "On War," retrieved January 14, 2006, from http://www.ccel.org/a/aquinas/summa/SS/SS040 .html#SSQ40A1THEP1.

3. Thomas Hobbes, *Leviathan*, in *From Plato to Derrida*, 4th ed., ed. Forrest E. Baird and Walter Kaufmann (Upper Saddle River, N.J.: Prentice Hall, 2003), chap. 14, 469–71.

4. However, Aquinas did not think it acceptable for a person to intentionally *kill* another in self-defense because he held that this is within the power only of a public authority.

5. H. L. A. Hart, *The Concept of Law* (New York: Oxford University Press, 1961).

6. Nicolo Machiavelli, *The Prince*, chap. 17, retrieved January 14, 2006, from http://etext.library.adelaide.edu.au/m/machiavelli/niccolo/m149p/m149p.html#c hapter17.

7. John Stuart Mill, "The Subjection of Women," in *Philosophers at Work: Issues and Practice of Philosophy*, ed. Elliot D. Cohen (Fort Worth, Tex.: Harcourt, 2000), 144.

8. Janice K. Wilkerson, "The Philosopher as Social Worker," in Cohen, *Philosophers at Work*, 165.

9. Hannah Arendt, *The Human Condition* (Chicago: University of Chicago Press, 1958), 140.

10. Gail M. Presbey, "Hannah Arendt on Power," in *Philosophical Perspectives on Power and Domination: Theories and Practices*, ed. Laura Duhan Kaplan and Laurence F. Bove (Amsterdam: Rodopi, 1997), 29–40.

11. Sometimes the negative language is only implied, however. For example, the expression "fight like a man" implies that failure to fight makes you unmanly. The beef industry's advertisement "Real people eat beef" does not explicitly use negative language, but it implies that, if you do not each beef, then you are not a "real person."

12. P. H. Nowell-Smith, *Ethics* (London: Penguin Books, 1964), chap. 11.

13. Nowell-Smith, *Ethics*, 159.

14. J. L. Austin, *How to Do Things with Words*, 2nd ed., ed. J. O. Urmson and Marina Sbisa (Cambridge, Mass.: Harvard University Press, 1975). See also John Searle, *Speech Acts: An Essay in the Philosophy of Language* (London: Cambridge University Press, 1974).

15. Austin calls acts performed *in* saying something *illocutionary acts*, and he calls acts performed *by* saying something *perlocutionary acts*.

16. This doesn't mean that to warn or advise someone, you need to use such explicit performatives like "I warn" or "I advise." For example, you can warn someone of impending danger by saying "He will shoot you if you try to stop him" where the "I warn you" is implied.

17. I am assuming that you poison the well only if the person you are attempting to dissuade perceives the well as having been poisoned and is thereby inclined to avoid drinking from it. This means that it is not enough, for example, to utter the words "Only a nerd would wear those glasses" in order to poison the well against wearing those glasses. You would also have to have successfully intimidated someone against wearing them. If the targeted person is not so intimidated, then there has been only an unsuccessful *attempt* at poisoning the well. You successfully poison the well only when you actually succeed at intimating the targeted person.

18. See Nowell-Smith, *Ethics*.

19. See note 11.

20. Daren Fonda and Rita Healy, "How Reliable is Brown's Resume?," *Time*, Online Edition, September 8, 2005, retrieved September 29, 2005, from http://www.time.com/time/nation/article/0,8599,1103003,00.html.

21. Plato, *The Republic*, bk. 1, retrieved January 14, 2006, from http://etext.lib.virginia.edu/toc/modeng/public/PlaRepu.html.

22. If you defined bullshit in terms of morally objectionable deception, you could of course avoid calling this bullshit; but I don't see what is gained by defining away the problem. It seems more honest to say that you would still be bullshitting your friend, however, for a good reason.

23. See the section "Antidotes to Poisoning the Well" in this chapter.

24. You should recognize this version of Kant as a version of the "golden rule" to treat others the way you would want others to treat you. Unfortunately, this subjective principle could justify treating others sadistically if you happened to be a

sadomasochist. However, my version is cast in terms of what you would *reasonably* tolerate of others. It also includes the provision that unacceptable bullshit can't be consistently acted on by everyone without its destroying meaningful interpersonal communication.

25. John Rawls, *A Theory of Justice* (Cambridge, Mass.: Harvard University Press, 1971), 136–37

26. Seneca, *Moral Epistles*, trans. Richard M. Gummere (Cambridge, Mass.: Harvard University Press, 1917), vol. 1, 185, cited in Sissela Bok, *Lying* (New York: Random House, 1989), 94.

27. Bok, *Lying*.

28. Bok, *Lying*, 97.

29. This is not to mention much more publicized bullshit schemes, such as the installing of "fake" journalists in the press corps, such as Jeff Gannon (a.k.a. Jim Guckert) or columnist Armstrong Williams, who went on the Bush administration's payroll to promote its No Child Left Behind education initiative.

30. This was in the context of discussing a book I had edited at the time on media ethics. This book deals largely with the manner in which the corporate news media cooperate with government to disseminate bullshit. See Elliot D. Cohen, *News Incorporated: Corporate Media Ownership and Its Threat to Democracy* (New York: Prometheus Books, 2005).

31. Carl Rogers, *On Personal Power* (New York: Delacorte Press, 1977), 9.

32. George Berkeley, *A Treatise concerning the Principles of Human Knowledge*, in *The English Philosophers From Bacon to Mill*, ed. E. A. Burtt (New York: Modern Library, 1977), chap. 33, 533.

33. Berkeley, *A Treatise concerning the Principles of Human Knowledge*, chap. 31, 532.

34. Aristotle, *Metaphysics*, trans. W. D. Ross, in *The Basic Works of Aristotle*, bk. 4, chap. 7, 749.

35. Karl Marx, *A Contribution to Critique of Hegel's Philosophy of Right*, introduction, 1843, retrieved January 15, 2006, from http://www.marxists.org/archive/marx/works/1843/critique-hpr/intro.htm.

36. Bertrand Russell,, "What Is the Great Value of Veracity?," in *The Quotable Bertrand Russell*, ed. Lee Eisler (Amherst, N.Y.: Prometheus Books, 1993), 312.

37. Believing according to evidence and not according to what you would prefer to believe is discussed in greater detail in chapter 11.

38. Aristotle, *Ethics*, bk. 4, chap. 7, 998.

39. Aristotle, *Ethics*, bk. 4, chap. 7, 999.

8

CONNECTING WITH OTHERS

In the previous chapter, I talked about the correspondence approach to truth. This popular, commonsense definition of truth says that beliefs are true when they correspond to reality (facts). There's also another, opposing view of truth assumed by many human beings in their dealings with other human beings. This other view turns this correspondence definition on its head. It says that something is real—a fact or true—when it corresponds to what *you* believe. On this view, it isn't your belief that must correspond to reality; it is instead reality that must correspond to your belief in order to be true.

If you believe something is true, false, right, wrong, good, bad, or indifferent, then that's the way it is. You are the reality guru; you don't bow to reality; reality bows to you. If you think that beef is what's for dinner, then that's what *should* be for dinner—for you and all of humanity. Your tastes are a law unto all. If you think that secondhand smoke doesn't harm a fly, then you can darn well smoke where you want—in your car, in your home, in your office—and anyone who doesn't like it had better take a gasping breadth of (your) reality—since that is the only *true* reality. If you like action thrillers and despise romantic comedies, then action thrillers are great, and romantic comedies suck—and you too *must* concur if you have any sense of what's worthwhile. If you think gay guys are immoral child molesters (or that they're nicer than straight guys), if you think success means a mansion and a flashy car (or a job as a "professional" or a college education or whatever), or if you think that Christianity (or Islam, Judaism, Buddhism, Hinduism, or whatever) is the only true religion, then you are right, and everyone else is wrong. On this view, reality is nonnegotiable. It's your way or the highway. If others agree with you or they can be brought around to your way of thinking by *your* "rational" arguments, then that's well and good.

Here's what this truth-decreeing rule stipulates:

> The World Revolves Around Me: If *you* believe (disbelieve) something, then what you believe is true (false) and indeed the one and only true reality. Therefore, everybody else should also share your belief.

It's not hard to find a hole in this rule. It makes you the center of the universe when you have no more of a claim on reality than does anyone else. In assuming this rule, you ignore the evidentiary requirement for justifying beliefs about the external world and treat yourself as though you had some special authority to turn your individual preferences and value judgments into objective reality binding on everyone else.

> Refutation: Your individual preferences, tastes, and beliefs about external reality—including your worldviews and value judgments—cannot be validated just because they are *your* beliefs. For example, what facts prove that your preference for action thrillers is more valid than the other guy's for romantic comedies? And just because *you* smoke doesn't mean that it is healthy for others to inhale your smoke. This is an empirical matter, not something that depends on what you decree to be true. This also points to a double standard, one for your self and one for others. While you disregard the beliefs of other people, you expect others to accept your own. This is not different in principle from other kinds of irrational bias, such as racial discrimination, in which a distinction without a difference—one's race—is used as a standard for providing selective treatment.

ANTIDOTES TO THE
WORLD-REVOLVES-AROUND-ME FALLACY

Antidote 1
In relating to others, transcend your ego-centered perspective by looking for the common interests and purposes that unite us all as human beings. (Lewis)

Human perception itself is to a large extent ego centered. When I perceive the rubber tree growing freely on my front lawn, it is my particular rendition of the tree. This rendition is no doubt filtered through a common set of concepts. Otherwise, people could not agree that it is a tree that is the object of perception. But my subjective rendition would still not be the same as yours. What aspects attract my attention, for example, that it is growing abundantly onto my neighbor's property is a function of my special values and interests, which are not likely to coincide entirely with yours. It is my tree, not yours, and while I might look on it with an eye toward keeping it groomed, you might not give a damn about whether it intrudes onto my neighbor's property.

Inescapably, we are all caught inside our own circle of subjectivity, so it is understandable why we tend to interpret reality according to our own purposes and values. But there is a danger of overemphasizing our differences. I am a philosopher, and much of what I perceive is processed through my unique training as a philosopher. But I am still a human being who, as such, has the same basic interests as you do. As philosopher C. I. Lewis stated,

> Although different individuals may, and to a certain extent verifiably do, intuit things differently, still the basic discrimination which one can make can also be made by another. Especially those distinctions and relations which concern our major purposes and hence are such as it is practically most important for us to discern in our adjustment of behavior to environment, will be made by different individuals in comparable ways.[1]

So the tree that grows on my front lawn may not be yours, but still you know what it's like to bear responsibility for something that affects others adversely.

Survival is certainly the nitty-gritty of human purposes, and it is manifested in the perception of danger when it is threatened by something and in common self-defensive behavior patterns. Human beings get hungry and want to eat, and we know what it feels like to have hunger pangs; when our bowels and bladders are filled, we want to empty them, and we know well what a cramp feels like and, oh yes, that relief that ensues when we've finally relieved ourselves. We know what it is to get overheated, to feel cold, to feel sick, and to be sleepy, and our behavioral responses to these common human circumstances are quite similar. People generally enjoy companionship, learning, and spiritual encounters, and while we may fulfill these desires differently, we are not so different in our purposes and responses to obstacles that get in the way of their fulfillment.

So we are different, but we are also similar in important ways. Looking for similitude can help you overcome the tendency to cast reality purely in your own terms, thereby overlooking the interests, desires, and values of others. Telling a person who has no palate for sushi that she has bad taste is no different than this person's telling you that you have bad taste because you like it. The point is that all of us like to eat food that tastes good to us. These foods may be different, but what is common is our propensity to prefer eating what tastes good to us.

Antidote 2

Engage your human powers of caring and empathy to take your relationship to a higher moral plane of beneficence, friendship, gratitude, and other human virtues. (Hume)

Because we are all humans with common human interests and purposes, it is possible for us to identify with the plights of other human beings when these interests and purposes are defeated and to empathize with them. In fact, for philosopher David Hume, it is from this universal human sentiment that moral virtues are themselves derived:

> No qualities are more entitled to the general good will and approbation of mankind than beneficence and humanity, friendship and gratitude, natural affection and public spirit, or whatever proceeds from a tender sympathy with others and a generous concern for our kind and species.[2]

For Hume, it is caring about our fellow human beings that creates friendship; leads us to help others in time of need; allows us to appreciate the kindness conferred on us by others; gives us the ability to love; leads us to set aside narrow, self-interest for some public good; and all other aspects of moral existence.

Joined by common human purposes, we humans have the ability to feel the sorrows, frustrations, and disappointments of others as well as their joys and elations in overcoming great obstacles. This is why we can cry when we see a movie or a news story depicting human misfortune and to feel uplifted by one depicting the overcoming of great obstacles. You don't have to have been poor to know what it feels like to lose your home and your job and to be out on the street. You are human, and you know how you *would* feel if this were to befall you.

It's not hard to refuse to care. You can always find excuses. "Why should I feel sorry for the homeless? It's their fault." But in insulating yourself like this from the suffering of others, you can easily lose sight of your own human frailty. This is not to say that having been down and out can't help you empathize. It can. There was a low point when, starting out, I rolled pennies just to buy a few gallons of gas to get down the road, and I know what it feels like to stand in a bread line. But there are many things that I haven't experienced myself. I have not been sold into slavery, but I love my freedom, and I can well imagine what it might be like to have every ounce of my autonomy stolen from me. Nor have I been in the subjective shoes of the Iraqi civilians whose country has been devastated by a war. But I value my life and those of my family, and I can imagine (although admittedly not nearly with the same vivacity of having lived through it) what it might be like to exist under such inauspicious conditions.

My late mentor Samuel L. Hart stressed the necessity of harmonizing the interests and desires of others with your own in the attainment of personal happiness:

> The essence of a morally good life is a satisfaction which makes for satisfaction of other people. To be inconsiderate, to strive for gratifications of needs at the expense of other people's desires, to make one's joy the suffering of another, to claim privileges for oneself which become burdens of our fellow men—these are the clearly discernible immoral doings. . . . Exigencies of living together call for principles of conduct which aim at harmonizing conflicting desires and interests.[3]

Here Hart speaks of *harmonizing* the desires of others with your own. We live in a world where consideration for the desires of others is ordinarily a condition of others' consideration for your desires. Such reciprocity is a practical condition of human happiness—your own as well as that of others.

I have elsewhere talked about being morally sensitive.[4] By this I mean having concern for the *welfare, interests,* and *needs* of others—what I have termed the WIN standard. You can certainly go through your life caring only about your own welfare, interests, and needs, but unless you put an effort into tending to those of others, you will miss the ingredients of a moral existence about which Hume so eloquently spoke. Friendship, benevolence, affection, gratitude, and public spirit, among other virtues, will be conspicuously absent from your life. I know that this is not how I would choose to live. I'd be a shell of humanity. I know this is also true of you. I know this because you and I are very much alike. We are *human*.

Antidote 3

As a way of connecting with another person, bust your gut to see the truth in what he or she is saying. (Belenky and Clinchy, Buber, Rogers)

Mary Belenky and Blythe Clinchy, among other feminist thinkers, have distinguished between two methods or procedures of knowing that bear significantly on how well you might fare in empathizing with the plights of others. These they call "separate" and "connected" knowing.[5]

Separate knowing is actually the classical approach to knowing embraced by philosophers. It is a methodology that seeks to discover truth by critique, careful logical analysis, and the demand for justification at every step. It is enshrined in the Socratic method of arriving at truth, which asks critical questions, summons reflective responses, and attempts to find flaws in these responses by posing counterexamples to them. It is a method that uses *doubting* as a strategy for discovering truth. Later in this chapter, I will talk about René Descartes' use of doubt as a procedure for discovering truth. His approach to acquiring knowledge is squarely in this tradition. Separate knowing is also used in the logic-based approach developed in this book. But, as you will see, logic-based therapy (LBT) also uses connected knowing.

In contrast to separate knowing, the focus of connected knowing is not on pulling things apart, analyzing them, and trying to find something wrong with what another is saying but rather on trying to *believe* what someone is saying. It is on busting your gut to see the truth in what someone is saying, on understanding it, rather than on trying to find holes in it.

Connected knowing doesn't mean simply believing what is easiest for you to believe, namely, those things toward which you already have an affinity to believe. To the contrary, it means overcoming your tendencies to doubt the credibility of what you are being told. This requires flexing your willpower muscle to tune in to what the other is saying without putting it on trial.

Connected knowing is essential for empathizing. If you approach another with doubt and incredulity, you will automatically drive a wedge between your subjective world and that of the other. But empathy requires putting yourself in the subjective shoes of another person. This requires attachment, not detachment. Doubting others *detaches* you *from* them, while believing others *attaches* you *to* them. This does not mean that you should go to the opposite extreme of the world revolving around you by losing yourself in the other. It was for fear of such overattachment that Martin Buber rejected use of the word "empathy" since he took it to connote "loss of the self in the process of experiencing the other." Instead, Buber emphasized experiencing the other "without forfeiting anything of the felt reality of his [own] reality."[6]

Nevertheless, other thinkers have managed to speak meaningfully of empathy while heeding Buber's caution. For example, for Carl Rogers, to empathize is to "sense the client's world as if it were your own, but without ever losing the 'as if' quality."[7] This means getting as close as possible to the client's subjectivity without losing yourself in it. On the other hand, it is also possible to lose *the other* by getting too caught up in yourself.

Antidote 4

In trying to connect with another person, avoid two extremes: underdistancing, where you get too emotionally caught up in your own practical interests, and overdistancing, where you are emotionally detached. (Bullough, Aristotle)

It is not infrequent to find the work of a philosopher in one area useful for addressing a problem in another distinct area. In particular, I have used Edward Bullough's work in the philosophy of art as a guide to connected knowing.[8] In his seminal work on relating to a work of art, this philosopher speaks of maintaining "psychical distance." Such a relation, he says,

> does not imply an impersonal, purely intellectually interested relation of such a kind. On the contrary, it describes a personal relation, often highly emotionally coloured, but of a peculiar character. Its peculiarity lies in that the personal character of the relation has been, so to speak, filtered.[9]

The filter of which Bullough speaks is a practical filter whereby you bracket off your own practical interests when you attempt to connect with another. Bullough offers this example:

> Suppose a man, who believes that he has cause to be jealous about his wife, witnesses a performance of "Othello." He will the more perfectly appreciate the situation, conduct and character of Othello, the more exactly the feelings and experiences of Othello coincide with his own—at least he ought to on the . . . principle of concordance.[10] In point of fact, he will probably do anything but appreciate the play. In reality, the concordance will merely render him acutely conscious of his own jealousy; by a sudden reversal of perspective he will no longer see Othello apparently betrayed by Desdemona, but himself in an analogous situation with his own wife. The reversal of perspectives is the consequence of the loss of distance.[11]

Similarly, if you try to connect with another person through your own feelings and experiences, you will need to exercise caution that you don't wind up seeing yourself in the same position as the person with whom you are trying to empathize. Otherwise, you risk losing the opportunity to connect with that person because the focus will then be off that person and on you instead. By losing distance between yourself and the other, you lose the opportunity to see and appreciate what *he* is saying.

Bullough's antidote to such reversal of perspectives is to avoid two extremes—overdistancing and underdistancing. By underdistancing, you lose the other in yourself. On the other hand, by overdistancing, you fail to get close enough emotionally to the situation to appreciate it. This would be illustrated by looking at *Othello* in a purely, intellectual, emotionally detached manner.

In fact, there are variable degrees of distance, and the key is to get as close emotionally to the situation as you can without losing distance. This is another fine example of Aristotle's "golden mean," that is, finding the mean between under- and overdistancing yourself. And, like all such avoidance of extremes, while there is no exact formula, it is largely a function of your own ability to maintain distance. As mentioned, this calls for flexing your willpower muscle in busting your gut to overcome your tendency to doubt and therefore to avoid overdistancing yourself. But this also requires tuning out to a considerable extent those personal desires and interests that would prompt a reversal of focus away from the other person and onto you.

This doesn't mean that your empathetic understanding of another's situation should be purely at the gut. It is a myth that empathy is improved when it is purely emotional and lacks cognition. For example, knowing that the person in question has just lost his wife after a relentless battle with cancer and that he was constantly at her side caring for her up to her last gasp for air, knowing that this couple were virtually inseparable from the time they met as teenagers, knowing that they have three small children—knowing these and other facts about the history and circumstances of this person could only add to your ability to connect and empathize with him. On the other hand, mere whining and weeping with the person does not help you connect with the person. This is not empathetic *understanding*, which is emotionally charged *knowing*.

Nor does maintaining the proper distance mean that you should not bring your own experiences and feelings to the table in empathizing. It means only that these should not take over and defeat your ability to keep your focus on the person rather than yourself. As I said, there is no mathematical formula for this, but being aware that you can defeat your ability to connect by getting too caught up in yourself is paramount.

In stressing connected knowing as an antidote to the world-revolves-around-me fallacy, I do not want to devalue the fundamental role of separate knowing in the LBT process. Like connected knowing, separate knowing is not a purely self-absorbed process. In LBT, there is a nonpossessive collaborative effort to find out the truth.

When philosophers get together to philosophize among themselves, they are generally not there to shoot down a colleague like a hunter out for a hide. It is more like "we're all out for the truth and in it together as seekers of truth." This is how separate knowledge enters into LBT when, through logical analysis, it seeks to expose and refute the irrational premises underlying self-destructive emotions and behavior.

Still, philosophers are human, and there are some who seem more interested in shooting holes in their opponents and leaving them out to dry than in trying to plug up the holes they find. These philosophers are to their intellectual opponents as a school of piranhas is to a piece of flesh. They are often very talented, intellectual assassins who hit and run. LBT is not hit-and-run philosophy. Instead, it takes its cue from the systematic philosophers of antiquity—like Plato, Aristotle, Kant, and the many others addressed in this book. Philosophers of this ilk are not happy simply to expose a problem—What is knowledge? What is truth? How does mind relate to body? What is right conduct?—they also strain every ounce of their intellectual genius to provide solutions.

The point is, in applying the tools of LBT, you will have occasion to use both methods of separate and connected knowing and to move back and forth between them. It is a somewhat artificial division to separate these procedures in the act of dealing with problems of living. Sometimes you will need to separate yourself by using a method of doubt, while other times you will need to connect by using a method of belief. Both require willpower to apply, and both can have beneficial results. In overcoming your tendency to see the world as revolving around you, you should push yourself to connect with others. But that doesn't mean that your empathy for the person will solve your problem. You may then have to take the understanding you gain through empathizing and use it to arrive at a reasonable, equitable solution. This typically requires logical analysis, that is, separate knowing.

Antidote 5

If you really wouldn't want to be trapped inside your own subjectivity, acknowledge the existence of others: take seriously their desires, values, preferences, and beliefs. (Descartes)

As I mentioned previously, the philosophy of seventeenth-century philosopher René Descartes epitomizes the method of separate knowing.

His challenge was to demonstrate the existence of the external world in the same way in which a mathematician demonstrates a theorem to follow from a set of axioms. He believed that if he began trying to doubt everything he could find reason to doubt and if he could find something that was beyond doubt, he could use it as an axiom (starting point) from which to demonstrate all other things in the world.

To help him along, he hypothesized that there was some powerful evil demon out to deceive him into believing everything people ordinarily believe about the world outside them.[12] Descartes therefore set out to find something about which even such a malignant power couldn't deceive him, and here's what he said:

> I have just convinced myself that nothing whatsoever existed in the world, that there was no sky, no earth, no minds, and no bodies; have I not thereby convinced myself that I did not exist? Not at all . . . let him [the evil demon] deceive me as much as he will, he can never make me be nothing as long as I think that I am something. . . . I must finally conclude and maintain that this proposition: *I am, I exist*, is necessarily true every time that I pronounce it or conceive it in my mind.[13]

With this insight, Descartes rescued himself from *complete* skepticism. As a philosopher, he could be sure that he existed as long as he thought he did. His own existence was revealed to him through his thinking like an illuminating light. In pondering his own existence, he proved it to himself. This proposition of his own existence was certain and indubitable as long as he thought it.

Now to see what Descartes was talking about, just try this little thought experiment. Try doubting that you exist. Keep telling yourself that you don't exist. Say five times, "I don't exist," and try believing it as you say it. What happens? The more you keep telling yourself you don't exist, the more apparent it becomes that you *do* exist.

On the other hand, try doubting that yours truly (Elliot D. Cohen) exists. Not hard to do, right? Surely you can doubt *my* existence in a way that you can't doubt your own. After all, your own existence is revealed to you through your thinking in a way that mine (or anyone else's) is not. The upshot of this is that your own existence has a more central place in your world than mine does. It is you, after all, not anyone else, who is revealed to you through your thinking. You are the center of your world, not me and not anyone else. Accordingly, it's a lot easier, from your subjective standpoint, to assign greater reality and importance to *your* beliefs than to mine, easier to ignore the other guy in favor of yourself, easier to put yourself first, and easier to perceive yourself as the hub of reality.

True, once Descartes had proven his own existence to himself, he did try to prove the existence of everything else in the world. First he tried to derive God's existence from his own existence, and then he attempted to use God, in His infinite goodness, as the underwriter of the rest of creation. As a benevolent being, God would not deceive us into thinking that the external world existed if it really didn't.[14]

Clearly, Descartes didn't want to remain stuck in a world where only his own existence was assumed, and, save for the philosophical challenge of escaping it, he had good practical reasons for wanting to escape it. Just imagine what it would be like to inhabit such a world. You would be a prisoner in your own mind, unable to defer to anyone else's judgment, unable to trust any judgment about external reality—about anything reaching beyond your own subjectivity. It would be a desolate and impoverished universe devoid of the diversity of legitimate, alternative viewpoints. The world would revolve exclusively around you.

Would you want to inhabit such an ego-centered world? If your ego is anything like mine, you would rather be dead.

I'm not saying that world-revolves-around-me thinking need go that far. You don't have to *really* deny the existence of other people and things to do this sort of thinking. But this is just a matter of degree, not of kind. To the extent that the world revolves around you—and we all, to some extent, think like this—is the extent to which you discount the reality of the external world, including other people. If you wouldn't want to inhabit such a world, then be more mindful of the subjective worlds of your compatriots. And instead of validating external reality on whether it conforms to what you think or desire, let it have its own independent existence. This will add considerable color to what would otherwise be a very bland world not fit for human habitation.

Antidote 6
If you really believe in external reality and that your life is not just a dream, look for truth beyond your own subjectivity. Otherwise you might as well be dreaming. (Berkeley, Locke)

Nor was Descartes alone in his desire to believe in the existence of the external world and to escape the futility of the world-revolves-around-me fallacy. Even the most skeptical of philosophers, David Hume, had to admit the practical necessity of believing in external reality.

Bishop Berkeley, who reduced the external world to bundles of ideas, still found a way to distinguish between true ideas that represented external reality and ones that didn't. Just imagine if the existence of the external world depended entirely on your perception of them. Things would go out of existence just by shutting your eyes. But Berkeley didn't care to inhabit such an unstable universe, so he did what any respectable bishop would do: He called on God. Objective reality persists, even when human beings cease to perceive it, because God is the omnipresent, grand perceiver, the divine motion picture camera that keeps the reality show running. So the milk in your refrigerator does not go out of existence when you shut the fridge door. Why? Because God's still perceiving it.[15] And your dreams can be distinguished from your veridical perceptions. Why? Because God's perceiving your real perceptions, while your dreams are just in your own mind. God to the rescue once again.[16]

For John Locke, the existence of an external world was not certain, but it was nonetheless "beyond bare probability." Said Locke: "We are provided with an evidence that puts us past doubting: for I ask anyone whether he be not invincibly conscious to himself of a different perception, when he looks on the sun by day and thinks on it by night, when he actually tastes wormwood or smells a rose or only thinks on that savour or odour?" Against his critics who claim that what we think is real may only be a dream, Locke answered, "It is no great matter whether I remove his scruple or no: where all is but dream, reasoning and arguments are of no use, truth and knowledge nothing."[17] When the world revolves around you, you might as well be dreaming. And, as the philosopher says, in a dream, there is no point to rational argument, truth, and knowledge. Do you believe in rational argument, truth, and knowledge? If so, awaken from your dogmatic slumber and greet the world outside you with open arms.

Antidote 7
Don't confuse believing that your values, preferences, and desires are true with their actually being true. (Chisholm, Descartes)

As I mentioned previously, in Descartes' attempt to acquire knowledge through the method of doubt (separate knowing), his own existence became evident to him. He could not doubt his own existence. Nor could he doubt his own doubts. Just try doubting that you *are* doubting. The more you try to doubt your doubt, the more evident it becomes that you have doubt. And the plot thickens. If you believe you believe something, how could you possibly be mistaken that you believe something? Notice there's a difference between *what* you believe and *that* you believe. If you believe that today is Monday, you can surely be mistaken about *what* you believe—it might, in fact, be some other day of the week. But how could you possibly be mistaken that you *believe* it's Monday? So here perhaps is something to which you—and you alone—have privileged access: your *own* thoughts. At least with respect to them, the world does appear to revolve around you.

My late doctoral adviser Roderick Chisholm used to refer to a person's thinking and believing as "the directly evident." According to Chisholm, something is directly evident when it fits the formula:

> What justifies me in counting it as evident that a is F is simply the fact that a is F.[18]

For example, it's directly evident to me that I *believe* there is presently a war in Iraq since what justifies me in counting it as evident that I believe this is simply the fact that *I believe it*. On the other hand, it's not directly evident to me that there *is* a war in Iraq because this statement is not about my thoughts at all but rather about the external world, and for this I need further evidence, such as the fact that I have heard numerous reports from politicians and journalists about such a war.

Similarly if you believe you feel cold, then it's true that you feel cold; and if you believe you feel dizzy, then it's true you feel dizzy,[19] and you can know your own desires and preferences in the same way. But this is a far cry from saying that your desires and preferences are *better* than anyone else's. You are captain of whether you *believe* they're better, but whether they *are* better is *not* directly evident to you. So, the range of things directly evident to you is very limited, indeed—your own existence and your own thoughts and not anyone else's thoughts.

That, at least, is what Descartes seems to have thought. Here then is the Cartesian punch line. If you want the world to revolve around you, you'll just have to content yourself with your feelings, sensations, desires, beliefs, preferences, hopes, and other mental events going on in your *own* psychic backyard. Just don't confuse this with what's going on in the external world. About the latter, you have no better access than anyone else.

Antidote 8
Since the world-revolves-around-me rule cannot consistently be made a universal law, dump it. (Kant)

In fact, when it comes to external reality, all human minds seem to come equipped with the *same* standard perceptual equipment. According to

Kant, the human mind comes equipped with concepts that fashion the raw data of sense experience into knowledge. For example, human minds see things in terms of time and space—so that the sensations you receive of yonder table are ordered in time and space. It's like you're wearing spectacles that take what you experience and fashion it into external objects. Reality is therefore constructed out of these two components: the raw data of your senses and the innate concepts of the mind. For Kant, concepts without sense experience were "empty," and sense experience without concepts was "blind."[20] Concepts are the forms that shape the content of your sense experiences into the external world. Form without content is empty, and content without form is blind.

Kant also thought that human beings perceive practical matters in terms of a *moral concept* that's standard equipment. In particular, as mentioned in chapter 8, he thought that human reason itself commands people to act in ways that can be consistently acted on by everyone. Recall that he put this in terms of the command to "act as if the maxim of your action were to become through your will a universal law of nature." So this is what it's like to wear moral spectacles: people can know right from wrong by seeing if their rules of action ("maxims") can be turned into "universal laws"—that is, if they can be consistently acted on by everyone.

Here's the bottom line. If the world revolves around you, then your maxim is automatically off limits for everyone else. Indeed, that's just what it means for the world to revolve around *you*: you make special exception of yourself. For example, if the world revolves around you, then, if you believe that human beings are not responsible for contributing to global warming, you are right, and everyone else who doesn't share your belief is wrong. You expect others to believe as you do, but you are not prepared to believe as they do. In other words, the world-revolves-around-me Rule couldn't be consistently acted on as though it were a universal law. So, for Kant, if you subscribe to this rule, your moral perception is defective.

And Kant would be right. Watch how much resentment you are likely to conjure up from your fellow human beings when they are subjected to your rule. They are likely to perceive you in less-than-flattering terms—hypocritical, narrow-minded, and selfish. After all, would you want to have *your* beliefs—preferences, values, and desires—summarily dismissed by someone who thinks the world revolves around him? I doubt it.

Antidote 9

Strive to be rationally tolerant of others in resolving disagreements with them. (Benedict, Herskovits, Socrates, Aristotle, Aquinas, Kluckhohn)

Self-indulgence that ignores the preferences and values of others suffers from a very serious, related moral transgression. This is the failure to respectfully tolerate differences between us. There appears to be a wide range of disagreement among different cultures about matters of right and wrong and good and bad. For example, in the Netherlands euthanasia (mercy killing) is widely accepted and legal, whereas in the United States it is not generally accepted and is illegal. There is also a broad range of disagreement of people *within* any particular culture. In the United States, for example, there is a strong emphasis on God and religion, but there are still people who are not religious, some of whom do not believe in God. These differences do not negate other agreements, however. For example, most of us, theists and nontheists alike, agree that it is wrong to kill or otherwise do harm to people who do not directly threaten your own life or the lives of significant others. As anthropologist Ruth Benedict stated,

> the recognition of cultural relativity carries with it its own values. . . . [In recognizing it] we shall arrive then at a more realistic social faith, accepting as grounds of hope and as new bases for tolerance the coexisting and equally valid patterns of life which mankind has created for itself from the raw materials of existence.[21]

These "raw materials of existence" are and can be interpreted differently by people who come from different backgrounds. As Melville Herskovits expressed it, "Judgments are based on experience, and experience is interpreted by each individual in terms of his enculturation."[22] It is only by thinking that your enculturation is somehow superior to the other person's that you can even begin to discount the other person's values and preferences.

However, anthropologists like Benedict and Herskovits have disclaimed an ancient philosophical tradition that would disagree with the popular slogan "It's all relative." Indeed, Socrates devoted his life to trying to debunk contemporaries of his known as Sophists, who were hardheaded relativists. According to one influential Sophist, Protagoras, "Man is the measure of all things." In contrast, Socrates thought that truth was independent of people's cultural beliefs. For example, according to the Socratic perspective, it would not be just to torture prisoners of war simply because the government—or even an entire culture—permitted it. Socrates would undoubtedly have condemned the U.S. treatment of prisoners in Abu Ghraib as unjust.

There are two extremes to avoid—inflexibility and pigheadedness on the one hand and the willingness to tolerate virtually anything on the other.

As Aristotle would remind you, in making practical decisions, the truth lies somewhere between the extremes, and therefore there are rational limits to what you should and should not tolerate.

Unfortunately, when the world revolves around you, no such rational line is drawn, or, if a line is drawn, you draw it in a way that even you yourself would not tolerate if applied to your own case. If your preference is for romantic comedies and your significant other's is for action thrillers, then there is no rational standard that could equitably validate your preference as superior. On the other hand, if your significant other wants to sneak into the movies without paying and you are unwilling, there *is*, in this case, a rational standard that could validate your refusal. Unfortunately, it is only by treating the first sort of case as though it were akin to the second that you would fail to respect the *rational* limits of tolerance.

Tolerance *as such* is therefore not necessarily a good thing. Tolerance for Hitler's preferences was not a good thing, for example. Tolerance, like all other principles, is not an absolute. It has rational limits. *Rational tolerance* is tolerance for the outlooks of other human beings within the limits set by rational standards, that is, by standards you as a rational being would also be prepared to apply to your own case.[23] Again, to be rationally tolerant means willingness to respect your significant other's right to prefer action thrillers, but it does not confer the right to sneak into the theater without paying in order to see one.

The main idea behind *rational tolerance* is illustrated by St. Thomas Aquinas's discussion on how morality can set rational limits to making law. In his famous *Treatise on Law*, Aquinas distinguishes between "determinations of natural law" and "deductions"[24] from it. By a "natural law," he meant roughly a universal moral principle binding across cultures from which human laws can be derived. For example, there is a natural law that says that harming another human being is wrong, from which you can deduce the wrongfulness of homicide.[25] On the other hand, he also says there's a natural law that evildoers should be punished. But it doesn't say just *how* a particular evildoer should be punished. This, says Aquinas, is a "determination" of the natural law.[26] That is, it is open to interpretation. For example, there is room for debate among lawmakers as to how much to fine a person for speeding, but that doesn't mean it would be permissible to put a speeder to death as punishment for his offense. To be sure, there is more than one reasonable alternative, but there are also rational limits.

Anthropologist Clyde Kluckhohn expressed a similar point about the limits of cultural relativity:

The human parade has many floats, but when one strips off the cultural symbolism, the ethical standards are akin. . . . To be sure, there must be room left for relativity as regards specific moral rules. . . . Even then, however, *both* within and between cultures moral behavior in specific instances and in all its details must be judged within a wide context *but with reference to principles which are not relative.*[27]

The point is that there can be room for alternative perspectives on an issue without concluding that there are no objective boundaries to them. Within the limits of rational tolerance, when your values and preferences conflict with that of another, there is room for flexibility.

In the case of conflict, one thing you could do is to try to compromise. For example, this time you can bite the bullet and see an action thriller, and the next time your significant other can yield to your preference. Another option is to find alternative activities to pursue for which you don't encounter a conflict. In the absence of any resolution to a conflict, rational people can always agree to respectfully disagree.

Antidote 10
Say no to gender roles that adopt self-serving/self-denigrating double standards. (de Beauvoir)

The inflexible "my way or the highway" perspective signalizes world-revolves-around-me thinking. On the other hand, there is a point to being *too* flexible. Like all contracts, compromises are valid (morally speaking) only when they are based on mutual consent. If you are not prone to world-revolves-around-me thinking but happen to be shacked up with someone who is, then you may find yourself making increasing accommodations in order to satisfy this individual. But here's the problem. The more you yield, the more you reinforce the inflexible demandingness of your partner.

Typically, those who think the world revolves around them do not last long in a relationship with like-minded individuals. That's a no-brainer. Their partners are usually individuals willing to make abundant self-sacrifices to keep the peace. This is an inherently dysfunctional situation since these partners eventually become increasingly resentful, while the self-absorbed partner becomes increasingly more demanding.

Let me illustrate with the case of Sam and Sue, a couple whose marriage of ten years ended in divorce. The dysfunctionality of this relationship was fueled by adherence to traditional values. Sue was brought up to believe that the man was the head of the household and that whatever he said was the final word. Sam was brought up to believe that the wife should be subservient to the man. At the beginning, Sue worked to put Sam through both undergraduate and law school and ended up sacrificing her own immediate aspirations to become a teacher. When the couple had children, Sue became a stay-at-home mom, while Sam worked at a cushy law firm. Sam drove a BMW, played golf on weekends with his associates, and not infrequently went on business trips while Sue stayed behind with the children. Sue did the housework, tended to the children, and had Sam's dinner on the table routinely.

Eventually, Sue learned from a friend that Sam was having an affair, and that's where she drew the line. Unfortunately, society had supported Sue in her servitude and Sam in his self-absorbed view of women.

I am not saying that the two had no control over the directions their lives took. To the contrary, such individuals were, in the famous words of John Stuart Mill, "willing slaves."[28] Still, the tendency of men to think that their marriages revolve around them and that women should try to accommodate them is not entirely without social influences. Feminist philosopher Simone de Beauvoir, writing in the 1950s about how women and men differ in their concepts of love, had this to say:

> In their most violent transports, [men] never abdicate completely; even on their knees before a mistress, what they still want is to take possession of her; at the very heat of their lives they remain sovereign subjects; the beloved women is only one value amongst others; they wish to integrate her into their existence and not to squander it entirely on her. For women, on the contrary, to love is to relinquish everything for the benefit of a master. . . . A woman is non-existent without a master. Without a master, she is a scattered bouquet.[29]

Oh, but that was in the 1950s, you say. "You've come a long way, baby!" Right? But it's the condescending "baby" that belies the truth, for this archaic perspective has unfortunately lasted into the twenty-first century. If you have doubts, consult any seasoned social worker who gets to see what goes on behind the closed doors of households spanning all economic brackets and races.[30]

There is presently a growing trend in America toward the acceptance of fundamentalist religious values upholding traditional gender roles in which men are heads of households and women are "obedient" to them. This trend is also hostile to gay relationships, which it perceives as perverse and "unnatural." As the social pendulum swings in this direction, there is danger that more women, not fewer, will become ensconced in such un-equal relationships with men and that more men will come to perceive their relationships with women as revolving around them. Against this social backdrop, it is important to keep in mind the inherent problems of the-world-revolves-around-me thinking both for those who are committed to this fallacious rule of living and those who become their codependents.

What to do? If you are in an unequal relationship, the first thing is to realize it. You can't fix a problem unless you acknowledge it exists. As pre-viously discussed, what tends to fuel such relationships is rationalization, a form of lying to yourself in order to make yourself feel better about ex-ploiting someone. "That's women's work!" is a good example of an excuse that has traditionally allowed "macho" men to get out of doing domestic chores like cooking and cleaning. "Women are more emotional and less ra-tional than men" is another, which has kept traditional women barefoot and pregnant, intellectually unfulfilled, underrepresented in professional ranks, and unfairly compensated for their work. For the sake of happiness, cast these self-defeating constructs and stereotypes to the flames. It takes two to tango: the exploiter needs someone to exploit, and the exploited need an exploiter. Saying no to such self-serving/self-denigrating relationships brings the curtain down on these colossal wastes of human potential.

As mentioned in chapter 8, it's a fallacy to assume that *someone* must be "the boss." True, a master needs a slave and vice versa, and a dictator needs a subject and vice versa, but that doesn't mean unequal relations are your only options. As I have stressed, a better option is partnership, where the world does not revolve around anyone, where each partner is au-tonomous, and where there are democratic, noncoercive divisions of labor and sharing of benefits and burdens. Say adieu to Mr. and Mrs. Nean-derthal.

NOTES

1. C. I. Lewis, *Mind and the World Order* (New York: Dover Publications, 1956), 111.

2. David Hume, *An Enquiry concerning the Principles of Morals*, sec. 2, pt. 1, retrieved January 15, 2006, from http://www.gutenberg.org/dirs/etext03/nqpmr10.txt.

3. Samuel L. Hart, *Ethics: The Quest for the Good Life* (Delmar, N.Y.: Caravan Books, 1972), 85.

4. Elliot D. Cohen and Gale S. Cohen, *The Virtuous Therapist: Ethical Practice of Counseling and Psychotherapy* (Belmont Calif.: Brooks/Cole, 1999).

5. Mary Belenky et al., *Knowledge, Difference, and Power* (New York: Harper-Collins, 1996).

6. Cited in Clinchy, "Connected and Separate Knowing," in Belenky et al., *Knowledge, Difference, and Power*, 231.

7. Carl Rogers, *On Becoming a Person*, (Boston: Houghton Mifflin, 1989), 284.

8. Mike W. Martin makes similar use of it in professional ethics. See his article "Professional Distance," *International Journal of Applied Philosophy* 11, no. 2 (winter/spring 1997): 39–50.

9. Edward Bullough, "'Psychical Distance' as a Factor in Art and an Aesthetic Principle," in *Aesthetics: A Critical Anthology*, ed. George Dickie and Richard J. Scalafani (New York: St. Martin's Press, 1977), 761.

10. This is the principle that says that your appreciation is directly proportional to how closely the feelings and experiences of the character in question matches your own.

11. Bullough, "Psychical Distance," 762.

12. Just for the record, Descartes is not having paranoid ideation. He doesn't really believe there is such a powerful evil demon out to dupe him. This is just a tool he uses to help him along with his method of doubt.

13. René Descartes, *Meditations*, in *Descartes: Philosophical Essays*, trans. Laurence J. LaFleur (Indianapolis: Bobbs-Merrill, 1976), "Second Meditation," 82.

14. Unfortunately, most philosophers do not believe that Descartes succeeded in his mission. This is because he appears to need God's existence as a basis to prove anything else, including God's existence itself. This would make his proof circular.

15. Berkeley's position is expressed in the following limerick:

> There was a young man who said, "God must think it exceedingly odd
> If he finds that this tree
> Continues to be
> When there's no one about in the Quad."

Reply:

> "Dear Sir: Your astonishment's odd:
> I am always about in the Quad.
> And that's why the tree
> Continues to be,
> Since observed by, Yours faithfully, God."

16. Remember, Descartes also brought in God to rescue the external world.

17. John Locke, *An Essay concerning Human Understanding*, in *From Plato to Derrida*, 4th ed., ed. Forrest E. Baird and Walter Kaufmann (Upper Saddle River, N.J.: Prentice Hall, 2003), bk. 4, chap. 2, sec. 14, 601.

18. Roderick M. Chisholm, *Theory of Knowledge* (Englewood Cliffs, N.J.: Prentice Hall, 1966), 28.

19. On the other hand, if you believe you're angry, that's another story. This is because anger involves behavioral as well as physiological changes in your body that are not themselves directly evident to you. Of course, if you think you're angry, then at least it's true that you *think* this.

20. Immanuel Kant, *Critique of Pure Reason*, trans. J. M. D. Meiklejohn, pt. 2, introduction, sec. 1, retrieved January 15, 2006, from http://www.gutenberg.org/dirs/etext03/cprrn10.txt.

21. Ruth Benedict, *Patterns of Culture* (New York: Pelican Books, 1946), 257, cited in *Ethical Relativism*, ed. John Ladd (Belmont, Calif.: Wadsworth, 1973), 9.

22. Melville J. Herskovits, "Cultural Relativism and Cultural Values," in Ladd, *Ethical Relativism*, 61.

23. Here I am reaching into my Kantian bag of tools to define a rational principle. I mean one that could be turned into a "universal law." See antidote 4.

24. *Summa Theologica*, "Treatise on Law," in *Introduction to St. Thomas Aquinas*, question 95, art. 2, 649–50.

25. Aquinas is assuming that killing someone always harms them, but some have questioned this. For example, Richard Brandt has maintained that a person in a serious medical condition such as an irreversible comatose may be "beyond injury." See Richard Brandt, "A Moral Principle about Killing" in *Applying Ethics: A Text with Readings*, 8th ed., ed. Jeffrey Olen et al. (Belmont, Calif.: Wadsworth, 2005), 202–7.

26. Aquinas, *Summa Theologica*, Treatise on Law, question 95, art. 2, 650.

27. Clyde Kluckhohn, "Ethical Relativity: Sic et Non," in Ladd, *Ethical Relativism*, 91.

28. See the discussion on bullying in chapter 8.

29. Simone de Beauvoir, "Women in Love," in *Philosophers at Work: Issues and Practice of Philosophy*, ed. Elliot D. Cohen (Fort Worth, Tex.: Harcourt, 2000), 137–41.

30. For example, the statistics on sexual abuse of women are alarming. See, for example, Melanie Randall and Lori Haskell, "Sexual Violence in Women's Lives: Findings from the Women's Safety Project, A Community Based Survey," *Violence Against Women* 1(1, 1995):6–31.

II

HOW TO ATTAIN
PRACTICAL WISDOM

9

EXERCISING GOOD JUDGMENT

So far, I have spoken about the *rules* by which you deduce destructive behavior and emotions. It's now time to discuss the *reports* that you can file under your rules. Even if you have a profoundly rational rule, you can still deduce a very irrational conclusion if the report you file under it is itself irrational.

For example, the rule that tells you to defend yourself if someone is about to harm you is itself quite rational. But what happens if you jump to a conclusion about another person's intention to harm you, and you launch a precipitous preemptive strike? Indeed, stories abound where people mistake pranksters (and even family and friends) for prowlers and regrettably kill or seriously injure them with a weapon. What is irrational is not the rule of self-defense but rather jumping to conclusions about impending harm based on insufficient evidence.

A (behavioral and emotional) rule basically says that if such and such a report is filed, then you should do or feel in such and such a way. So such a rule doesn't tell you to do something unless you file a report under it. For example, consider the following rule:

If you're overweight, then you should diet.

This rule doesn't tell you to diet unless you report being overweight. But whether it's a good idea to diet will depend on how realistic this report really is. If you have sufficient evidence to think you're overweight, then your conclusion to diet can, indeed, be a useful one. On the other hand, if you're not—if, for example, you're anorexic—then your conclusion can be hazardous to your health.

Aristotle would say you possessed *practical wisdom* or prudence if you were able to file realistic reports and use them to attain constructive goals. When these rational reports are filed under rational behavioral and emotional rules, you can deduce constructive actions and emotions.

As Aristotle expressed,

> The work of a man is achieved only in accordance with practical wisdom . . . for virtue makes us aim at the right mark; and practical wisdom makes us take the right means.[1]

The practically wise (or prudent) person files rational reports under rational behavioral and emotional rules. The philosophical antidotes furnished in part 1 of this book have provided such rational behavioral and emotional rules. These "virtues" (or "right rules") can help you "aim at the right mark," while the antidotes presented in this part of the book can help you "take the right means." Together, both sorts of antidotes can help you attain profound happiness.

A person who possesses practical wisdom is *open minded*. This means being able to take an objective, unbiased perspective in exploring and choosing alternative solutions to a practical problem. It involves having a discerning eye for creative solutions. Aristotle called such discernment *good judgment*, and he distinguished between two sorts: *sympathetic judgment* and *correct judgment*. The former, he said, "discriminates what is equitable and does so correctly," while the latter "judges what is true" with an eye toward acting.[2] For Aristotle, to judge correctly in this latter sense meant to judge of things that have practical significance, such as judging whether a bridge is strong enough to support your weight before you cross it.

The exercise of good (practical) judgment is a powerful antidote to one of the most dangerous and self-defeating human tendencies. This is the tendency to *oversimplify reality*. Two of the most common ways in which people tend to oversimplify reality are by *pigeonholing* and *stereotyping*. Both of these forms of judgment oversimplify reality by failing to discern significant aspects of it. They underlie a host of traits of character that impede human flourishing, including narrow-mindedness, intolerance, inflexibility, prejudice, bigotry, and lack of creativity.

In *pigeonholing* you oversimplify your range of options. Two ways you can do this is by thinking of things in all-or-nothing terms or by seeing reality as black or white with no shades of gray in the middle. For example, try filling in these blanks:

1. If you are not happy, then you are _____.
2. If you are not smart, then you are _____.
3. If you are not large, then you are _____.
4. If you don't win, then you _____.
5. If something is not good, then it is _____.

Were you inclined to give any of the following answers?

1. sad
2. stupid
3. small
4. lose
5. bad

Be careful. If you were so inclined, Aristotle would tell you that you were confusing two different types of statements: contraries and contradictions. *Contrary statements* are opposites that allow for other possibilities. For example, the statement "I am sad" is the contrary of "I am happy." This is because you can be neither happy nor sad, such as when you are fair to middling.[3]

On the other hand, a *contradiction*, says Aristotle, is "an opposition which of its own nature excludes a middle."[4] For example, the statement "I am *not* sad" contradicts "I am sad." That's because either you're sad or you're not. Unlike the case of contraries, there can be no other options in the middle. One of the two statements must be true and the other false. End of story.

So, in thinking of contraries as though they were contradictions, you ignore the options in the middle. For example, you don't have to be stupid just because you're not smart. You can be of average intellect. And you don't have to be small just because you're not large. You can be medium.

Now the danger of such pigeonholing is that it narrows your range of rational responses to a situation. Recently, a student in my ethics course came to see me with a problem she had in taking the course. She disclosed that she was a "black-or-white" person, whereas this course was "opinionated." This student wanted me to provide her with the correct answers to some of the most perplexing social problems. Is a legal option for active euthanasia (mercy killing) good for society? Does human cloning violate a person's right to uniqueness? How much, if any, of our civil liberties should we be prepared to give up in "the war on terrorism"?

Unfortunately, hard-and-fast solutions to the problems of living, no less *ethical* living, are not ordinarily possible. This student was experiencing anxiety over having to confront the ambiguities of living. What she wanted was the truth, but all she got was opinions. She had a difficult time seeing that "true" and "false" and "yes" and "no" were contraries, not contradictories, and that neither one had to apply. Instead, there were rational options "in the middle" about which reasonable people could disagree.

In matters of life (and death), unwillingness to tolerate such ambiguity can be very dangerous. For example, when, referring to "the fight against terror," President George W. Bush once said of other nations that they were "either with us or against us." This left no room for being neither "with" nor "against" us. Consequently, France (among other nations) became "the enemy" when it refused to see the U.S. invasion of Iraq as an acceptable move in "the war on terrorism." In attempting to pigeonhole reality into such stark black-or-white categories, Bush missed a clear distinction between a terrorist organization that can reasonably be said to be "against us" (like al-Qaeda or the Taliban regime in Afghanistan) and the French. The result was no less than alienation of an allied nation that had fortitude to stand on principle. It made no sense to rename French fries "freedom fries."

Here then is the refutation:

> In pigeonholing reality, you make the logical mistake of thinking of contrary statements as though they were contradictions. In so doing, you exclude options that could be important in helping you make more realistic decisions. For example, in thinking that people are either saints or sinners, you either idealize them or demonize them rather than accepting the fact that they are neither but instead fallible creatures capable of *both* virtue and vice.

While pigeonholing oversimplifies reality by putting it into narrow categories, *stereotyping* broad-brushes it by lumping people into general classes without regard to individual differences: "All blondes are dumb," "All Italians are in the Mafia," "All gays are child molesters," "All blacks have rhythm," "All Jews are rich," "All old people are senile," "All southerners are racists," "All poor people are ignorant," and so on. Notice that the respective terms "dumb," "Mafia," "child molesters," "rhythm," "rich," "senile," "racist," and "ignorant" have either favorable or unfavorable emotive vibes. Calling someone "dumb" is an insult, while it is generally thought desirable to have "rhythm." But, positive or negative, all stereotypes are degrading insofar as they devalue individuality. They ride roughshod over what makes persons uniquely who they are and therefore fail to deal equitably with them.

Yet at the same time, such oversimplifications are attempts to cope with a complex universe that would otherwise appear as unmanageable. An unfamiliar face can appear as a threat to your security. Picking out in advance some general aspect of the unfamiliar can help you gauge your response. A stereotype directs you in one direction or another: "He's a Christian, so he must be trustworthy" or "He's an Arab, so he must be a terrorist." The one invites you to come hither, while the other sounds the danger alarm.

Media critic Walter Lippmann was the first to use the term "stereotype" to characterize such oversimplifications of human groups. In his classic book *Public Opinion*, he succinctly described the way stereotypes function in perception:

> For the most part we do not first see, and then define, we define first and then see. In the great blooming, buzzing confusion of the outer world we pick out what our culture has already defined for us, and we tend to perceive that which we have picked out in the form stereotyped for us by our culture.[5]

This human tendency to stereotype probably emerged as part of an evolutionary process of self-protection in dealing with the "great blooming, buzzing confusion of the outer world." It is no accident that every human culture has embraced stereotyping in one form or another. It is the human attempt to plot a reliable and stable course through the thickets of life.[6]

But in this attempt to cope with the unknown, we have devalued much of what enriches human interpersonal relationships, in particular, respect for the intrinsic worth and dignity of humankind. Instead, it has left a cultural path of bigotry and unfair discrimination. This is what is irrational about stereotyping. It does not live off the coin of evidence. Instead, it feeds off human insecurity and therefore judges *in advance* of evidence.

There's no denying it. If you are human, then you stereotype to some extent or other. It's not a matter of whether but how much. Since such prejudgments are fueled by culturally transmitted ignorance, you are not likely to respect the individuality and dignity of others unless you yourself reclaim your own dignity and individuality. I have already talked about the dangers of jumping on the bandwagon. As Lippmann intimated, stereotypes are part of such a cultural bandwagon. Realizing the inherent irrationality of going along for the ride is the first step in resisting your tendency to stereotype.

Stereotyping is driven by a mind-set, that is, by blind adherence to a rigid categorizing of human beings. As mind-set driven, it is immune to contrary evidence. If a counterexample to your stereotype is encountered, then it's merely accommodated. "Okay," you say, "he's just an exception. Most of them are . . ." Instead of abandoning the stereotype in light of evidence to the contrary, you adjust its level of generality so that you can continue to hold on to it. This is what makes stereotypes so hard to eradicate. Like fungi, they thrive in the dark, unenlightened regions of the human mind, where the light of evidence is not allowed to enter.

When exposed to this light, the refutation of stereotyping becomes evident:

> Stereotyping is conceived in fear and sustained by a mind unreceptive to contrary evidence. Its own offspring is prejudice—the refusal to judge others equitably on their own merit. From racial, gender, sexual, religious, and class discrimination to countless other forms of cultural oppression, this manner of trying to attain stability in confronting the blooming, buzzing universe has proven self-defeating. Instead of improving human existence, it has provided a breeding ground of hatred, distrust, resentment, divisiveness, and sundry other forms of destructive strife among humankind.

Potent antidotes to stereotyping can help you transcend such oppressive, self-defeating treatment of others by helping you cultivate a habit of "sympathetic judgment"—judging others equitably. On the other hand, potent antidotes to pigeonholing can help take you from narrow-mindedness and rigidity to "correct" judgment—perceiving practical concerns in a realistic, constructive, and creative light.

ANTIDOTES TO PIGEONHOLING

Antidote 1
Instead of looking at life in black-or-white, all-or-nothing terms, think of it as a work of art in progress with unlimited possibilities and opportunities to be creative. (Tomas)

Perception through a pigeonhole is limited to a very small portion of your perceptual field. With this cognitive limitation, you can expect to miss much in the way of reality. Like stereotypes, pigeonholing is a way of making life appear tidier since you don't have to deal with the gray areas. It's either black or white, true or false, or right or wrong. Unfortunately, reality is not so tidy, and if you are not prepared to deal with the ambiguities of living, then you are bound to make some sorry mistakes.

Pigeonholing is anticreativity. Your creativity is inversely proportional to the extent to which you pigeonhole reality. The more you pigeonhole reality, the less creative you will be. Did you know that a protein, not a bacteria, virus, or fungus, is the cause of mad cow disease? If no biological researchers were prepared to break with the traditional wisdom that said that only organisms are infectious, they wouldn't have discovered that prions, a type of protein, were the cause of this disease. If Einstein had pigeonholed reality into two separate slots of matter and energy, he wouldn't have figured out that $E = MC^2$. If people assumed that you had to be a bird to fly, then aviation wouldn't have gotten off the ground.

Listen to philosopher of art Vincent Tomas's account of artistic creativity:

> When we congratulate an artist for being creative . . . it is not because he was able to obey rules that were known before he painted his picture or wrote his novel or poem, so that thereby he succeeded in doing what had been done before. We congratulate him because he embodied in colors or in language something the like of which did not exist before, and because he was the originator of the rules he implicitly followed while he was painting or writing.[7]

Tomas contrasts the creative artist to the academic artist or writer who simply follows the same rules as the creative artists and achieves similar success. The difference is that the former, unlike the latter, was the originator of the rules. The Picasso imitator can grasp Picasso's cubistic style, but she is not creative for it. Picasso himself might have spent his time imitating nature instead of trying to abstract from it, but that wouldn't have made him special. Bach didn't have to spin multiple lines of music into a polyphonic network but could have stuck to the conventions of his time, but he chose to invent new rules for making music.

According to Tomas, the creative artist differs from the rifleman who aims at a definite target in that she does not know what her target is although she knows she is aiming at something. As a result, she is able to exercise some critical control on her creative activity. Thus, some notes and chords are not "right," whereas others are. Some brushstrokes and colors "work," and some don't. Yet when she hits her target, she knows she is there.

Now this creative process seems to me to apply to the canvas of life. Here you don't have to have the innovative genius of a Picasso or a Bach to be creative, but still there is a fundamental difference between "painting by number" and a creative approach to living. On the canvas of life, the lines aren't already drawn for you so that all you have to do is paint inside them according to a fixed set of directions. Rather, the activities of life are constrained only by the broad parameters set by laws of nature and social convention, within which there is room for an infinite number of permutations. Even social and cultural constraints can be changed by a creative process of challenging the status quo. This is what makes life so intriguing. It's only by artificially perceiving the vast array of colors of life through black-and-white lenses that this awesome potential for creativity is missed. Life is an amazing venue for creativity.

This is how it was for me in deciding what I wanted to do with my life when "I grew up," and curiously I am still trying to find out. I have already mentioned how I came to be an applied philosopher. One obstacle I had was transcending the academic tunnel vision that characterized my professional training. Either you do "pure" philosophy, or you do no philosophy at all. Either you do Anglo-American analytic philosophy (for example, the British empiricists and the American pragmatists), or you do continental philosophy (for example, the existentialists). If you do philosophy, you can't (at the same time) do psychology. These were the options I perceived, compliments of my indoctrination, all carved out and ready to go like a takeout order at McDonald's.

My choice was to do applied philosophy, to draw from both analytic as well as continental philosophy, and to do both philosophy and psychology simultaneously. The creative product of this decision was logic-based therapy. It is the bastard child of pure philosophy. It is a product of an interracial marriage of psychology and philosophy. It is the birth child of two families that have traditionally been in a feud: the analytic, linguistic approach to philosophy and the phenomenological approach.[8]

An instructive example of how pigeonholing can stifle creativity is in parenting. There are two extremes in child rearing that seem to lead to problematic results. One is to assume that children have equal rights with parents, and the second is to assume that children have no rights (except, of course, to adequate parental care and protection). The first option tends to render family life and education more difficult by making children capricious and unruly. The second option is oppressive, and children's potential for becoming self-reliant, responsible adults tends to be stifled.

While there is no formula for how to avoid these extremes, it seems clear that an approach to parenting that recognizes reciprocal rights and duties of children is a far more efficient way of preparing children for the adult world. Unfortunately, I have known many parents who fall into the two extreme categories mentioned here. Some have been "liberationists" who have viewed children as small adults having equal rights to make their own decisions and to act on them. Others have been strict authoritarians who have emphasized parental authority in determining what children can think and do.

But you don't have to be a strict authoritarian to provide a stable framework for children to develop, nor do you have to be a liberationist. Children need *both* structure and freedom. It is implausible to argue that young children have a right to hold full-time employment. It is equally implausible to argue that they should only be "seen and not heard." As Kant would advise, parents have a duty to provide an atmosphere that fosters children's development as rational, autonomous, beings. In being rational role models, in listening to children's concerns, and in speaking rationally to them, parents can help foster such an environment. On the other hand, the classic authoritarian parental saw "Do it because I said so" fosters blind obedience and stifles autonomy.

Like Tomas's analysis of creativity suggests, you don't always know exactly what you are aiming at in trying to be a good parent. But, speaking as a parent, I have generally known when I have screwed up, and I have also recognized when I have succeeded in doing something right. I have also found that what works with one child may not work with another. For example, some children at a given age may be more capable of handling responsibility than others. Parenting may be more like creating an original work of art than it is a science. The process of child rearing resists a formulaic approach such that all you have to do is X, Y, and Z, and, presto—out pops a well-adjusted, happy child.

Flexibility and openness to alternatives in dealing with parental challenges is more likely to succeed than taking an all-or-nothing approach. As with any creative process, in starting out you may have only a general, somewhat vague notion of what it means to be a good parent. Nevertheless, this idea can still guide you in aiming at and recognizing success. Pigeonholing (in any of its extreme forms) is likely to prove a bad parental philosophy—unless you want to raise pigeons.

Pigeonholing can also be a bad *spousal* philosophy. I have already talked about the illogic of assuming that *someone* must be the boss in a marriage. Better to have a partnership where two adults share in an equitable division of labor. Whether this state of familial equity is achieved can have serious implications for the welfare of children.

Most unequal power arrangements between parents—where, for instance, the man is the head of the household and the women is his subject—are dysfunctional. Indeed, this is typically the case in households where there is domestic violence. When children see that daddy can beat up on mommy, they themselves often end up perpetrators of abuse or else victims. On the other hand, where children see their parents working constructively and respectfully together as equal partners, children have a model to emulate that can be conducive to their own future happiness.

How such a partnership is arranged—who cooks, cleans, cares for the kids, stays home, goes to work, and so on—is amendable to many creative options. Traditional role models and arrangements may not even be viable when economic constraints on earning power require that two parents enter the workforce. In pigeonholing the roles of parents, you will inevitably miss innovative possibilities. This can make the difference between a functional, stable household and one fraught with familial discord.

Antidote 2
Consider that the antidote to your problem may lie in the synthesis of thesis and antithesis. (Hegel)

Aristotle's idea that there is a middle ground between contraries is well entrenched in the philosophy of Georg Wilhelm Friedrich Hegel. Hegel believed that reality unfolded in a dynamic, logical process he called dialectic. All of human history, Hegel believed, was an embodiment of an intellectual progression of ideas in a process of opposition and resolution. First there's a thesis, then it is opposed by an antithesis, and then there's a synthesis.[9]

I have often observed Hegel's dialectical process at work in the way history unfolds. For example, consider what life was like in the 1950s. It was generally taboo to speak of sex in public and even to show a toilet bowl on television; women were expected to be homemakers, and men were expected to bring home the bacon; whites were segregated from blacks; and homosexuals were hiding out in their closets.

Then there was the sexual revolution beginning in the 1960s, which represented a backlash against traditional sexual values; freedom fighters fought racial oppression in the South, and Martin Luther King Jr. preached peaceful nonviolent protest to racism. The culture of drugs took root, antiwar protests and student activism on college campuses became common, social consciousness replaced the laissez-faire attitude of the 1950s, and the gay rights movement began. The pendulum had indeed swung to the other extreme.

Then, beginning in the late 1970s through the 1990s, there seemed to be a synthesis of the 1950s and the countercultural movement that began in the 1960s. Women no longer burned their bras in effigy, and racial unrest simmered down, but there was now emphasis on affirmative action programs aimed at bringing more women and minorities into the workforce. There was still drugs and sex, but the emphasis now was on sex education and drug awareness and rehabilitation programs. Gays became more accepted in the mainstream with actors, politicians, and other celebrities coming out of their closets.

Now it seems to me that the pendulum is once again swinging to the other extreme. There is a strong politically conservative front moving toward what could well be the next antithesis to the prior synthesis. If Hegel is right, this will eventually usher in a new synthesis. And this process will continue on and on as we approach higher and higher levels of reality.

Freeze the camera on the words "higher levels of reality." For Hegel, progress is to be found in the synthesis. It is here that the oppositions are resolved and there is movement toward greater freedom and human happiness. This is important. It's not in the contraries, in the opposition between black and white, that you will locate higher truth but rather in the compromise that affects a synthesis.

This does, however, require some qualification. I don't mean to suggest that each successive synthesis is necessarily a good thing in some absolute sense. For example, in applying Hegel's dialectic to economics, Karl Marx claimed that feudalism was a synthesis between primitive communism (thesis) and slavery (antithesis), but he didn't think feudalism was in itself a good thing. While it resolved problems of production and subsistence inherent in both a primitive communal economy and slavery, it still left other problems to be resolved in future syntheses. For Marx, the antithesis of feudalism was capitalism, and the final synthesis was a classless society. This last synthesis was, for Marx, good in itself. But that was just Marx's preference. If such a synthesis were to occur—and that's a big "if"—many of us who value a free market would still look forward to another round of good old Hegelian dialectic.

This said, a higher-level synthesis may be *better* at least insofar as it resolves the problems formerly opposed by a prior antithesis. This doesn't mean that such a synthesis resolves all problems—since there would then be no room for future resolutions. Indeed, in contrast to Marx, Hegel believed that the dialectical process continues on and on without end.

I'm not about to deny what seems true. Syntheses are often hard won. In the establishment of women's rights, for example, we needed bra-burning radical women, even ones who despised macho men with a vengeance. Otherwise, their protests would have fallen on deaf ears, and positive change wouldn't have occurred. Radicalism of sundry varieties has usefully served to get the attention of society. Since society is stubbornly resistant to change, it often takes such a radical opposition in order to effect a synthesis for the better.

But that doesn't mean you should pigeonhole reality. Indeed, a black-or-white, all-or-nothing thinker wouldn't have had the creativity to come up with a radical position that could really work. There can be extremes even of extremes. When Martin Luther King Jr. preached nonviolent protest based on unconditional love of other human beings, even one's enemies, his position was truly a radical departure from other forms of protest. Yet he knew that violence and hatred just tended to breed more of the same, so he creatively sought new avenues for ushering in social change. This was going to extremes, to be sure, but in the context in which it was practiced, it was also a rational response to the oppression of blacks in America. So it was extreme—"radical," but it was not an "extreme of an extreme." It was not so radical that it wouldn't work. In fact, it was ingenious.

Here then is a Hegelian antidote for the tendency to see things in terms of black or white, all or nothing. Look for the synthesis to the opposition. Consider the possibility that a better solution to your problem may lie *between* opposites instead of within them. For example, take the opposition between master and slave. According to Hegel, neither the master nor the slave is free. The master is dependent on the slave, and the slave is dependent on the master. The antidote (synthesis) for Hegel was to recognize that freedom is not possible in relationships of domination. This means that you are better off, because freer, when you avoid relationships with unequal power differentials. This is why partnerships would represent a synthesis between such unequal relationships. In a partnership, the focus is on mutual respect for one another's autonomy. As Hegel suggests, this is also why totalitarian and dictatorial forms of government are inferior to democratic ones.

Antidote 3
Look for a yin in every yang and a yang in every yin. (Taoism)

So many philosophies. Is there not a philosophy that even *defends* pigeonholing as an approach to reality? The famous Taoist idea of yin and yang might well come to mind. Isn't this a philosophy that prescribes thinking in terms of opposites?

According to this well-known Chinese philosophy, everything can be seen in terms of opposites—either yin or yang. "Yang" means "sunny," whereas "yin" means "shady." Yang is active and masculine. Yin is passive and feminine.

But if you think this makes things simple, then you have the wrong idea about this doctrine. First of all, according to this view, opposition is always relative and temporary. There is always the seed of yin in yang and of yang in yin. For example, hot cools off and turns cold, and cold warms up. There are also subdivisions of yin and yang so that there is a yin and yang in every yin and likewise a yin and yang in every yang. For example, hot can be warm or scorching, and cold can be cool and icy.

In addition, there are many different things that are included under yin and yang. For example, yang includes left, odd, light, the sun, summer, day, heaven, and south. In comparison, yin includes right, even, dark, the moon, winter, night, earth, and north. So the doctrine of yin and yang is not so simple after all.

The point is that in applying this theory of opposition, you will still need to be careful not to pigeonhole your yins and yangs. The distinction is both narrow and broad. Right turns to wrong and wrong to right. George W. Bush's foes—those who are "against" him—have the seeds of becoming his friends and allies, and his friends—those who are "with" him—have the seeds of becoming his adversaries. Opposition is relative, transitory, and therefore not an ultimate, permanent feature of reality.

Stare for a while at the drawing shown in figure 9.1. Can you see the image flip from a duck to a rabbit? So is it a really duck or a rabbit?

Figure 9.1

Ludwig Wittgenstein, the originator of this image, called it a "duck-rabbit." The duck turns into the rabbit and the rabbit into the duck. That's the way it is with opposites. The appearance is just that. Wait a moment, and it changes.

I said before that the yang is masculine and the yin feminine. Being masculine has the seeds of femininity and vice versa. Nor am I here referring to sex change operations and drag queens. I am talking about human character. Human beings, at least well-adjusted ones, are not purely one or the other—they have both feminine and masculine characteristics. These characteristics complement one another. A man who can be sensitive and compassionate does not cease to be a man, and a woman who can be dispassionate does not shed her female gonads. The simple black-and-white dichotomy that says men are men and women are women misses the invaluable aspects of *being human*. If you live by such fixed and rigid dichotomies, you will inevitably fail to change gears when the need arises. On the open highway (of life), it is sometimes fine to cruise in high gear. But sooner or later, you will encounter traffic. Then you will need to slow up and proceed with care.

ANTIDOTES TO STEREOTYPING

If you tend to pigeonhole reality, you're also likely to stereotype people. This is not a mere contingent fact about pigeonholing. It's actually a truth about how we use language. For example, "*All* men are after just one thing" is equivalent to "Either you're after sex *or* you're not a man." The first stereotypes with the word "all," while the second pigeonholes with "or." The first uses "all" to say what the second says using "or." But, as is true of all forms of pigeonholing, when you stereotype people, you inevitably end up overlooking some very important aspects of (human) reality.

Antidote 1
Instead of relating to others as though their essences preceded their existences, get to know them as individuals. (Sartre)

Stereotyping dehumanizes people by treating them like manufactured items. To determine if a product has a successful track record, you need only look up the product number. Variations in individuals are not ordinarily considered important. For example, when a dairy product is recalled, the entire lot number is recalled. The manufacturer doesn't typically sift through each item in the lot to see if it is different than the rest.

In stereotyping, you classify persons as though they belonged to a certain product model and treat them accordingly. You don't judge the individual on her own merit but instead according to its model. Blacks are or tend to be criminals, so you suspect them in the commission of crimes and find them guilty as charged. Since Jews are intelligent, successful, rich, and faithful, you encourage your daughter to marry one. Since Arabs are terrorists, you shutter at boarding a flight with an Arab on board. In stereotyping individuals, you fail to relate to them as individuals and as persons in their own right; instead, you process them as though they came off an assembly line.

I have counseled married couples who have related in this way. For instance, Bob and Carla, as I will call them, were married for one year when they came to see me at the prompting of Carla. The presenting problem was "problems in communicating." While this case ultimately presented other challenges, it was accurate to say that the couple did indeed have such a problem stemming largely from cultural and socially transmitted stereotypes.

For example, Carla came from New England, and Bob carried with him the stereotype of New Englanders as indiscrete, outspoken, and crude. Consequently, he described her as having a "New England mentality." In addition, he classified her as having a "union mentality," by which he meant that she was mercenary and demanded compensation for whatever she did. As a result, Bob tended to discount many of the requests and grievances she expressed. After all, she was just trying to negotiate a deal in her boisterous New England style.

On the other hand, Carla, with the support of her enculturation, conceived of men as heads of households who "wore the pants." As a result, she expected Bob to take the reigns of family matters and to make the decisions. When Bob failed to fit the mold she had conceived for him, she became disheartened.[10]

In working with this couple, I applied Sartre's idea (discussed in chapter 5), that "existence precedes essence." Here, in a concise phrase, was an antidote to a marriage based on treating each other as fixed, rigid essences or, what amounted to the same thing, as stereotypes. When Carla spoke, Bob did not hear *her* speak. Instead, as Lippmann would say, he defined first and perceived second. It was not her words he perceived but those of some fixed archetype of New Englander and union member. Similarly, in relating to Bob, Carla expected the strong arm of a man to lead her. She saw him not as an individual but rather as an instance of manliness. When Bob did not fit this macho archetype,[11] Carla became frustrated.

In an effort to encourage the couple to perceive each other as individuals, I gave them each a homework assignment to list the features of each other they liked and those that they didn't like. The subsequent session, both returned with extensive lists. On the one hand, Carla liked Bob's looks; on the other, she disliked his tendency to sit on her furniture with a sweaty body after coming in from doing yard work. On the one hand, Bob liked the way Carla cooked; on the other, he disliked immensely her smoking. So began an honest, open dialogue that wasn't between fixed essences but rather between two distinct individuals.

If you also have "communication problems" with a significant other, it may be due at least in part to your relating as "essences" instead of as unique "existences." Essences cannot share their personal experiences with one another; they cannot connect with each other, attain intimacy, and be *with* each other. This is possible only for persons who authentically relate to each other *as* themselves and *for* themselves without stereotypes intervening, impersonalizing, dehumanizing, and detaching one another from their concrete beings.

Antidote 2

Assess human worth, freedom, and dignity—your own and that of others—not in terms of race, gender, ethnicity, or any other contingent aspect of humanity but in terms of membership in one transcendent community of ends. (Yamato, Kant, Marx)

Not only do stereotypes promote unfair discrimination against individuals, they also subdue and control those subject to them. The targeted populations, such as persons of color in the case of racial stereotypes, are socialized to believe that these stereotypes are, in fact, true. According to author Gloria Yamato, this process of *internalizing* a racial stereotype can have profound effects on a person's self-concept:

> Internalized racism is what really gets in my way as a Black woman. It influences the way I see or don't see myself, limits what I expect of myself or others like me. It results in my acceptance of mistreatment, leads me to believe that being treated with less than absolute respect, at least this once, is to be expected because I am Black, because I am not white. . . . The color of your skin may be used as an excuse to mistreat you, but there is no reason or logic involved in the mistreatment. If it seems that your color is the reason; if it seems that your ethnic heritage is the cause of the woe, it's because you've been deliberately beaten down by agents of a greedy system until you swallowed the garbage. That is the internalization of racism.[12]

According to Yamato, the first step to overcoming such racism—from the perspective of both the oppressor and the oppressed—is to acknowledge that it exists. People, she says, become so used to it that they don't even question it. She admonishes whites (among others) who want to quit prejudice to do so not for the sake of the victim but for the sake of those who discriminate.

As Marx admonished, those who use a popular stereotype (or "ideology") to oppress others are also losers since they become slaves to their oppression. It's therefore a no-win situation for both those who discriminate and those who are discriminated against. Breaking the shackles that bind the oppressed as well as the oppressor requires that you realize first that you are yourself a slave to your stereotype. Freedom means freedom to relate to others without oppressing them. Your personal happiness depends on it. A man who subjects his wife because women are inferior to men deprives himself of a marriage based on mutual respect. People who harbor racial prejudice embroil themselves in hatred, hostility, and avoidance instead of cultivating meaningful, constructive relationships with others.

For victims of racism who have internalized it, Yamato has clear advice:

> Remember always that you and others like you are completely worthy of respect, completely capable of achieving whatever you take a notion to do. . . . Celebrate yourself. Celebrate yourself. Celebrate the inevitable end of racism.[13]

You have already seen the importance of unconditional self-acceptance. It is also an antidote to internalized racism and other forms of stereotype-driven, social oppression that insidiously dismantles self-respect.

As Kant would remind you, *all* human beings have an unconditional worth and dignity by virtue of their being *persons*—rational, self-determining beings. This value is not a function of your race, gender, ethnicity, or religion. It transcends whether you are rich or poor, young or old, or any other contingent aspect of human existence. The transcendent value of a human being is unconditional and inalienable and cannot be augmented or diminished by any of these extrinsic factors. As a "community of ends," we are, all of us, united as one:

> For all rational beings stand under the law that each of them should treat himself and all others never merely as means, but in every case at the same time as an end in himself. Thus there arises a systematic union of rational beings through common objective laws. This is a community which may be called a community of ends.[14]

Stereotypes are an affront not only to *your* personal dignity and value as a human being but also to everyone else's. This is because we are all members of the same "community of ends" and so subject to the same law to treat each other with dignity and respect. Stereotypes violate the moral law. Obey the moral law.

Antidote 3
Transcend the limits of your personal experiences by exercising your innate ability to feel for your fellow human beings. (Scheler)

I write in the aftermath of Hurricane Katrina, which ravaged New Orleans, leaving people destitute and dependent on government for their lives. The majority of these people were poor blacks, many of whom did not have the means to evacuate prior to the storm. While these people were struggling for their lives, Michael Brown, head of the Federal Emergency Management Agency, was sending e-mails discussing his fashionable clothing and inquiring about dogsitters.

When thousands of New Orleans residents were corralled up and transported to the Houston Astrodome without adequate toilet facilities, food, water, and essential medical resources, Barbara Bush, ex–first lady and wife of former President George H. W. Bush, said,

> What I'm hearing, which is sort of scary, is they all want to stay in Texas. Everyone is so overwhelmed by the hospitality. And so many of the people in the arena here, you know, were underprivileged anyway, so this is working very well for them.[15]

Uprooted, traumatized, divested of their livelihoods and personal possessions, separated from family, and existing in subhuman living conditions, Barbara Bush worried that this displaced population might seek asylum in Texas. They were "underprivileged anyway" . . . "working very well for them"? Detaching herself from the ordeal, Barbara Bush relied on a stereotypical perspective that perceived being poor—and black—as used to living in dirty, crowded quarters without adequate food and water.

True, Barbara Bush never had to contend with spending time in the Astrodome, but surely she knew what it meant to experience a loss. Indeed, in her early years she had lost a daughter to leukemia. So why couldn't she get past her stereotypes to appreciate the plights of these fellow human beings?

According to Max Scheler, all human beings are cable of going beyond their personal experiences in commiserating with others. This capacity is, in fact, an innate human potential, "a moral unity of mankind, over and above the actual contacts of its members." He stated,

> Given the range of emotional qualities of which man is intrinsically capable, and from which alone his own actual feelings are built up, he has an . . . *innate* capacity for comprehending the feelings of others, even though he may never on any occasion have encountered such feelings (or their ingredients) in himself, as real unitary experiences.[16]

So you have an innate ability to feel for others even if you have not ever been in a situation such as Hurricane Katrina. As a human being, you have the innate ability to comprehend human suffering—your own and that of others. This ability is like seeing in color. Even if you never saw a violet object, you still have the ability to see this color even before it enters your visual field. Likewise, you have an innate capacity to understand and to feel for others in plights not directly experienced by you. Indeed, said Scheler, you could experience "genuine fellow feeling" for a mortally terrified bird even though you know nothing of what it's like to be a bird.

Scheler was not speaking of empathy, by which you experience the suffering of another as though this suffering were *yours*. He is instead was talking about a form of caring that is more appropriately called *sympathy*. In this, you have an emotional grasp of another person's feelings without *yourself* experiencing the same emotion. For Scheler, insofar as you get caught up in and take on the other person's emotion as your own, your focus shifts to yourself and how *you* feel instead of how the other person feels. This, he said, has a tendency to downgrade the moral worth of the attitude, which is raised only through transcending your personal interests to become united with the other.

You don't have to be black or poor or female to experience such sympathy for others any more than you have to be a bird to feel for its mortal terror. According to Scheler, this ability is innately part of being human.

Clearly, such self-transcendence is impeded by stereotypes. When you bring another human being under a stereotype, you sever your bond with that individual by subtracting the concreteness of his being. Instead of an individual who is before you, there is a *kind* of person. You cannot commiserate with such an abstract concept. Nor can you commiserate with a stereotype of a certain group of humanity. In so separating yourself from the concreteness of your fellow human beings, you disable your innate capacity to relate on a self-transcending, emotional level. This appears to be how Barbara Bush managed to disengage herself from the concrete reality of the displaced residents of New Orleans. They were, for her, stereotypes, not real persons like her.

An antidote to stereotyping is thus to *re*engage yourself by letting go of your stereotypes, unleashing your innate human potential to feel for others. In practical terms, this "letting go" means identifying and refuting the stereotype that insulates you from genuine fellow feeling. In accomplishing this, you need to exert your willpower, to turn away from what you may have unreflectively internalized through your enculturation. "*I* am human, *you* are human, *we* are human" is the language of unity. "*I* am human and *you* are dirty, ignorant, and lazy" is the language of *dis*unity. Embrace the former and disavow the latter. Disavow your stereotypes that insulate you from your fellow human beings and instead unite.

Antidote 4
Instead of believing on insufficient evidence, question all that you believe. (Clifford)

Evidence is to a stereotype what garlic is to a vampire. If you want to destroy your stereotype, then expose it to evidence. Some stereotypes arise as a result of hastily generalizing from past experience. You read in the paper about a gay child molester, so you generalize this to all or most gays. A woman rear-ends you, so you come away thinking that all or most women are shitty drivers. You are burglarized by a black man, so you conclude that all or most blacks are criminals.

However, in the majority of cases, the logic of stereotyping is more like this. You *already* have the ideas that gays are child molesters, that women are shitty drivers, and that blacks are criminals. You were told these things by peers and significant others when you were a child, and you have already internalized them. When the case arises that satisfies your stereotype, you say, "See, it's really true."

The bottom line is that our stereotypes are based on inadequate evidence, and, as mentioned earlier, we typically refuse to consider evidence that disconfirms them. This means that you can avoid stereotyping if you change your attitude toward evidence. Become an evidence freak. Demand evidence before you commit something to belief.

In his classic essay "The Ethics of Belief," W. K. Clifford argued that people have a duty to question all that we believe. Says Clifford:

> It is not only the leader of men, statesman, philosopher, or poet, that owes this bounden duty to mankind. Every rustic who delivers in the village alehouse his slow, infrequent sentences may help to kill or keep

alive the fatal superstitions which clog his race. Every hard-worked wife of an artisan may transmit to her children beliefs which shall knit society together, or rend it in pieces. No simplicity of mind, no obscurity of station can escape the duty of questioning all that we believe.[17]

According to Clifford, no person's belief is a private matter. It is woven into a social network of beliefs that becomes an heirloom for future generations to guide their lives. This, he says, is an "awful privilege, and an awful responsibility, that we should help to create the world in which posterity will live."[18] When you believe unfounded stereotypes, you breach this awesome duty by subjecting not just yourself but also future generations to inadequate basis of action. As stereotypes are socially transmitted from one generation to the next, in propagating them you become an accomplice in undermining the lives of others—your children, their children, and others who are subjected to such distortions of reality.

Clifford emphasized the importance of cultivating a *habit* of questioning all that you hear before committing it to belief. Even if you believe something correctly on insufficient evidence, this still weakens your ability to assess truth in the future. In the end, not just you but others are bound to suffer from shoddy habits of belief, including society itself. "The danger to society," he says, "is not merely that it should believe wrong things, though that is great enough; but that it should become credulous, and lose the habit of testing things and inquiring into them; for then it must sink back into savagery."[19] Help save society from the savagery of believing on insufficient evidence. Cast off your stereotypes and believe only that for which you can muster adequate evidence.

NOTES

1. Aristotle, *Ethics*, bk. 6, chap. 12, 1034.

2. Aristotle, *Ethics*, bk. 6, chap. 11, 1032.

3. Of course, you can't be both happy and sad, at least at the same time. This is what makes these statements opposites.

4. Aristotle, *Posterior Analytics*, in *Basic Works of Aristotle*, ed. Richard McKeon (New York: Modern Library, 2001), bk. 1, chap. 2, 112.

5. Walter Lippmann, *Public Opinion* (New York: Penguin Books, 1946), 61.

6. See, for example, Gordon W. Allport, *The Nature of Prejudice* (Garden City, N.Y.: Doubleday, 1958).

7. Vincent Tomas, "Creativity in Art," in *Art and Philosophy: Readings in Aesthetics*, 2nd ed., ed. W. E. Kennick (New York: St. Martin's Press, 1979), 131–32.

8. A phenomenological approach, as distinct from a linguistic one, uses introspection—examination of your own consciousness—as a way of discovering reality.

9. Georg Wilhelm Friedrich Hegel, *Phenomenology of Spirit* (New York: Oxford University Press, 1979).

10. Strictly speaking, Carla's concept of what a man should be was more properly a gender role than it was a stereotype. Stereotypes are overgeneralized claims about the way people *are*, whereas gender roles are normative rules about how men *should* be. Nevertheless, for Carla her acceptance of this gender role had the same result as a stereotype; that is, it prevented her from accepting Bob as an individual.

11. In fact, it turned out that Bob was gay. For more details of this case, see my article "The Philosopher as Counselor," in *Philosophers at Work: Issues and Practice of Philosophy*, ed. Elliot D. Cohen (Fort Worth, Tex.: Harcourt, 2000).

12. Gloria Yamato, "Something about the Subject Makes It Hard to Name," in *Race, Class, and Gender*, ed. Margaret L. Andersen and Patricia Hill Collins (Belmont, CA: Wadsworth, 1995), 73.

13. Yamato, "Something about the Subject Makes It Hard to Name," 75.

14. Immanual Kant, *Foundations of the Metaphysics of Morals*, 2nd ed., trans. Lewis White Beck (Upper Saddle River, N.J.: Prentice Hall, 1989), sec. 2.

15. "Barbara Bush: 'Things Worked Out "Very Well" for Poor Evacuees of New Orleans,'" *Editor & Publisher*, September 5, 2005, retrieved November 3, 2005, from http://www.editorandpublisher.com/eandp/news/article_display.jsp?vnu_content_id=1001054719.

16. Max Scheler, "Fellow Feeling as Original Human Unity," in *Philosophies of Love*, ed. David L. Norton and Mary F. Kille (Totowa, N.J.: Rowman & Allanheld, 1971), 280.

17. W. K. Clifford, "The Ethics of Belief" (1877), chap. 1, retrieved November 4, 2005, from http://www.infidels.org/library/historical/w_k_clifford/ethics_of_belief.html.

18. Clifford, *The Ethics of Belief*, chap. 1.

19. Clifford, *The Ethics of Belief*, chap. 1.

10

CONTENDING WITH PROBABILITY
IN AN UNCERTAIN WORLD

I just entreated you to believe on adequate evidence. But the ten-million-dollar question is, When is evidence *adequate*?

If the reports you file under your behavior and emotional rules are based on shoddy evidence, then the ways in which you respond to your personal and interpersonal life situations are likely to be regrettable. That's right—junk in, junk out. You know what happens to a news reporter who has insufficient evidence for her claims. Look what happened to Judith Miller, formerly a reporter for the *New York Times*. She gave credibility to the Bush administration's claim that there were weapons of mass destruction in Iraq prior to launching its "preemptive" war. Readers of the *New York Times* trusted that Miller's reports were credible, but the newspaper ended up having to apologize for shoddy reporting and subsequently gave Judy her walking papers—she "retired."

Whether you are reporting on affairs of state or about intimate details of your own personal life, *jumping to conclusions* on the basis of shoddy evidence can have dangerous consequences—for you, other people, and even an entire nation. "Jumping" here is not a physical activity like jumping off of a bridge—although the result can sometimes be the same. It here refers to a mental (cognitive) activity of determining the *probability* that one statement is true based on the truth of another statement or set of statements. This is what philosophers typically call *drawing an inference*.[1]

When you infer things, you assume certain *rules*. You have seen how you can infer your emotions and behavior from irrational rules and wind up in emotional and behavioral hot water. You can also infer your reports from irrational *reporting rules*—that is, rules that tell you how to file your reports.

There are at least five types of reporting rules:

1. *Generalization rules* for generalizing about the world
2. *Predictive rules* for predicting the future
3. *Explanatory rules* for explaining things
4. *Causal rules* for determining the causes of things
5. *Contrary-to-fact rules* for speculating about what could-a/would-a/ should-a happened

The first two types of rules are supposed to help you infer things about unobserved cases based on observed cases. Generalization rules give you instructions for inferring things about *all* or *most* members of a group on the basis of what you know about just *some* members. Prediction rules give you instructions for inferring things about the *future* on the basis of what you know about the *past*. Both kinds of rule, if they are rational, can yield *foresight*. This is the ability to assess the probability of whether the future will resemble the past—whether uniformities you have observed in the past provide good reason for thinking they will continue in the future. These rules therefore address one of the most common and inevitable sources of anxiety for human beings: confronting the unknown.

The last three types of rules aim at helping you draw inferences about *why* things have happened. Explanatory rules and causal rules try to help you understand the reasons or the causes of events that have taken place in the world. If they do what they are supposed to do, they can help bring law and order to what would otherwise seem a precarious, chaotic universe. Contrary-to-fact rules aim at enlightening you about what could otherwise have taken place had things happened differently than they actually did happen. These rules try to help you avoid wild, self-defeating speculation.

This chapter will look carefully at the first two types of reporting rules—rules of generalization and prediction. The next chapter will address the last three.

GENERALIZATION RULES

If you make hasty generalizations, you're likely to infer horseshit. For example, it is not uncommon for people having a bad experience with a man (or a woman) to generalize to all or most members of the same gender. "They're all like dogs," says a woman burned by an adulterous husband, vowing never to get involved with another man again. "Women are such bitches!" says a guy whose wife just reprimanded him about leaving the toi-let seat up.²

Have you ever sworn off purchasing a certain brand of product after one bad experience? "All Fords suck," says a disgruntled owner of a Jaguar with a fuel emissions stench, excessive engine noise, and a water leak into the interior. "All Italian restaurants are filthy," says a patron of a local Italian restaurant after reading in the newspaper about a vermin and roach infesta-tion problem in the kitchen.

Each of these inferences assumes an irrational reporting rule that bids you to hastily generalize from an insufficient sampling of group members.

Hasty Generalization: If *some* members of a group have an undesirable feature, then *all* (or *most of*) the other members also have it.

It's not hard to figure out why this rule is so popular. Like other animals, human beings are hardwired to protect themselves from dangerous condi-tions in their environment. But, in the attempt to protect yourself, you may do just the opposite. Thus, a guy who swears off going to doctors because of *a* bad experience with *one* doctor may end up dying from an undiag-nosed medical condition. It's not that generalizations are *never* justified. In-deed, all generalization, even the reliable kind, samples just *some* members of a group and then generalizes to all or most members. As you will see, what is important is that this sample adequately represents the group. To have an antidote to hasty generalization, you will need to know the differ-ence between hastily generalizing from an unrepresentative sample and gen-eralizing from a sample that adequately represents the group.

PREDICTIVE RULES

Wouldn't it be nice to have eyes in the back of your head? Wouldn't it be even nicer to be able to see into the future? Countless times we act, only to regret the consequences of our actions. Even when we are careful about our predictions, we still invariably act in ways we later regret. It's the na-ture of the universe. No wonder all of us are to some extent anxious about the future. Flying high in April, shot down in May, there's always the un-foreseen and the unforeseeable and always the possibility that even the best laid plans can go astray. So managing the future is of the utmost impor-tance for all of us. Since we don't have—at least given the state of current technology—a direct window into the future, we have to rely on the past as a basis for making predictions about the future. Learning from prior mistakes, we can try to avoid them in the future. But no matter how much we may have learned about the past, there is still a gap between what we know here and now and what we can expect in the future. In the midst of great angst about bridging this gap, it is no wonder that humans have gone to extremes in predicting the future. In responding to the unexpected dangers that "lurk" in the future, some *fatalistically* perceive their prospects for the future, while others *wishfully* seek consolation though an overly optimistic outlook.

There are three related kinds of fatalistic rules that many people use in making predictions:

Murphy's Law
> If something *can* go wrong, then it will.

Magnifying Risks
> If there's any chance of something's going wrong, then it *probably* will.

Insisting on the Past
> If anything has gone wrong in the past, then it *must*, as a matter of *lawful necessity*, continue to do so in the future and there's nothing whatsoever you can do about it.

Each rule in this triage is virulent and self-destructive. Murphy tells you to *definitely* expect something to go wrong just because it's possible, and magnifying risks inflates the probability. Insisting on the past conceives a fatalistic cosmic order operating in the universe such that whatever has gone wrong in the past must inescapably do so in the future.

First, Murphy's Law is not really a law at all. Laws are universal, which means that they don't admit of exceptions. If the universal law of gravity and whatever can be inferred from it did not hold true, then we would no longer call it a law. Murphy's Law does not hold water. For example, it was possible that the last time you drove your car on the highway, your brakes failed, you had a blowout, your steering wheel locked up, and countless other things went wrong. Indeed, all these things could have gone wrong singularly and at once, but that didn't happen. Therefore, Murphy's Law is a crock—not really a law at all.

Moreover, not everything that has a chance of going wrong is *probable*. There was a chance of rain yesterday, but it was only a 10 percent chance, which meant that there was a 90 percent chance of it *not* raining. Statistically, there's a remote chance that you will be struck by lightning in your next thunderstorm. In fact, this chance is higher here for me in sunny

Florida than in other parts of the country. Nevertheless, I am willing to bet that I won't struck by lightning the next time there's a thunderstorm in my vicinity. No, I'm not 100 percent certain of this—that would be irrational. However, I am reasonably confident and would be willing to bet my bottom dollar on it.

Nor would I cancel my next flight simply because there's always that chance of a plane crash. I was once on a flight that had problems landing because of a malfunctioning landing flap. While fire engines watched cautiously from the ground in the event the brakes caught fire on landing, the plane did manage to finally land without incident. But just because there is a chance the next flight out of here will crash doesn't mean it's probable.

Nor does it mean that because the landing flaps didn't work properly on this flight, the same thing *must* happen on my *next* flight. In fact, I have since flown successfully on many occasions without the same thing happening. In insisting on the past, you forfeit rational judgment and discretion in favor of fatalistically locking yourself into a universe that invariably keeps you from accomplishing your worthwhile goals and aspirations. You cook your own goose every time you tell yourself that you are destined to fail because you did so in the past. For example, you tell yourself that you mustn't ever get married again because your first marriage failed or that you must stay at a dead-end job because that's how it's always been for you in the past. In such cases, it's not some all-pervasive cosmic necessity locking you into gloom and doom. No, instead, the cosmic force sealing your fatalistic prophecies is none other than *yourself.*

But going to the other extreme won't give you a more realistic handle on the future. Whereas being fatalistic about the future can keep you from making positive changes in your life, so can being overly optimistic. You can keep yourself stuck in the same old same old by doing wishful thinking. Here's what this rule says:

Wishful Thinking
    Even though something has consistently gone wrong in the past, things will be different in the future.

This is the opposite of insisting on the past. In accepting this rule, you would be *ignoring* the past. You would be telling yourself that things will be different in the future even though nothing has really changed as long as you wish hard enough for a change to occur. News flash: If you don't do anything in the present to change your situation in the future, then all the wishing in the world won't help to make things different. The universe is uniform to this extent. You can expect like results under like conditions. If you don't make any relevant changes for the future, then (other things being equal) it's reasonable to expect the past to repeat itself. Not that the past *must* repeat itself. That would be fatalistic. Still, the probable outcome is that you'll remain in the same rut if remedial changes don't occur.

For example, victims of domestic violence often tell themselves that things will be different in the future. "I know he's beaten me in the past," says the victim about the perpetrator. "But I just know things are going to be different this time—after all, he told me how sorry he was." Yes, but then how many countless other times did he apologize, and then didn't history still repeat itself?

Did the perpetrator seek counseling? Did he make verifiable attempts to get help or to make certain changes in his life? Did he stop drinking, attend AA meetings, admit his problem, or work cognitively and behaviorally on it? Unless the answer to such probative questions is affirmative, it's just wishful thinking to expect constructive change to occur in the future.

REFUTATION OF
DISTORTING PROBABILITIES

It should now be evident why filing reports on the basis of the previously mentioned fallacious generalization and prediction rules is a bad idea. Here's why in summary:

> Refutation: In hastily generalizing, you jump the gun on negatively pre-judging members of a group and short-circuit objectivity in relating to them. In making predictions on the basis of Murphy's Law, magnifying risks, insisting on the past, and wishful thinking, you create needless anxiety about the future and sabotage your opportunity to make constructive changes in your life.

Antidotes to Distorting Probabilities
ANTIDOTES TO HASTY GENERALIZATION

Antidote 1
Think like a scientist, not a dogmatist: base your generalizations on probability, not certainty. (Hume)

The first philosopher to have raised, in a clear concise way, a problem about generalizing about the world was David Hume. "What," inquired Hume, "is the nature of that evidence which assures us of any real existence and matter of fact beyond the present testimony of our senses or the records of our memory?"[3] What Hume wanted to know was how you can justifiably come to a conclusion about all or most members of a group with countless members merely on the basis of observations of just some of them.

For Hume, the answer was that such an inference was not really justified at all. It is, he thought, a psychological fact that people get into the habit of making these inferences, but as far as being justified, they weren't. For example, even if you observed millions of human beings and noticed that all had hearts and kidneys, you still wouldn't have observed all human beings—past, present, and future. So how could you say all human beings (at least living ones) have hearts and kidneys? For Hume, in order to make this claim, you would have to assume that nature is uniform and that all unobserved humans would always match the observed ones. But what right do any of us have in making this assumption? According to Hume, the only way to prove this assumption would be to base it on observation of past regularities. But that would mean that you would have to make the same assumption in trying to prove it. But that would mean trying to prove something by assuming just what you're trying to prove. That would be to spin in a vicious circle. If there's anything antiphilosophical and irrational, surely this would win the door prize.

Hume's point is very important. Before him, philosophers thought that people could be *certain* about their generalizations from experience. In setting the record straight, however, Hume defined what it means to take a scientific outlook. This is the view that the laws of nature gleaned from our observations are not necessary truths about which we can't be mistaken. Instead, they are more or less *probable*, depending on how much evidence you have for them. So, while it is a biological law that all humans have hearts and kidneys, this is not absolutely certain. It is always possible for someone human to come along who somehow gets by without a heart and kidneys. I say this is possible but not likely.

The scientific point of view holds that all generalizations from experience are subject to the possibility of future disconfirmation. This is what distinguishes a scientific view from a dogmatic one. If you want to be scientific, then you need to give up the quest for certainty in favor of contenting yourself with probability.

Probability is a function of evidence. The more humans you observe to have hearts and kidneys, the more probable the generalization gets, but this probability can never reach certainty. In his classic philosophy primer, philosopher William Halverson formulated the rule of generalizing concisely:

> The more often two things have been observed to be conjoined in nature, the more probable it is that they always are conjoined.[4]

Here is what it means to take a scientific perspective. From the scientific point of view, generalizations based on small samples are ordinarily to be given a low probability rating. Since this probability rating translates for practical purposes into how reasonable it would be to *act* on the generalization, a scientific outlook would reject acting on low probability ratings. This scientific attitude would also admonish you not to be cocksure of yourself even if you have considerable evidence for your generalization.

Are you a dogmatist or a scientist? Scientists are open minded, but not just anything goes—you need evidence. Dogmatists are closed minded and do not care much for evidence. For example, people who stereotype other people are not scientists but are instead dogmatists. For your own happiness and the happiness of others, think like a scientist, not a dogmatist.

Unless you intend to live in a bubble, you should learn to play the probabilities and to be realistic in assessing them. If you want a risk-free world, then maybe you will find it eventually in heaven, but don't expect to find it here on earth.

Antidote 2
Beware the human propensity for bias in making generalizations. (Mill, Salmon)

When you make hasty generalizations, you jump to conclusions before having a sufficient number of cases to justify your conclusion. So a big question is, How do you know when you have *enough* cases to support your generalization?

This can get tricky because your sample could be very large but extremely biased. For example, if you wanted to know how many Americans were in favor of Bush's attempt to privatize social security, you wouldn't want to ask only rich people who have experience and money to invest in the stock market. You would also want to ask the poor and middle-class folks who don't have money to risk. Even if you asked thousands of rich guys about this proposal, it would still not be sufficient because it would be biased.

As logician Merrilee Salmon points out, "The real question is whether the sample is large enough to capture, or represent, the variety present in the population."[5] So the answer to the question of whether a sample is sufficient in number depends on how many instances it takes in order to get a representative sample.

The problem of generalizing from biased samples is a serious one, especially when it comes to generalizing about people. If like most of us you hold stereotypes, it is a good bet that you have tried to support them with cases that fit only a small fraction of the group.

Here's how bias often comes about. The media portray a certain group in a stereotypical way by singling out only a small fraction of the group and uses it to represent the entire group. For example, while this may be slowly changing, gays have been portrayed as "flaming," so you get the idea that all or most gays are this way. Then when you see a gay guy who fits your stereotype, you rest your case. As such, you don't bother to look beyond your socialized bias for instances of gays that don't fit your stereotype. And if confronted with such instances, you rationalize, "Oh, he's just an exception."

Not all generalizations about people are biased, however. "Most people want a roof over their heads" appears true across a great diversity of human populations. It is also possible to take unbiased polls about what *most* people in a given township, state, nation, or even the world community think about a particular issue. For example, it appears that most people in the United States at the time of this writing believe that they were deceived by the president about the real reasons for waging a "preemptive" war in Iraq. If it were not for our being able to make such unbiased generalizations, democracy in terms of "rule by the majority" would not work. We couldn't have democratic processes for electing—and impeaching—government officials and for giving legal effect to the collective will of the people.

True, it is notoriously difficult to make generalizations about *all* people in very large groups since there are bound to be some exceptions. Nevertheless, as John Stuart Mill noted, for practical purposes, you ordinarily need generalizations only about most members of a group. For example, a statesman, says Mill, needs to know only how most people will react to a certain political arrangement in order to come to a conclusion about it.

The popular saw "That's only a generalization" said for purposes of dismissing any and all generalizations is therefore absurd. The real question is whether your generalization is based on *sufficient* evidence. This means that the sample you are generalizing from should not be biased, and it should be large enough to accurately represent the diversity among group members.

ANTIDOTES TO PREDICTIVE FALLACIES

Antidote 1
As probability is relative to data and the future is never certain, change your circumstances now to increase the probability of your future prosperity. (Russell, Lewis)

What I have just said about generalizing also applies to making predictions about the future. In making predictions, knowledge about what has happened in the past affords you a basis for making them. But watch out for how strictly you construe this statement. The more two things have been associated with one another in the past, the more *probable* it becomes that they will be so connected in the future. For example, you have no doubt come to associate lightning and thunder so that in seeing lightning, you can well predict with high probability that thunder will soon follow. But this is a matter of probability, not of certainty. As the esteemed philosopher Bertrand Russell has expressed,

> It must be conceded, to begin with, that the fact that two things have been found often together and never apart does not, by itself, suffice to prove demonstratively that they will be found together in the next case we examine. The most we can hope is that the oftener things are found together, the more probable it becomes that they will be found together another time, and that, if they have been found together often enough, the probability will amount *almost* to certainty. It can never quite reach certainty, because we know that in spite of frequent repetitions there sometimes is failure at the last, as in the case of the chicken whose neck is wrung. Thus probability is all we ought to seek.[6]

Notice how Russell carefully said "almost certain," which means it will never be certain. You can never be certain about the future. No matter how probable, it is never certain that the future will resemble the past. Like the chicken that, after becoming accustomed to being fed, finally has its neck wrung, the future doesn't *have to* resemble the past.

Further, Russell also noted that "probability is always relative to certain data." For example, he said that it would be probable that all swans are white for a man who has seen many white swans and never a nonwhite one. However, in learning that color is variable in many animal species, the probability that all swans are white will be greatly diminished.

Now if you fatalistically accept the rule of insisting on the past—that if anything has gone wrong in the past, it *must* irretrievably continue to do so in the future—it should not be hard to see the error of your ways. First, this "must" is antiscientific and dogmatic. Even *if* things have consistently gone wrong in your life *in the past*, this would justify you only in thinking that it is *probable* that things will go wrong in your life in the future. But let's be honest. Unless you are vastly different than me, there will have been at least some things—and probably a great many things—in your life that have gone right. If you have eaten food and received nourishment; if you have gotten in your car and traveled successfully to work, school, or the grocery store; if you have gone to the bathroom, taken a shower, or brushed your teeth; or if you have successfully accomplished these and so many other mundane tasks, it's simply false that *everything* in your life has consistently gone wrong.

Nor will it do to say that everything important in your life has gone wrong. If your vital organs are presently functioning to keep you alive, then there is something very important that has not gone wrong. I entreat you to make a list of all the things in your life that you would regard as important that have *not* gone wrong.

But maybe you are disturbed about not having fulfilled yourself in some special way. Maybe you have dreamed of graduating college, going into a certain profession, or getting married or of having children, or maybe you are telling yourself, "It hasn't happened for me," and you are deeply frustrated, even deeply depressed.

Okay, but remember that fatalism is fatally flawed. The future is not sealed by the past. If it were, there would be no point in trying to predict it. As C. I. Lewis keenly pointed out, "a predicted future which should follow fatally upon what is presently given, is a future it would be pointless to foresee, since . . . nothing could be done about it."[7] But you *can* do something about the future. Always remember that the probability of a future event is relative to data. If you change the data, you can change the probability of the outcome. For example, if you enroll in college, you change the probability that you will graduate. If you actually complete some credits, you increase that probability even more. The more steps you take toward your goal, the greater the evidence there is for meeting your mark. In sitting on your rump and fatalistically insisting on the past, you are not likely to succeed in attaining your goal. But that's precisely because *you* make success improbable by not doing anything about it. You can alter the probabilities by making suitable changes in your life. The ball is in your court.

Antidote 2
Turn Murphy's Law on its head: Increase the probability of things going right in your life by basing your judgments about your future on sufficient evidence. (Aristotle)

The same thing can also be said about Murphy's claim that if something can go wrong, it will. Lots of things can go wrong but don't. So the association between what *can* go wrong and what actually *does* go wrong is not really lawful. Still, there are lots of things that can go wrong and actually do. As Aristotle pointed out long ago, given the infinite number of ways in which things can go wrong and the relatively few ways they can go right, you will need to exercise careful judgment if you want them to go right. According to Aristotle, there are many ways to fall into vice but only one to act virtuously—many ways, for example, to fail to be courageous in a given situation but only one to meet the targeted "golden mean." Said the philosopher:

> It is possible to fail in many ways (for evil belongs to the class of the unlimited . . . and good to that of the limited), while to succeed is possible only in one way (for which reason also one is easy and the other difficult—to miss the mark easy, to hit it difficult.[8]

Like an archer, we are more likely to hit our mark if we know what we are aiming at. In shooting blindly, we are likely to miss the target altogether.

So Murphy's Law has at least this grain of truth. If you shoot aimlessly at the proverbial target of life, you will probably miss your mark. One important way to shoot aimlessly is to judge on insufficient evidence. The probability that things will go wrong for you is marked high if you judge on insufficient evidence. Here then is a more reasonable formulation of Murphy's idea: If you don't judge on sufficient evidence, things are likely to go wrong for you. This is *negative* Murphy. But here is the new, improved, *positive* Murphy: To increase the probability of things going *right* for you, base your judgments on sufficient evidence.

A young woman whom I counseled had a history of unsuccessful dating activities. She had attempted to meet men by playing the bar scene every few weeks and by relying on friends to occasionally set her up with someone. After a few years of trying unsuccessfully to meet someone she liked, the young woman jumped to the conclusion that she would never have a successful relationship and therefore decided simply to give up trying.

This young woman had decided on insufficient evidence. Her dating history was indeed meager, to say the least. But by taking herself out of circulation, she was fulfilling her own prophecy. I pointed out that the chances of meeting someone were increased substantially by increasing the number of eligible men she dated. So she agreed to increase her prospects by increasing her dating activities. For example, she enlisted in online dating services, started going to socials on a weekly basis, and allowed herself to be set up by friends and relatives. About six months later, she was involved in a steady relationship that appeared promising. In increasing her sample of eligible men, she increased the probabilities of meeting someone. In this way, she stood Murphy's Law on its head and showed that things can, indeed, go right for you if you play the probabilities instead of letting "fate" take its course.

Antidote 3

Be prepared to accept some risk in making your life choices. But before jumping to conclusions about increased risks, consider first the evidence to account for them. (Plato, Chisholm, Sartre, Clifford, Hart)

An attenuated form of Murphy's Law is *magnifying risks*. This turns small risks into great big ones—if there's *any* chance of something going wrong, it *probably* will. While Murphy's Law tends to deduce a defeatist response ("Why even bother!"), magnifying risks also generates considerable anxiety about trying. It is the unknownness about the future that people tend to fear. When you go headfirst into this unknown with the belief that the odds are stacked against you, the climate is ripe for awfulizing and *can't*-stipating yourself into an emotional frenzy. So how can you save yourself some sweat?

First of all, the amount of risk you report should be a function of the *risk factors* you objectively confirm. For example, it's always possible to get a blowout on the highway, but without any evidence of predisposing factors, the probability is low. Don't automatically conclude that something is *too* risky because there is *some* risk involved. Look first at the risk factors before jumping to conclusions.

As my esteemed mentor Roderick M. Chisholm admonished, whenever you make inferences about the probability of things, you shouldn't omit any premises that you think would affect the probability of your conclusion.[9] This is because something could be low risk in relation to one set of evidence but not in relation to another. For example, if you see that the tire has wear bars or is breaking apart or even if you learn that the model has been recalled because of a material defect, then that's a different story.

This doesn't mean you should drive yourself crazy looking for risk factors. Looking on the Internet to see the track record of a tire—or of an entire car—before you purchase it can sometimes give you valuable information (on recalls, crash test results, and other safety-related data), but at some point you will need to come down from cyberspace and make your decision in physical space. It is impossible for us mere mortals to be omniscient. So, if you demand perfect knowledge before reaching a verdict, you will make your decision by indecision. That's why even criminal investigations require proof of guilt beyond a *reasonable* doubt. Hey, it's not perfect, but it's the best we've got to go on.

Nor can statistics *alone* function as an adequate "guide of life."[10] Knowing the percentage of traffic fatalities on the highways due to blowouts will not tell you whether you or any other *particular person* is at risk of being among those fatalities. The same is true of statistics regarding plane crashes. Knowing the stats about an airline or even about a particular kind of equipment will not tell you anything about the operating condition of the *particular plane* you are boarding.

I once boarded a plane, only to be told that one of the engines was defective and that the mechanics would be addressing the problem. Before boarding, I was not aware of any special circumstances that would put this particular flight in a high-risk category. But after the captain informed the passengers of the engine problem, I had reason to think otherwise. While the other passengers sat patiently in their seats, I got up, approached the crew, and requested a different flight. I told them that I didn't mind waiting for them to address a relatively minor problem but that an engine was a risk factor I didn't care to bet my life on. The pilot and crew agreed with me, and I was permitted to book a different flight. In the end, the plane was grounded, and the rest of the passengers clamored for a flight home.

It wasn't that I was unprepared to take *some* risks. Plato would remind you that the physical world is one of uncertainty. Theoretically, it's only *highly probable* that the book you are now reading is real and that you are not instead dreaming it into existence. That's the sort of talk that has often made philosophers the butt of much ridicule. Nevertheless, if you want a risk-free environment before you are willing to live in it, then you are not being realistic.

Want to make financial gains? Want to fall in love and have a meaningful interpersonal relation based on trust? Want to invest in a college education? Then you need to take risks. Sometimes the unexpected happens, for better or for worse. Someone I knew went in for routine surgery and never came out alive. There are no guarantees that things will turn out as expected. That's life.

Remember, Sartre said that we're "condemned to be free" (see chapter 5). That also means we're condemned to take risks. Freedom to choose is equivalent to *freedom to take chances*. So you might as well assess the risks intelligently. Trying to rationalize risks away is one extreme; exaggerating them is another. Both approaches to risk assessment are pragmatically bankrupt. In doing the former, you set yourself up to take senseless risks.

In doing the latter, you can frighten yourself into not taking sensible risks. In the end, it's up to you to decide *which* risks to take, not whether to take any at all.

Distortion of risks sometimes comes in the form of *slippery-slope pre-dictions* that predict a progression of snowballing negative consequences. "If I don't get to sleep tonight, I won't be able to think straight tomorrow. I'll mess up on my job interview. I won't get that great job. I'll never find an-other job like that again. I'll be stuck at my dead-end job for the rest of my life." And at the end of this chain of spiraling negativity, you are bound to add something alone these lines: "This would be so awful, and I just couldn't stand it!" The devil here is in the thinking itself, not in the verac-ity of what it predicts. In fabricating this probability for gloom and doom, you deduce intense, self-defeating anxiety. You prevent yourself from get-ting to sleep by disturbing yourself.

This is not to say that *some* anxiety is always a bad thing. It isn't—at least when there's *really* something to be anxious about. As my old profes-sor Samuel L. Hart keenly stated,

> The fear felt in a threatening situation is invaluable . . . the adjustive value of emotions decreases with their reality-incongruence which is at the root of violent and persevering passions. Such passions, instead of serving thought, subjugate it; instead of making thought abide by the threatening situation, force it to dwell on imaginary situations. The per-sistence of strong emotions deprives consciousness of its intentional rep-resentative features, the most essential elements in our rational moral conduct.[11]

According to Hart, feelings like fear play an important role in directing your consciousness to aspects of your environment that could either help or hamper you. A mild form of anxiety can keep you on your toes when you are driving on a busy highway. It can keep a soldier on his toes who is stand-ing guard. In situations where there is real danger, such anxiety can be adap-tive. However, this constructive function is thwarted by intense emotions such as intense anxiety deduced from slippery-slope predictions.

Keeping yourself from going off into such self-destructive reveries is very important. Sticking to the *evidence* is of the essence in such situations. Don't forget W. K. Clifford's admonition about your *duty* to question all that you believe (see chapter 9). For example, where is the evidence for thinking that you will *never* find another job if you flub up this interview? "What horseshit!" you exclaim as you roll over and go to sleep—counting philosophers instead of sheep.

Slippery-slope predictions can also be *refuted* by appealing to *past experience*. For example, in 1994, Oregonians passed a law by public referendum, the so-called Death with Dignity Act, which permitted physician-assisted suicide for competent Oregon residents who were terminally ill—expected to die within six months, as documented by a qualified physician and confirmed by a second qualified physician. The act permitted doctors to prescribe medication to qualified patients who requested it both orally and in writing for purposes of ending their lives.

However, politicians opposing the act questioned its constitutionality, and it was tied up in the courts until 1997, when Oregonians voted again by public referendum to reinstate the act. Opponents feared the act would prove discriminatory against minorities and poor people and that it would cause a landslide of people requesting suicide and ultimately a demoralizing and catastrophic disregard for human life.

At the time of this writing, the act has been in force for about eight years, and none of the feared consequences have occurred. There have been a relatively small number of patients availing themselves of this legal option, and they have been largely middle-class white folks. Still, the U.S. attorney general has managed to challenge the act in the U.S. Supreme Court on grounds that it violates a federal law controlling illegal drugs.

While the government can always find ways to force its own moral values on Americans, the experience gleaned from this act refutes speculations that assisted suicide, when carefully circumscribed, is likely to have the said catastrophic consequences on respect for human life. Past experience has now disconfirmed such probability estimates. That's why the attorney general has tried a different approach!

Politicians as well as private citizens would do well to consult the evidence of past experience in formulating their policies and life choices. For example, oppression of human freedom is predictably counterproductive. Many and sundry dictators of times past have tried it, only to effect their own undoing. Oppressive regimes have often had their time to bask in the sun at the expense of human suffering, but in the end they have all paid the piper. Those who think otherwise are either ignorant of history or delusional (or both).

Antidote 4
In facing situations involving risk to self or others, seek the "golden mean" with regard to feelings of fear and confidence. (Aristotle)

In chapter 3, I talked briefly about a former client of mine who was a male psychiatric nurse. Each evening after work, this fellow would experience considerable anxiety over the prospects of things going wrong the next day on the job. He had told himself that his job was extremely important since other people's lives depended on him and that if he slipped up, this could have serious consequences for his patients.

True, it was possible that he might have screwed up and that a patient could have been seriously harmed, but this was not likely. After all, he was competent, and there were other support staff on duty besides him. Yet he demanded perfection, telling himself that he must always be in control,[12] and he magnified risks regarding things going out of control and resulting in serious injury to patients. Consequently, he experienced extreme anxiety each evening.

This case clearly raised issues about the ability to rationally control fear. From the perspective of character ethics, my client was behaving cowardly. He was too fearful of something happening under the circumstances. On the other hand, according to Aristotle, rational management of fear requires *courage*.

Courage, said Aristotle, "is a mean with regard to feelings of fear and confidence." Regarding the things people fear—disgrace, poverty, disease, friendlessness, and death—he said, the brave person

> will face them as he ought and as the rule directs, for honor's sake; for this is the end of virtue. But it is possible to fear these more, or less, and again to fear things that are not terrible as if they were. Of the faults that are committed one consists in fearing what one should not, another in fearing as we should not, another in fearing when we should not, and so on; and so too with respect to the things that inspire confidence. The man, then, who faces and who fears the right things and from the right motive, in the right way and from the right time, and who feels confidence under the corresponding conditions, is brave; for the brave man feels and acts according to the merits of the case and in whatever way the rule directs.[13]

In fearing doing harm to his patients, my client seemed to fear something worthy of fearing. But since his patients were not in any immediate danger, his fear was untimely. In addition, his low level of confidence was not commensurate with his training and ability. Evidently, then, my client did not show courage in confronting his circumstance. Rather, he was *too* afraid.[14]

This doesn't mean you should go to the other extreme of becoming overconfident. As Aristotle says, such people are fearless only because they don't really think there is anything to be afraid of. In contrast, the brave person is aware of the danger and does not discount it. Driving is a good example. As soon as you start to think that you deserve the Driver of the Year Award, you have set yourself up for an accident. A courageous driver does not discount the dangers inherent in driving. On the contrary, such an individual keeps these dangers in mind so as to exercise care in addressing them.[15]

So the trick is to be neither over- nor underconfident and to be neither too afraid (cowardly) nor not afraid enough (rash). As I mentioned, risk assessment should take account of the risk factors involved in the activity in question. To be fearless in the face of grave danger is as foolish as it is cowardly to be frightened off by small risks.

Recently, Congressman John Murtha, a thirty-seven-year Marine Corps veteran and colonel, came forth and advised that the United States withdraw its troops from Iraq in the near future. A decorated war hero who received a Bronze Star and two Purple Hearts for his service in Vietnam, he had recently visited Iraq to assess the progress for himself. Referring to the Bush administration's handling of the conflict as "a flawed policy wrapped in illusion," he warned that the continued presence of the United States in Iraq was "uniting the enemy against us."[16] Finding the conditions in Iraq even more dangerous than they were in Vietnam, he spoke out of concern for the needless loss of human life.

In response, Vice President Cheney accused Murtha of not having "backbone." However, as a young man, Cheney himself had received several deferments that kept him out of military service. Now here he was accusing a decorated military hero of cowardice. As Aristotle wisely stated, "People who are ignorant of the danger also appear brave . . . but those who have been deceived about the facts fly if they know or suspect that these are different from what they supposed."[17] Who, then, had more "backbone," the man who had faced similar danger in the jungles of Vietnam or the man who himself fled from danger but had no difficulty sending others into harm's way?

While Murtha had originally approved of the war in Iraq, he was not afraid to admit that a mistake had been made. The prospective welfare of others—Iraqi civilians as well as Americans—took precedence over trying to save face. On the other hand, in failing to even consider the possibility that remaining in Iraq was too costly, Cheney displayed overconfidence in an area in which he had no direct experience. Cheney's dogmatic adherence to taking risks he was not qualified to assess and his dogged refusal to listen—or at least to respect—others who were so qualified made him anything but courageous.

Ignorance is often at the root of underconfidence and overconfidence in managing risks. For example, in making predictions about risks of disease, people often over- or underreact. Some people think that they are invincible and hence take few health precautions. For example, I know of one fellow who boasted how he drank from his friend's cup with full knowledge that he had the flu. This poor fellow ended up almost dying from the flu. It is such laxness and overconfidence in the management of health risks that can lead to widespread epidemics and even pandemics.

Sexual activity is a good example. Promiscuity is foolhardy given the risks of sexually transmitted diseases such as HIV. On the other hand, there are some people (fewer today than twenty years ago) who worry about catching HIV by shaking hands with someone with the disease. Again, as Aristotle rightly surmised, ignorance is often at the root of mismanaging fear and confidence.

So educating yourself about risks before you assign them is usually a good idea. For example, consulting the Internet to find out the transmission modes of HIV and the types of sexual activity that are high risk can be useful. This said, beware the tendency to misinterpret data and to under- or overstate risks. For example, deep-mouth kissing isn't usually high risk, but if you deep-mouth-kiss a person with HIV who has bleeding gums, you can contract the disease that way. On the other hand, worrying about getting HIV from a peck on the lips or by getting someone's saliva on your lips is irrational.

Antidote 5

If you're spinning in a self-destructive, vicious cycle, get pessimistic about your future. Expose the blind, perverse craving for security that keeps your life in limbo. Then do what you can to increase the probability of a brighter future. (Schopenhauer)

On the other hand, you should avoid the extreme of wishful thinking—thinking that even though something has consistently gone wrong in the past, it'll still improve for the future. While fatalism crushes your future prospects by locking you into gloom and doom no matter what you do, wishful thinking crushes them by deluding you into thinking that you needn't make any changes for things to change. In either case, you end up stagnating, stewing in the witch's brew.

As Russell made plain, the more times two things have been conjoined in the past without exception, the more *probable* it is that they will be conjoined in the future. This means that if you don't make suitable changes in your life and if something has repeatedly gone wrong in the past under these conditions, then it's probable that the same thing will happen in the future. But again, to say this does not mean that it is certain. Change your circumstances in relevant respects, and you can change your future.

Many people persist in habits that repeatedly lead to undesirable results. Like a punching bag that is knocked down and pops back up, only to be knocked down again and on and on in a vicious cycle, these people naively trust that the next time they get up from being knocked down (or from knocking themselves down), things will be better for them the next time around. The victim of domestic violence—who gets beaten, then gets treated royally, then walks on eggshells, and then gets beaten again—rides this merry-go-round nonstop. "Things are going to be different this time," she proclaims when she enters the calm after the storm, but this is just a prelude to further cycles of abuse until permanent change—sometimes in the form of the death of the victim—halts the process.

Some students manage to earn tenure as undergraduates by taking the same optimistic perspective about the future after they fail, again and again, to pass courses they need to graduate. Over and over, these students persist in study habits that are bankrupt, but optimistically they chug along until permanent change finally sets in—often in the form of giving up completing and dropping out without a degree.

I have had some students who kept reemerging every few years for a period as long as a decade, taking more courses toward their "major," which changed each time they got closer to graduating. Their enthusiasm was reinvigorated each time they reemerged, but it went flat again and awaited a new cycle that kept them in perpetual limbo.

Similarly, some people devote their lives to job hunting and career seeking but never ultimately find their niche. And yet it always seems to them like "things will be different this time," until the bomb predictably drops, and they are once again back in hot pursuit.

Some people go through the process of dating, courting, getting serious, and then breaking it off, only to find someone else whom they optimistically pursue, only to find a reason to call it quits.

What all these cycles have in common is wishful thinking. Wishfully, they ignore the evidence of the past, only to repeat it in the future. I often feel like screaming, "Open your eyes. You're lying to yourself"—living in bad faith as Sartre would say. You are unfree, spinning like a top on its axis until you will inevitably drop. That is when your time will be over and you will have blown it. Wake up and smell the evidence.

These cases make a strong case for determinism—that the will is entirely controlled by external conditions—since why would someone *freely* choose such a life for themselves? But if this resembles you to some extent, here is also a challenge to your willpower muscle. How capable are you of getting off this merry-go-round and living authentically?

Whether willpower is itself under external control is not the issue. You really don't have to get deep into the waters of metaphysics to acknowledge the human ability to alter self-destructive patterns of behavior. As mentioned earlier, this is verified every time people manage to change their self-destructive ways. Whether you are a determinist or a firm believer in free will—a so called libertarian—you cannot realistically deny the fact that such change is genuinely possible and does in fact occur.

So what antidote can you use to direct your effort of will in overcoming your inertia that keeps you in a vicious self-destructive cycle?

The most salient response is to require adequate evidence for your beliefs. Make it your avocation to question anything and everything that is not backed by sufficient evidence. If the conditions of the past have repeatedly produced consistent undesirable results, saying that "things will be different" flies in the face of reason. It rises to the height of absurdity on stilts. It portends more of the same unless something significant in your life changes.

Arthur Schopenhauer believed that everything is accounted for by the "principle of sufficient reason."[18] This principle says that everything has a reason for its existence. When the same reason is present, you can expect the same results. You can't get around this by rationalizing the future. Schopenhauer also thought that reality unfolded in terms of a blind craving for self-preservation that self-defeatingly inclines toward death and destruction. According to Schopenhauer, the way to overcome this blind chaotic force is to resist it. Spinning away your life in a self-destructive circle does provide a certain sort of perverse stability. At least, at some level, you always know where you're heading. That is why abuse victims often doubt their ability to break away from their abusers. They tell themselves how difficult it would be to make it on their own and how fortunate they are to have someone who provides for them. So they find it comforting to be optimistic and to rationalize staying in the abusive relationship.

Here then is the work of a blind craving that ultimately will do you in if you let it. Schopenhauer would tell you to resist this craving by using your intellect. One way to do this is to contemplate the destructiveness of your ways—to expose this chaotic perverse craving for security for what it is, namely, an inherently destructive and "evil" force that is taking you down. Your optimism that things will be different is thereby juxtaposed with and overshadowed by the reality hidden underneath your rationalization. It is such a jolt to the system that can help awaken you. Wake up and smell the evidence.

This is not a call to become pessimistic for its own sake. Nor would I suggest carrying Schopenhauer's pessimistic view to the extremes that he himself did—everything in nature was the work of this evil destructive force, and the universe was the worst of all possible worlds according to him. But it is not irrational to be pessimistic about cases in which you are needlessly throwing away your happiness.

As Bertrand Russell suggested in commenting on Schopenhauer's philosophy,

> His pessimism made it possible for men to take to philosophy without having to persuade themselves that all evil can be explained away, and in this way, as an *antidote*, it was useful.[19]

Indeed, not all evil *can* be "explained away" by telling yourself that things will be different, and, in such cases, to be optimistic is irrational. In these situations, to be pessimistic about your future if you keep it up is just being realistic. This doesn't mean you should depress yourself. To be depressed means to give up. Pessimism here means being ready for constructive action.

Thus, the unsuccessful student can attempt to cultivate new study habits or to stay on task. The perpetual dater can give up the search for the perfect person (whom she'll never find on earth) and to take some risks and building a lasting relationship. The abuse victim can seek help from trained professionals.

Wake up. Turn off your *blind* optimism. It is a dangerous rationalization. Get real by getting pessimistic about your situation and the probability that things will genuinely be different. Then you should do something to change your prospects for future happiness. Give yourself something to *really* be optimistic about.

Profound happiness is in your power, but it calls for work on your part. Each time you flex your willpower muscle, you make it easier to flex it again. Eventually, you can overcome the inertia that keeps you in a downward trend. Building up this forward-moving momentum toward constructive change is like a perpetual motion machine. Despite the inevitable vicissitudes along the highway of life, once you are in gear, you are likely to continue to move forward, making gradual progress toward increased prosperity. Wishful thinking will anchor you to a state of inertia. Flex your willpower muscle and put yourself in gear.

NOTES

1. More precisely, philosophers typically refer to such *probabilistic* inferences as *inductive* inferences.

2. I have talked about the dangers of stereotyping in chapter 9. While many of these gems are routinely passed down like family heirlooms and are "programmed into us" as part of our enculturation, it is reasonable to suppose that at least some of them—and perhaps most of them—have *originated* as a result of such shoddy inferences.

3. David Hume, *An Enquiry concerning Human Understanding*, ed. Charles W. Handel (New York: Liberal Arts Press, 1955), 41.

4. William H. Halverson, *A Concise Introduction to Philosophy* (New York: Random House, 1981), 83.

5. Merrilee H. Salmon, *Introduction to Logic and Critical Thinking*, 2nd ed. (New York: Harcourt, 1984), 91.

6. Bertrand Russell, *The Problems of Philosophy* (New York: Oxford University Press, 1972), 65–66.

7. C. I. Lewis, *An Analysis of Knowledge and Valuation* (La Salle, Ill.: Open Court, 1971), 3–4.

8. Aristotle, *Ethics*, bk. 2, chap. 6, 958.

9. Roderick M. Chisholm, *Perceiving: A Philosophical Study* (Ithaca, N.Y.: Cornell University Press, 1969), 26.

10. Chisholm, *Perceiving*, 27.

11. Samuel L. Hart, *Ethics: The Quest for the Good Life* (Delmar, N.Y.: Caravan Books, 1972), 41.

12. As mentioned earlier, he also had a problem with approval damnation. Actually, his control issues stemmed from his demand for approval.

13. Aristotle, *Ethics*, bk. 3, chap. 7, 975–76.

14. I also doubt that my client's *motive* would have satisfied Aristotle's standards of courage. This is because he appeared to be motivated largely by his demand to be thought well of by his employer, whereas for Aristotle the proper motive of courage was to do right for its own sake.

15. This is sometimes referred to as "defensive driving."

16. James Kuhnhenn, "A Hawk Says Get Out," *Philadelphia Inquirer*, November 18, 2005, retrieved January 15, 2006, from http://www.philly.com/mld/inquirer/13196809.htm.

17. Aristotle, *Ethics*, bk. 3, chap. 8, 979.

18. Arthur Schopenhauer, *On the Fourfold Principle of Sufficient Reason*, trans. E. F. J. Payne (Peru, Ill.: Open Court, 1974).

19. Bertrand Russell, *A History of Western Philosophy* (New York: Simon & Schuster, 1945), 759 (emphasis added).

11

UNDERSTANDING THE WHYS AND WHEREFORES OF EXISTENCE

"Why are there pandemics like AIDS and natural disasters like tsunamis?" "Why do bad things happen to good people?" "Why do I sometime have runs of bad luck?" "Why haven't I met the love of my life?" "Why did it have to rain on my entire vacation?" "Why did he hurt me like that?" This list of "why" questions can be extended ad nauseum. Getting immersed in *groundless speculation* about why such undesirable events happen can and often does lead to needless, self-defeating anxiety, anger, guilt, and depression.

Nevertheless, asking "Why?" goes to heart of what it means to be rational. Socrates made this question the cornerstone of his dialogic philosophical method. Scientific inquiry always begins (and ends) by asking why. It is therefore not a matter of whether to raise the question. Rather, it is a matter of just *how* to address it.[1]

In chapter 10, you saw how self-defeating it can be to file reports on the basis of fallacious rules of generalization and prediction and how, in taking rational, philosophical antidotes to these destructive tendencies, you can decrease your stress and increase your happiness. In this chapter, you will see how you can avoid many of the stresses associated with *blind conjecture* and how you can instead attain greater happiness through a *scientific* approach to living.

Broadly speaking, a scientific approach to living means basing the answers you give to the whys and wherefores of life on rules of reporting that show you how to *rationally* arrive at and confirm your answers. As mentioned in chapter 10, there are three related types of rules in this category: explanatory rules, causal rules, and contrary-to-fact rules.

EXPLANATORY RULES

Explanatory rules tell you how to go about explaining facts about which you are especially curious or puzzled. "Why didn't I get that job?" asks a disgruntled job applicant. And then she self-consciously explains, "I bet it's because I'm overweight."

"Why isn't he home yet?" says a panicked mom who is waiting for her teenage son to come home from a school social. "It's 2:00 A.M. and he was supposed to have been home two hours ago." And then she explains this fact with the things she fears the most: "Maybe he's gotten into an automobile accident."

"Why wasn't he friendly to me?" wonders an employee after her boss gives her a lukewarm "hello" in passing. "Maybe," she explains, "he's angry at me or, worse, is intending to fire me."

In these and sundry other cases like them, the explanation we often favor is the one we fear the most—fear of rejection, fear of losing someone or something we covet, or fear of betrayal. This attests to the tendency of human beings to be insecure. Motivated by self-protection, we often overlook the obvious, upset ourselves unnecessarily, and waste valuable time ruminating over unlikely possibilities.

This isn't to say that people don't go to the other extreme and favor the most benign explanation. Sometimes people stubbornly cling to the explanation that is the most optimistic despite evidence to the contrary. For example, despite strong reason to believe her son was taking drugs— she discovered a stash hidden under his bed—a mother accepted her son's explanation that the drugs belonged to a friend. And in another instance, a mother dismissed her nine-year-old daughter's persistent complaint that her stepdad was touching her private parts with the explanation, "You're just jealous and are trying to break us up." But even in such cases, where evidence was rationalized away in favor of a more benign, less threatening explanation, it was still fear that drove the choice of explanations—in the one instance a mom's fear that her child might be addicted to drugs and in the other instance a wife's fear that her husband was a child molester.

These are unsavory explanations, and it is understandable why someone might prefer to believe the more benign explanation. But the logic of explanation is one of probability, not of fear or preference. Probability is a function of evidence and is not augmented or diminished by what you might fear or prefer to believe. The logic of explanation is the logic of science, which speaks in objective terms of weighing evidence.

Here then are two reporting rules to avoid if you are to be scientific about explaining things:

The Feared Explanation
> To the extent that you *fear* one explanation more than another, that explanation is the more probable.

The Pet Explanation
> To the extent that you *prefer* one explanation to another, that explanation is the more probable.

Both of these rules confuse the probability (believability) of an explanation with its practical import. True, if your child were killed in an automobile accident, this would have profoundly greater (negative) effect on your life than if he were simply late because of a traffic jam. But this is no reason to give it a higher probability rating or to think of it as more credible. Yet this is exactly what many of us do. In becoming overwrought with fear, we react as though the probability of an especially unpalatable explanation were somehow catapulted to heights transcending any of its less threatening competitors.

How scientific are you about explaining things? Do you base your explanations on fear, or do you lean toward the explanation that's least threatening and that fits best with what you want to believe? You are not alone. The history of human attempts to make sense of the universe is rife with examples of subscribing to such explanations. Why, for example, do you think human beings have perennially blamed plagues and other natural disasters on the wrath of the gods? Out of fear for our lives. Maybe the gods can be appeased by making sacrifices to them. So we try to get back in their good graces and save ourselves.

True, the more control human beings have attained over nature, the less they have come to rely on such supernatural explanations. Fear of bringing a plague down on us has been supplanted largely by confidence in our power to control nature. Nevertheless, even today there are many who believe in God largely out of fear of going to hell, and there are still others who believe that diseases like AIDS are the result of the wrath of God on homosexuals and other "sinners."

It was such religious fanaticism that led to the persecution of Galileo in the seventeenth century. The Catholic Church wanted to keep human beings, who were "created in God's image," at the center of the universe. However, Galileo (like Copernicus before him) had evidence to support that the earth revolved around the sun and not vice versa. The Church viewed this as heretical since it denied that earth was at the center. The Church's desire to hold on to its pet explanation—the one that squared best with its religious dogma—led it to rationalize away any evidence that conflicted with it.

CAUSAL RULES

Do you avoid walking under a ladder or getting in the path of a black cat? Do you step over the cracks in a sidewalk or knock on wood to ward off bad luck? Do you fear seven years of bad luck if you accidentally break a mirror? Do you fear spilling salt? Do you paddle or get paddled on your birthday? These and many other superstitions have arisen as attempts to ward off evil spirits, appease the gods, and otherwise deal with supernatural powers in order to remain safe and free of misfortune. To the question as to why someone would go through such motions, you say, "To avoid bad luck." But there is no evidence to show how things like breaking a mirror can cause you to have bad luck. Here, the judgment of cause and effect is motivated by fear, not evidence.

How, then, did the judgment come to be made in the first place? For example, what has breaking a mirror to do with bad luck? The ancients thought that when you broke a mirror that contained the reflection of a person, you also injure that person. Why would anyone make this connection in the first place? Surely, the image looks like the person, so that could be at least part of the reason. But there's a deeper explanation for why such superstitions are sustained over time.

Many years ago, I broke a mirror. In the years that followed, I experienced a stretch of bad luck. It was therefore easy for me to think that it was that damn mirror that caused the bad luck. After all, the bad luck came after that cursed mirror smashed into thousands of tiny pieces.

But the problem with this reasoning is that there were lots of things that came before the bad luck. For example, I received my doctorate, relocated to a different state, began a new job, and so on. I might as well have concluded that it was my moving to Florida that caused my stretch of bad luck. But that's absurd.

I recently heard a call-in on a television talk show in which the caller pointed out that since the time we were in Iraq, there haven't been any further terrorist attacks, meaning that the U.S. troops in Iraq were preventing terrorist attacks here at home. But it is equally true that there haven't been any terrorist attacks since the chief adviser to Vice President Cheney, Scooter Libby, was indicted on perjury charges, since the outing of CIA operative Valerie Plame, since Bill Clinton's biography came out, and since Hurricane Katrina slammed into New Orleans.

When I was an undergraduate, I used to wear a certain shirt to take my exams. I can recall taking my first test as a freshman. I happened to be wearing this shirt when I took the test and ended up getting the highest grade in the class. After that, I continued to wear the shirt and consistently got top-notch grades. After a while, the shirt became tattered, but I still continued to wear it—that is, until my dog Pepper got hold of it and ate it. When the shirt finally reappeared in a pile of dogshit, I no longer cared to wear it. I owe a special debt of gratitude to Pepper for having shown me the error of my ways. Divested of my test shirt, when I took my next test, I still did equally as well.

So here is one popular causal rule that holds no water:

The After-This-Because-of-This Rule[2]
   If one event comes after another, then the first is the cause of the second.

The most that can be said for this rule is that the cause does usually come before the effect. But that's just not enough to make a rational cause-and-effect judgment. As John Stuart Mill once pointed out, if that were all there was to making such judgments, you might as well say that night causes day since the second is *always* followed by the first. But that would be stupid.

I mentioned before how some people think that HIV is the result of God's wrath brought down on gays for their sinful behavior. On the other hand, those who take a scientific perspective would tell you that the disease is caused by a virus spread by contact with the blood or body secretions (such as semen) of an infected individual, the primary means of transmission being unprotected sex and needle sharing. The first explanation is not testable and is immune to falsification. In this respect, it is antiscientific. But notice that they are not contradictory. Indeed, it is possible to think of a view that is not bigoted and that still takes account of science. For example, you could say that God does not want people to be promiscuous, so he created causal laws that discourage this kind of behavior. These laws include getting sexually transmitted diseases like HIV if you are not discreet in your sexual activities.

Notice that this third view doesn't discount the science of HIV. In fact, if you suppose that the will of God is reflected in the laws of cause and effect that govern the spread of diseases, then this hypothesis even becomes scientifically testable. Unfortunately, some people who take religious perspectives view religiosity and a commitment to God as being incompat-ible with a commitment to science. They think that you can choose one or the other and that in making any concessions to science you're copping out on God. Similarly, some who take a secular scientific view see religious ex-planations as antiscientific and think that any concession to such explana-tions is tantamount to surrendering their commitment to science. So, on the one hand, there are religionists who declare war on secularists; on the other, there are secularists who declare war on religionists. Following are the respective rules of each camp:

Religious Fanaticism
In order to be true to your faith in God, you must always denounce secular scientific explanations and opt instead for religious ones.
Secular Fanaticism
In order to be true to your commitment to science, you must always de-nounce religious explanations and opt instead for secular, scientific ones.

Notice that both of these rules rest on the same assumption: that religion and science are incompatible. This is the causal fallacy. It is also a form of pigeonholing. Either you're religious, or you're a heretic; either you're sci-entific, or you're some sort of religious nut. It's all or nothing. But as I have emphasized (with considerable help from Aristotle), such extremism leads to a distorted view of reality and lowers your prospects for personal and in-terpersonal happiness. Moderate religiosity is not lunacy, nor is a scientific outlook that is open to moderate religiosity. Those who substitute prayer for science and wait for God to act fail to realize that God and the causal order of nature are not on competing teams and that whatever help we can muster from science is a product of a natural order that is part of "creation." Creationists who scorn scientific explanations commit the same fallacy as secularists who scorn religious explanations.

I am not saying that you have to believe in creationism in order to avoid a fallacy. Nor am I saying that you have to believe in God at all. The point is logical, not substantive. Science and religion are not black and white. They can be compatible. There are shades of gray—moderate reli-gious perspectives—that make both scientific and religious sense. Failure to realize this has created unnecessary schisms between fanatics on both sides.

So, does this mean that I think you should be able to teach religious explanations in natural science classes? No, not any more than I think you should be able to teach evolution in religion classes or economics in a hu-man anatomy class. But do I think that taking *both* classes can potentially give you a more coherent, complementary, and enlightening philosophical perspective about the universe? Yes.

Just as both creationism and evolution deal with the beginning of the universe, economics and human anatomy deal with human nature but in different, mutually compatible ways. The trouble usually starts with literalist interpretations of creationism where the religionist insists that all human beings literally came from two people by the names of Adam and Eve. Those who insist on such a literal interpretation will perceive an irreconcilable incompatibility between creationism and evolution. If these same religionists are not prepared to acknowledge the possibility of hypotheses that are compatible with science (even if they don't themselves accept them) and if they consider such views to be heretical, sinful, or abominations of God's word, then they are religious fanatics. But this is just what I mean by carrying religion to antiscientific extremes. And the same can be said for anyone who is equally as intolerant on the secular side.

CONTRARY-TO-FACT RULES

Unscientific claims can also take the form of contrary-to-fact speculation. Did you ever notice how much of what people say is about things that never really happened? We often speak about what we could-a/would-a/should-a done, not what we actually did do, and we do so with such great confidence, as though something that never really happened *would* have happened just the same. We replay reality in our minds, not as it *did* happen but rather as it could-a/would-a/should-a happened.

"Had I taken the highway instead of the back road, I wouldn't have been late." "Had I taken more vitamin C, I would have fought off that miserable bug." "We could have beaten their asses if our star quarterback hadn't gotten injured in the first quarter." "Had Gore been president, the terrorist attacks on 9/11 wouldn't have happened." "If only I had bought those stocks when they were low, I would be on easy street today." "Had I not worn that sexy, red dress, he never would have done that to me." "Had I tried harder, I would have fought him off." "Had I been home when he had the heart attack, I would have been able to save him." "I should have been there for him, and he would be alive today!" And so on.

Speculate all you want about how things could have been different, but at the end of the day, reality will be as it is. As I will discuss, this does not mean that all contrary-to-fact claims are groundless. But the plain fact is that many of them are used as ways to retreat from reality, not to confront it. For example, not uncommonly, survivors of sexual abuse blame themselves rather than the perpetrators, especially when the latter are intimate relations such as their fathers. "I must have done something to deserve it," says the victim, therein proclaiming her guilt. And it's just a stone's throw from here to self-damnation: "I'm worthless trash." This is not realistic.

Going to the opposite extreme, human beings often make contrary-to-fact claims in order to prop themselves up and soothe their psyches. True to his macho enculturation, the guy who wants to save face might blame a fender-bender on his wife. Here he can make convenient use of a contrary-to-fact judgment. "Had you not distracted me by talking to me, I wouldn't have gotten into that accident. It's *your* fault!" How convenient to be able to replay reality the way you want it. Excuses, excuses. Too many of these can leave you living in la-la land.

Here's a rule to watch out for:

> Could-a/Would-a/Should-a Thinking
> If you or others had acted differently, the world wouldn't be flawed in the way it is now.

This rule leaves too much room for groundless speculation. Yet it's easy to allow yourself to be sucked into such speculation. For example, in my weaker moments, I have told myself that if I hadn't climbed to the top floor of the Home Depot Auditorium in Fort Lauderdale to see Jerry Seinfeld two years ago (after a hectic day of being on my knees rebuilding my kitchen cabinets), I wouldn't have torn the meniscus in my knee. But who knows? It takes only a slight twist after a significant strain to tear this ligament, and if it didn't happen in seeing Jerry, it could have happened on a different occasion. Not that I'm crazy about Seinfeld, but it wasn't really his fault.

REFUTATION OF BLIND CONJECTURE

It should now be evident that conjecture on the basis of flimsy evidence is a bad idea. Here's why in summary:

> Refutation: In subscribing to rules of feared or pet explanations, you mislead yourself and others and preempt viable solutions to human problems. Similarly, in basing your causal judgments on after-this-because-of-

this thinking, you commit yourself to frivolous rituals and superstitions and send yourself down dead ends in addressing your problems. In going to extremes with religious or scientific fanaticism, you needlessly dismiss rational and potentially fruitful approaches to problems of living. In rationalizing your mistakes, misdeeds, and lack of success by making groundless assumptions about what could-a/should-a/would-a been, you forfeit the opportunity to learn from the past, and in using contrary-to-fact claims to condemn yourself, you set yourself up for depression, victimization, and other self-destructive states of being. In short, in relying on reporting rules that sponsor jumping to conclusions on the basis of inadequate evidence, you defeat your own purposes by diminishing your prospects for personal and interpersonal happiness.

Antidotes to Blind Conjecture

ANTIDOTES TO EXPLANATORY FALLACIES

Antidote 1

In arriving at an explanation, apply a critical, scientific method instead of responding out of fear or according to your subjective preferences. (Popper)

In chapter 10, I entreated you to be pessimistic *to the extent that this is realistic.* This latter qualification is of profound significance. Extreme fear has a tendency to lead a person to look on reality with jaundiced eyes.

This is the thrust behind what I have called *fearing an explanation.* You think the worst, and then suddenly you think it's real. The gulf between the possible and the actual somehow is bridged by the imagination in moments of extreme fear, especially when the stakes are high. "Oh my God!" exclaims the mom who hears the word "accident" out of her teenage son's mouth as her grip around the phone receiver tightens. The first thought is the worst—fear that her baby has been seriously injured. Reassurance that it was just a fender-bender soothes the anxiety, and the mom's pulse rate slowly begins to return to normal.

At the moment where there is even the slight possibility of grave harm to someone (or something) of inestimable value, it is admittedly no easy task to distance yourself enough from the situation to make a rational judgment. No easy task, but it is nevertheless in your power. It is a matter of building up the requisite willpower. The more you work at it, the more likely you are to cultivate the habit of mind fundamental to reaching grounded inferences.

According to Karl Popper, what separates a great scientist like Einstein or Newton from an amoeba is the possession of a *critical method* for solving problems. The amoeba learns by a genetically determined trial-and-error process whereby it adjusts its movements to overcome obstacles in its environment. While the scientist also engages in a trial-and-error process, it differs by being one grounded in a rational method of problem solving.

So how do you rise above the level of a single-celled creature and become more like old Einstein?

According to Popper, a critical method for solving problems consists of three steps:

1. The starting point is always a problem or a problem situation.
2. Attempted solutions then follow. These always consist of theories, and these theories, being trials, are very often wrong: they are and always will be hypotheses or conjectures.
3. In science, too, we learn by eliminating our mistakes, by eliminating our false theories.[3]

Consider the mom who awaits her teenage son's arrival home. Out with the car, he is later than usual—about two hours too late. "Where is he?" she thinks. This is the problem she has defined for herself. The question arises because there are facts that perplex her. He is not home when he said he would be home. He is normally not this late coming home. He is not answering his cell phone. So the mother wants an explanation.

If she thinks the worst—that he was in an accident and is maybe even dead or comatose—she will feed a dreaded fear she might have had ever since he got his driver's license. The fear intensifies the more she savors the unsavory thought until it becomes larger than life and explodes in her mind's eye. It trumps all other possibilities, which fade into the background, as her dreaded explanation is inducted into the hall of probability. This is what I mean by the fallacy of *the feared explanation*.

I once knew an art professor who bragged about grading women according to their bust sizes. "Abhorrent," you say. "It is dreadfully unfair since students should be judged on the quality of their work and the grades they *earn*." Doesn't choosing an explanation on the basis of fear resemble grading on the basis of sexual desire? Both confuse relevant criteria with emotions. In the latter case, grades should be assigned according to mastery of the subject matter; in the former, probability should be assigned according to evidence.

Like new students who haven't yet proven themselves, each possible explanation needs to be tested before it can be evaluated. Otherwise, you are making ungrounded prejudgments. To apply a *critical method* as an antidote, you would therefore have to consider the other possible explanations according to their rightful probabilities.

So the second step in Popper's method is to take notice of the other possibilities. Whatever you can think of that explains all the facts would be viable candidates. Maybe the teen has been making out all night in the backseat of his car and hasn't yet come up for air—having turned off the ringer on his cell phone so as not be disturbed. Maybe he decided to join a group of peers after the social at the local Starbucks. Maybe he ran out of gas on the highway and left his cell in the car when he went to get gas. Maybe he was abducted by space aliens who have scrambled the cell signal.

According to Popper, the third step is to eliminate explanations until you get to something that holds water. For example, you could call Starbucks to find out if he's there. If he isn't, then you have eliminated (or at least disconfirmed) the Starbucks hypothesis. You could call highway patrol. You could call Stephen King to find out if there are any space aliens in town for a cosmic convention. Or you could simply wait a while longer to see if the teen calls or walks in the door—thus eliminating the fatal accident hypothesis.

For the parent who waits by the door with pounding heart, stricken with fear, the homecoming is likely to be received with a mixture of both relief and anger.

"Where were you? I was worried sick about you! Couldn't you have at least called to let me know you were all right?"

"Oh, sorry mom," says the teen in a polite, composed tone. "We were just chilling in front of the school. I guess I didn't hear the phone on vibrate. My woofers were really turned up."

Moral: Instead of panicking listen to Karl Popper.

Popper's approach is to see if an explanation can be shown to be false rather than if it can be confirmed. The explanation that wins is the one that can't be falsified. What is distinctive in this approach is Popper's rejection of the idea that we should try to *confirm* explanations before accepting them.

Popper's main reason for stressing falsification over confirmation is that even highly uncritical theories can be claimed to be confirmed. Did you ever get a fortune cookie that said something like, "You will soon come into good fortune." There are so many ways this prophecy could come true—anywhere from having a good day at work to winning the lottery—that it's not surprising that it comes true. Or suppose that your car keeps stalling. You could of course explain the malfunction with the metaphysical assertion that there are invisible undetectable gremlins in your gas tank. That ought to do it, right? So every time it stalls, you can say, "See I told you; it's those damn gremlins at it again!" The problem is that there's simply no way to falsify this explanation because these critters are invisible and undetectable.

Popper thought the psychoanalytic theory of famed psychologist Sigmund Freud was likewise incapable of being falsified. For example, how can you falsify the belief that little boys have Oedipus complexes—that they want to bump off their dads and sleep with their moms? Or how can you falsify the claim that little girls have "penis envy"—that they feel castrated and want to be "fancy" like little boys? If you asked a little boy if he was sexually attracted to his mom, he wouldn't have a clue, and most little girls would not admit to wanting a penis.

Nevertheless, devout Freudians perceive no problem in confirming their own theory. And where evidence seems to suggest otherwise, they always have at their disposal a deep dark caldron called "the unconscious." The true motivation of a person, they claim, is repressed, buried deep in the unconscious, where not even the person can get at it—unless he cares to enter a rigorous program of psychoanalysis until he's old and gray.

In this way, human beings incline toward trying to make conflicting evidence fit their own pet explanations. This is what the Church did in the seventeenth century when Galileo challenged its earth-centered view of the universe. In order to account for the positions of the planets according to its pet theory, it postulated a highly complex network of suborbits known as epicycles. However, this juggling act resembled the gymnastics that people sometimes go through when they are caught in a lie. They heap excuse on excuse in an effort to explain away any inconsistencies. But the big problem with this is that it's much *simpler* to tell the truth.

Antidote 2
If you have a choice between two explanations, both of which equally well explain all the facts, then choose the simpler one. (Ockham, Beardsley and Beardsley)

It's simpler to tell the truth because true beliefs fit together in a coherent system. As soon as you have to start adding proviso on top of proviso in trying to explain away apparent inconsistencies, that's when what you're saying starts to lose credibility.

Further, the more provisos you add to an explanation, the more chances you have of being proven wrong. Simpler explanations tend to be more probable because they make fewer assumptions, and the fewer assumptions you make, the *less* chance you have of being proven wrong. That's why seasoned philosophers are always cautious about committing themselves to more than they need to in order to prove their point.

So when you have two alternative accounts that both seem to explain the same facts, it would appear more rational to choose the simpler one. This idea that the simpler explanation tends to be the truer one was a favorite principle of the thirteenth-century philosopher William Ockham, who often used it in philosophizing. "Pluralitas non est ponenda sine necesitate," he said: "Plurality should not be posited without necessity."

In fact, the giving of unnecessarily elaborate accounts of reality can be a symptom of some mental disorders. For example, according to philosophers Monroe and Elizabeth Beardsley,

> Certainly one of the key symptoms of the psychosis called paranoia is a persistent tendency to choose and act upon one of the less simple of available hypotheses. The paranoiac, when he leaves his house and sees someone dressed like a mailman coming down the street, does not simply infer that it is the mailman. He is convinced that it is his wife's lover in disguise, or that it is a foreign spy who is following him and probably has been hiding in his garage all night, hunched over a short-wave radio, while assembling a brace of plastic bombs. The paranoiac's delusions must, in general, also include the belief that he is threatened (which is why he himself is generous), but the credit he places in his fantasies is not deterred by their elaborate complexity, far in excess of what would be required to explain his observations.[4]

In this respect, say Beardsley and Beardsley, the preference for the simpler explanation over the more complex one is "almost a defining characteristic of rationality." This doesn't mean that you should always choose the simpler explanation. One explanation might be simpler than another but might not adequately explain all the facts. Nevertheless, *other things being equal*, it would be more rational to choose the simpler over the more complicated explanation.

So here is an antidote you can use to guard against trying to save your pet explanation by heaping proviso on top of proviso. If this is what you are doing, you might as well fess up. Sure it would be nice if the explanation you prefer turned out true. It would be infinitely better, for example, if no one's children took drugs and if no father ever touched his daughter's private parts. But shitty things cannot always be realistically explained away by making excuses. As you have already seen in our discussion of the world-revolves-around-me rule, external reality does not bow to your beliefs and preferences. You just can't prefer an explanation into reality.

ANTIDOTES TO CAUSAL FALLACIES

Antidote 1

In making judgments about what causes what, rely on evidence gleaned from scientific analysis and experiment, not on magical thinking and fear. (Popper, Bacon, Mill)

Causal explanations are vulnerable to the same dangers of uncritical assessment. In this sphere, magical thinking instead of rational, scientific thinking can keep you in a suspended state of needless and self-destructive anxiety. For example, in breaking a mirror, you say to yourself, "What have I done! Seven years of bad luck!" Then, as soon as something shitty happens, you attribute it to having broken the mirror.

According to Popper, the distinction between scientific thinking and such magical thinking has serious implications for the type of society you live in. For Popper, primitive societies, which he called "closed" societies, are rooted in magic and superstition, while progressive societies, which he called "open" societies, are rooted in rational, scientific thinking.[5] When fear and superstition is rampant in society instead of a rational, scientific outlook, the climate is fertile for dictatorial regimes to set themselves up as the arbiters of truth.

According to Popper, in an open society, people question the claims made by their leaders and demand evidence from them. The residents of such a society place great stock in freedom of speech and have the means available to throw out leaders who attempt to use their power to stifle democracy. They are inclined to reject supernatural explanations as bases for social policies, and they are tolerant and respectful of others who do not share their religious preferences, knowing that such disagreement cannot be settled by scientific thinking.

Popper's distinction between open and closed society is important to keep in mind in responding to political authority. For example, after the 9/11 terrorist attacks, the government attempted to link Saddam Hussein with the attacks. More than 60 percent of Americans believed that Saddam Hussein was responsible for 9/11 and accordingly supported Bush's invasion of Iraq. However, the government did not provide the American people with evidence to this effect. In fact, it was always curious why none of the terrorists who were involved in the attacks were Iraqis. It was also curious why a secular tyrant like Hussein would have been willing to cooperate with a nonsecular terrorist like Osama bin Laden. The Bush administration failed to address these facts before the American public because it had no way of honestly addressing them. Instead, the American people, including Congress itself, were encouraged to simply have faith in their government. This faith was tested when Bush asked Congress to surrender its constitutional authority to declare war, giving him the authority to invade Iraq at his discretion. With few exceptions, our elected representatives in Congress blindly surrendered to just one man an awesome power that was delegated by our forefathers to the entire corpus of Congress. Many of those who uncritically deferred to Bush have now come to regret it.

Fearing another terrorist attack, Congress was also willing, sight unseen, to support the surrender of vital civil liberties of Americans by signing the USA PATRIOT Act into law. This act included provisions for secretly entering private residences (the so-called sneak-and-peek provision) and the federal authority to attain copies of personal records of American citizens—including a list of the books purchased and the videos rented. These provisions were so broadly defined that the suspicion of terrorism without probable cause was deemed sufficient grounds to engage these expanded legal powers. Unfortunately, the efficacy of such measures in fighting terrorism has not been satisfactorily demonstrated to the American people.[6]

Blind faith is not a substitute for critical thinking in a democratic society. This lesson is one repeated throughout history. Governments that have used fear and intimidation instead of rational argument to accomplish their goals have invariably been oppressive. Looking at things from this social perspective, I hope you can see why it is important for citizens who value their freedom to cultivate firm habits of rational, critical assessment.

Do you think (or have thought) that 9/11 was caused by Saddam Hussein? Do you think that America is now safer because of the PATRIOT Act? If you believe these things, then you are not alone. It is easy to buy in to such uncritical causal judgments, especially when media sources try to connect these things and politicians, in their public speeches, mention them in the same breath.

Do you believe that God had a hand in declaring war on Iraq? Do you think that natural disasters such as Hurricane Katrina are due to the wrath of God? Do you partake in common superstitions like fear of breaking a mirror? Do you put yourself through strange rituals or activities from carrying a lucky rabbit's foot to wearing a lucky garment (like my infamous "test shirt," for example)? Again, you are not alone. But a serious problem with subscribing to such magical powers is that it weakens your propensity for rational causal judgment.

Rational judgment about what causes what is not a matter of placing your faith in some magical or supernatural cosmic power or authority. These are the ways of the closed society, and they won't suffice to contribute to a free, democratic lifestyle. To the contrary, they will keep you in a state of anxiety about what will happen to you next.

David Hume was very clear about this point in one famous paragraph of his *Inquiry concerning Human Understanding*:

> When you look about us toward external objects, and consider the operation of causes, we are never able, in a single instance, to discover any power or necessary connexion; any quality, which binds the effect to the cause, and renders the one an infallible consequence of the other. We only find that the one does actually, in fact, follow the other.[7]

For example, he says that when one billiard ball strikes another, we see the second billiard ball move, but we can't discover anything that *necessarily* links these two motions together as cause and effect. We just discover, from repeated experience, that the one motion is constantly followed by the other motion. There is no special power, no necessity that binds them together.

This was Hume's way of saying that cause-and-effect relations are based on experience and cannot be known without such evidence. You can think all you want about Saddam Hussein and what an "evildoer" he was, but you cannot, without empirical evidence, link him to 9/11. There's no magical power that connects the two.

But even if two events are constantly conjoined, that doesn't mean that they are related as cause and effect. As John Stuart Mill astutely pointed out, even if you have always observed one event to be followed by another event, that doesn't mean that the first is the cause of the second event. For example, night is always followed by day, but that doesn't mean that the first causes the second.

So how do you know if two events are really related as cause and effect?

Since my undergraduate days when I first read Francis Bacon's *Novum Organum*, I have been impressed at how he was able to figure out that heat was caused by motion. In order to show this, he set up three tables. The first was a list of diversified things, all of which contained heat. This table included such things as the rays of the sun, fiery meteors and thunderbolts, animal bodies, and horseshit and other forms of excrement. Then he set up a second table of things similar to the first but in which heat was absent.

This table included such things as the rays of the moon, stars and comets, and vegetables and plants. Third, he set up a table that compared degrees of heat in the same subject, such as the varying degrees of heat felt from the sun depending on the season, of the heat in living animals versus dead ones, and of heat in fresh versus old shit.

Based on these tables, Bacon excluded all things that were not found where heat was present or that were present where heat was absent and all things that were found to increase when heat decreased or to decrease when heat increased. For example, he found light and brightness not to increase or decrease in proportion to the quantity of heat.

When Bacon finished his analysis, he concluded,

> From a survey of the instances, all and each, the nature of which heat is a particular case appears to be Motion. This is displayed most conspicuously in flame, which is always in motion, or in boiling or simmering liquids, which also are in perpetual motion. It is also shown in the excitement or increase of heat caused by motion, as in bellows and blasts.[8]

Bacon was right, too, since heat is none other than molecular motion.

John Stuart Mill later elaborated on Bacon's method by arguing that simple observation is not always enough to show a cause-and-effect connection. You may also have to experiment.[9] For example, to confirm that you are allergic to a food, you may just have to eat more of it. This is the basis of allergy testing. The doctor scratches you with a bunch of different allergens to see which one causes a skin reaction in you.

Superstitions and other claims about magical powers can be unmasked when you take a critical, scientific approach to causation. There are simply no such experiments that can show that breaking mirrors causes seven years of bad luck—or any bad luck for that matter. Superstitions, all of them, are the result of fear, sustained by after-this-because-of-this thinking, not scientific thinking.

Antidote 2

In ascribing causes to things, don't allow your commitment to religion to become fanatical and destroy your ability to make rational judgments. Similarly, don't allow your commitment to science to become fanatical and destroy your ability to tolerate any religious views. (Hume, James, Sartre, Aquinas, Buber)

What about God? Is it antiscientific, magical thinking to hold God responsible for what happens to you? Is such thinking in the same boat as superstition?

Over the years, I have listened attentively to many folks who have talked passionately to me about "miraculous" events in their lives that they believed could not have been adequately explained by science according to natural laws of cause and effect. For example, a former student once spoke in class of an automobile accident in which he "miraculously" escaped death. In the instant before his car collided with another vehicle, he sensed a presence in the vehicle watching over and protecting him. His vehicle was demolished, but he was found virtually unscathed outside his vehicle. My student said he believed it was God who somehow had saved him. He described how the paramedics and police were unable to explain how he managed to escape the accident with little more than a scratch and a few bruises. My student said he was an atheist prior to this experience, but afterward he claimed to have formed a new and ever so strong personal bond with God.

I do not doubt that my student spoke candidly and honestly about his experience. Still, his explanation of what had happened to him was not testable according to the scientific method. So was it reasonable to believe his hypothesis?

In any miracle, something is supposed to have happened that contravenes the natural causal order as we know it. Such events defy what we have in our past experience observed to be true. In the case at hand, my student claimed that God intervened to somehow transport him from the vehicle and thereby to spare his life. Such an explanation defied past experience of how the laws of nature operate in such cases, and this shed doubt on the credibility of my student's interpretation of what had really happened.

According to our skeptical friend David Hume, it is "experience only, which gives authority to human testimony; and it is the same experience which assures us of the laws of nature." The one set of experiences—our own stock of past experiences—nullifies the other—the testimony of others—and therefore "we may establish it as a maxim that no human testimony can have such force as to prove a miracle."[10]

But Hume was talking about believing *the reports of others* about purported miraculous events. This still leaves open the question of whether the witness to a purported miracle was justified in believing his *own* report. Regardless of whether anyone else was justified in believing my student's supernatural report, was my student *himself* justified in believing it?

Here's my spiel: To take things to the extreme of disallowing yourself the option of believing in the miraculous nature of your own encounters would be as dogmatic as the religionist who disclaimed anyone's right to *disbelieve* in God. But what if my student's mother chose to believe in the miraculous nature of her son's survival? Should we look askance on her? But, then again, what if you or I chose to believe in the miraculous nature of what had happened instead of sticking to the laws of nature?

William James admonished,

> A rule of thinking which would absolutely prevent me from acknowledging certain kinds of truth if those kinds of truth were really there, would be an irrational rule . . . we have the right to believe at our own risk any hypothesis that is live enough to tempt our will.[11]

Your religious beliefs—the ones that are "live" enough (significant enough to you) to "tempt your will"—are your entitlement, but whatever risk you incur in believing—or not believing—is yours alone. These risks should not be forced on others who don't share your same religious commitments. This harkens back once again to the value in overcoming the common human tendency toward the world-revolves-around-me fallacy, which almost invariably leads to unhappiness—your own and those whose lives you touch.

But in believing in miracles, would you be surrendering your commitment to science?

Yes, to the extent that you would be suspending your commitment to believe only what can be tested in the light of past experience. But the rule should not be lost in the exception. Miracles, if they occur at all, are extremely rare. If you were to claim miraculous events sprouting up on a regular basis, then you would have lost the rule in the exception, and this would destroy your credibility. This is precisely what happens to fanatical religionists whose religiosity consumes their practical judgment and sense of reality. But extremes aside, I don't think that belief in miracles in proportion to the degree in which we might expect to find them if they really existed would destroy your prospects for happiness. Indeed, such belief might even enhance your spirituality without destroying your prowess for making practical decisions.[12] The religionist who sits by and allows his child to die of a disease while he waits for God to intervene would be a good example of someone whose belief in miracles has exceeded practical (and moral) limits.

Being devoted to God does not mean sitting back and letting God determine your life or that of significant others. It does not mean waiting for something miraculous to happen. Nor does it mean waiting for a sign from God before you know if something is right or wrong. As Sartre admonished, it is you who ultimately interprets those signs anyway.

The intimate and harmonious relation between God and the natural order—the world that science attempts to describe—is firmly recognized in the writings of many religious scholars from all walks of religion. For example, Aquinas believed that "the natural law is the rational creature's participation in the Eternal Law [the law of God],"[13] and, therefore, human beings, he thought, served God by exercising their rational judgment. Coming from a different perspective, here's how Buber conceived the relation between God and nature:

> God's speech to men penetrates what happens in the lives of each one of us, and all that happens in the world around us, biographical and historical, and makes it for you and me into instruction, message, demand. Happening upon happening, situation upon situation, are enabled and empowered by the personal speech of God to demand of the human person that he take his stand and make his decision. Often enough we think there is nothing to hear, but long before we have put wax in our ears.[14]

According to Buber, God speaks volumes to us through nature. Nature is the realm of science. God and science are not competitors but are in harmony with one another. For example, Bishop Berkeley believed that God gave human beings natural laws—the laws of cause and effect—so that we could use them as guides in life. A scientific approach to life need not be at odds with a healthy commitment to God. Be a religion–science compatibilist. Recognize and tolerate the possibility of religious–scientific outlooks that are coherent (even if you don't yourself accept them). In this era in which some creationists have taken up the defense of God against believers in evolution and some evolutionists are denouncing religion altogether, this isn't small potatoes.[15]

ANTIDOTES TO COULD-A/WOULD-A/SHOULD-A THINKING

Antidote 1
To see if your contrary-to-fact claim is credible, take a philosophical approach: consider what it assumes and whether you can rationally defend it. (Chisholm, Lewis, Socrates, Russell)

Commitment to the laws of nature (for example, those of physics) and commitment to God are not inconsistent. That's a no–brainer. Too bad the fanatic doesn't get it. But philosophers haven't always agreed about what a law of nature is in the first place. Of course, it's a universal statement like "*All* humans are creatures with hearts and kidneys." But some statements use "all" and they aren't laws, such as "All of the words on this page are in English." So how do you distinguish between universal statements that are laws and ones that are not?

Here's one reasonable answer given by my mentor Roderick M. Chisholm: Laws of nature, he said, imply contrary-to-fact statements. For example, if ET were a human, then he would have a heart and kidneys. Isn't that the truth? On the other hand, it's hardly true that if the word "hombre" were a word on this page, it would be in English. The first universal statement implies contrary-to-fact statements, while the second doesn't. That's why the first is a law and the second is not.

C. I. Lewis, Chisholm's teacher, astutely pointed out that even our concept of reality depends on contrary-to-fact claims. He stated, "If we did not believe that if something *were* tested, at a time when in fact it is *not* tested, certain specifiable results *would* accrue and not others, we should not believe in objective reality or facts which obtain independently of being experienced."[16] For example, what does it mean, in practical terms, for there now to be food in your fridge even though the door is closed and you cannot perceive it? For one, it means that if you *were* to open the fridge door (even though you're not opening it right now), you *would* perceive food. For Lewis, the idea of the continued existence of the physical world (food in the closed fridge, for example) would make no sense unless you could rest your case on such contrary-to-fact statements.

So do you see how important contrary-to-fact statements really are? You can't just discount all of them. The could-a/would-a/should-a claims of ordinary living are many. We routinely use them to make excuses for ourselves (and for others), to ascribe blame, and to express regret about how things could-a/would-a/should-a been. It is in this practical arena that the imposters are often found. The key, therefore, is to separate the rational from the irrational ones.

A contrary-to-fact statement tells you to *suppose* something true that is contrary to what really is true. On the basis of this supposition, it draws a *conclusion*. Take the statement, "If I were to open my fridge door, I would see the milk I placed in there yesterday." This statement makes the following inference:

Suppose (contrary to fact): I open my fridge door.
Therefore, I see the milk.

However, to get to the conclusion that I see the milk, there are obviously certain *assumptions* I need to add. For example, I would have to assume that nobody took the milk out of the refrigerator (for example, drank it or threw it out). If you are the only one who ordinarily has access to your fridge, then this assumption may not be hard to defend. If so, then your contrary-to-fact statement about seeing the milk would be quite reasonable—otherwise, not.

This method of exposing the assumptions behind your contrary-to-fact inferences goes to the core of what it means to think philosophically. Socrates is known for having said, "The unexamined life is not worth living," and here is a case in point. If you simply *assume* things without examining what you have assumed, you are likely to suffer considerable emotional pain and vexation. Bertrand Russell vividly expressed the same point. The person, he says, who fails to cultivate a philosophical approach to life (which means questioning rather than simply assuming things) "goes through life imprisoned in the prejudices derived from common sense, from the habitual beliefs of his age or his nation, and from convictions which have grown up in his mind without the co-operation or consent of his deliberate reason."[17]

Consider a rape victim who unreflectively tells herself, "If I didn't wear that sexy red dress, he wouldn't have raped me." This is her inference:

Suppose (contrary to fact): I don't wear that sexy red dress.
Conclusion: I don't get raped.

Does this conclusion really follow? Yes, it does! This is because you have to assume a lot more:

Assumption 1: When I don't wear my sexy red dress, I don't look sexy.
Assumption 2: Rapists are turned on by someone only when they look sexy.
Assumption 3: Rapists commit rape only when they get turned on sexually.

If someone looks sexy in a red dress, then she probably also looks sexy in other things too, which makes assumption 1 false. But assumptions 2 and 3 are also false. Rape is a crime of power and control, not sex. That's why old ladies wearing housedresses also get raped. Accordingly, a rape victim who makes these assumptions and fails to examine and refute them subjects herself to needless suffering.

One of my former clients who found out that her husband was gay stated, "Had I been more of a woman [been more sexual], he wouldn't have preferred another man to me." This was her inference:

Suppose (contrary to fact): I am more sexual with my husband.
Conclusion: My husband doesn't prefer another man to me.

In order to get from her supposition to her conclusion, she had to assume that gay guys can go straight if a woman is willing to devote herself to him sexually. But, save for an occasional gay man who claims to have been "changed," the probability that even a hot-to-trot, sexy heterosexual woman could get a gay guy to go straight is slim to none. Once my client realized this, she was eventually able to stop blaming herself.

Here's another example for the road. Out on a drive to a social, a friend of mine cut too close to the side of the road and grazed a mailbox. Alarmed and embarrassed, he snapped at his wife, who sat beside him. "If you weren't talking to me, I wouldn't have hit that mailbox." How did I know he said this? I was in the backseat. His inference:

Suppose (contrary to fact): You don't talk to me while I was driving.
Conclusion: I don't hit the mailbox.

To get to the conclusion from this supposition, my buddy needed to assume at least these two things:

Assumption 1: Nothing else distracts me.
Assumption 2: I can hit a mailbox only if someone or something distracts me.

Assumption 1 is at least questionable. This is because I was also talking—gabbing away as it were. Assumption 2 is bigger hogwash since we imperfect human beings not uncommonly make perceptual miscalculations, and sometimes our minds wander. In fact, my friend admitted to having gotten little sleep the night before.

When you put these shoddy assumptions together, what do you get? A heap of horseshit. This poor fellow needlessly became self-defensive and tried, albeit unsuccessfully, to shift the responsibility away from himself onto his wife, to which his wife responded, "That's an existential cop-out! Bad faith, as Sartre would say." She was the wife of a philosopher and had learned the lingo. As for my friend (the philosopher), he wasn't being very philosophical.

Antidote 2

Don't get stuck in the past by ruminating over what could-a/would-a/should-a been. Look to the future with the wisdom of the past. (Sartre)

Irrational could-a/would-a/should-a thinking is not uncommonly combined with other irrational rules to deduce self-destructive emotions. One frequent example of this is its use with damnation. For example, as mentioned earlier in this chapter, survivors of sexual abuse often blame themselves for the abuse and come to see themselves as unworthy persons. It is no accident that many women who become prostitutes have been sexually abused as children. These women have come to perceive themselves as unworthy of respectful, nonexploitative relationships.

People who lose loved ones not infrequently live with irrational guilt arising from self-blame. These people sometimes tell themselves that had they acted differently, their loved ones would still be alive today. Others needlessly anguish over divorce; still others lament unfortunate events, replaying them over and over again in their minds, telling themselves how it could have been so different.

It's not always the contrary-to-fact claim itself that contains the fallacy. Sometimes it's awfulizing and *can't*stipating yourself over it that inflames the problem. For example, it may not be unreasonable for someone who lost a loved one to tell herself how different it would (or might) have been had this beloved person lived. Still, it's usually a bad idea to wallow in what could-a/would-a/should-a been. As Sartre emphasized, "Reality alone is what counts," and to think otherwise is to define yourself negatively as a "disappointed dream, as miscarried hopes, as vain expectations."[18] It's generally more constructive to look to the future, enlightened by the past, than to ruminate over what could-a/would-a/should-a been in the past. Back to the future.

NOTES

1. The "Why?" question itself can be ambiguous. Sometimes in raising it, we are looking for an explanation, other times a justification, and sometimes it's just not clear what is being sought. The serial killer Ted Bundy said that his having been exposed to pornography played a part in the commission of his crimes. Many criminals come from abusive backgrounds. While these facts can provide explanations, they hardly suffice as rational justifications for committing murder. In contrast, the question "Why should there be laws against theft?" asks for a justification. "Because

we couldn't live a satisfactory life in common if stealing were permitted" provides a rational (moral) justification, not an explanation, for having such laws. This chapter is concerned primarily with "Why?" in the explanatory, not the justificatory, sense.

2. There's a Latin expression, *post hoc ergo proctor hoc*, which is often used to refer to this fallacious rule. It means "after this, therefore because of this."

3. Karl Popper, *All Life Is Problem Solving* (London: Routledge, 1999), 7.

4. Elizabeth L. Beardsley and Monroe C. Beardsley, *Invitation to Philosophical Thinking* (New York: Harcourt, 1972), 46.

5. Karl Popper, *The Open Society and Its Enemies* (Princeton, N.J.: Princeton University Press, 1971).

6. In addition, the PATRIOT Act moved us closer to even more atrocious abridgement of constitutionally protected freedoms. As of this writing, the federal government is conducting warrantless, widespread wiretapping of personal phone calls and e-mail messages. At least the "sneak and peak" provision of the PATRIOT Act required a warrant. See James Risen and Eric Lichtblau, "Bush Lets U.S. Spy on Callers without Courts," *New York Times*, December 16, 2005, retrieved January 15, 2006, from http://www.commondreams.org/headlines05/1216-01.htm. President George W. Bush explained his preemptive attack on Iraq by claiming to have been following the instructions of God. See Rupert Cornwell, "Bush: God Told Me to Invade Iraq," *The Independent*, October 7, 2005, retrieved January 15, 2006, from http://www.commondreams.org/headlines05/1007-03.htm. But I entreat you to tell me what experiments would confirm that it was God who directed him to wage war on Iraq? Replacing rational judgment with faith in matters of state portends a dangerous state of affairs. The basis for a nation to go to war must at least be falsifiable, as Popper would say. You can falsify weapons of mass destruction in Iraq—we did that—but you can't falsify a president's claim that God directed him to make a preemptive strike on a sovereign nation. Such decisions fall within the scope of human responsibility, which cannot be explained by appealing to God any more than "the Devil made me do it" can be used to honestly defend against a charge of murder. This is a *human* decision.

7. David Hume, *An Enquiry concerning Human Understanding*, ed. L. A. Selby-Bigge (New York: Oxford University Press, 1951), sec. 7.

8. Francis Bacon, *Novum Organum*, in *The English Philosophers from Bacon to Mill*, ed. E. A. Burtt (New York: Modern Library, 1977), 114.

9. John Stuart Mill, *A System of Logic* (San Francisco: University of the Pacific, 2002).

10. Hume, *An Enquiry concerning Human Understanding*, in *From Plato to Derrida*, 4th ed., ed. Forrest E. Baird and Walter Kaufmann (Upper Saddle River, NJ: Prentice Hall, 2003), sec. 10, pt. 2, 772.

11. William James, "The Will to Believe," in *Historical Introduction to Philosophy*, 4th ed., ed. Albert B. Hakim (Upper Saddle River, N.J.: Prentice Hall, 2001), 557.

12. The same could hardly be said for other magical beliefs such as superstitions. Their spiritual value is null.

13. St. Thomas Aquinas, *Summa Theologica*, "Treatise on Law," question 91, art. 2, 618.

14. Martin Buber, "I and Thou," in *Philosophers at Work: Issues and Practice of Philosophy*, ed. Elliot D. Cohen (Fort Worth, Tex.: Harcourt, 2000), 537.

15. The point is that creationists can still believe in evolution and evolutionists can still believe that God got the show on the road, for example, that God was the transcendent cause of the infinite series of natural causes and effects.

16. C. I. Lewis, *An Analysis of Knowledge and Valuation* (La Salle, Ill.: Open Court, 1971), 216.

17. Bertrand Russell, *The Problems of Philosophy* (New York: Oxford University Press, 1972), 156.

18. Jean-Paul Sartre, "Existentialism," in Cohen, *Philosophers at Work*, 447.

12

CONCLUDING REMARKS:
YOUR PROFOUND HAPPINESS

The contributions that philosophy can make to your mental health and profound happiness should now be evident. Its antidotes can be potent medicine against the most common and destructive ways human beings torment themselves and others. I hope you have already begun to internalize many of these vital capsules of wisdom. I hope you will use them like a golden sword wielded against the personal, interpersonal, and societal demons that have perennially obstructed the road to human happiness, individually and collectively as a society.

So many things adverse to human happiness—from self-oppression to mass genocide—can be linked to the eleven cardinal fallacies to which I've devoted this book. We live in an age that is technologically savvy, an age in which we can access a vast sea of information with the click of a mouse, an age that is beginning to unlock many great mysteries of nature. But this progress may mean very little unless we are able to face our own demons. The ability to live forever might give us only more time to drive ourselves insane. The ability to travel faster and to visit other galaxies might give us only more room to plunder and destroy. If we are not willing to look deeply into the sorts of issues that the great philosophers have wrestled with and to make sense of them, then all such technological progress will be for naught. We might as well have remained in the Dark Ages.

The potent antidotes of antiquity can provide light where there would otherwise have been darkness. They can illuminate the worth of freedom and democracy against the dark shroud of tyranny. They can help cultivate respect for human dignity and individuality to overcome blights of blind conformity and hatred of self and of fellow human beings. They can show you how to overcome irrational fears, to triumph from misfortune, to turn fear into courage, to see beauty where there once seemed ugliness, to connect with others instead of alienate them, to be temperate and in control instead of *can'ts*tipated, and to be forward moving and sanguine instead of stuck in a bleak, fatalistic outlook. In short, they can help you attain a life of transcendent virtue and profound happiness.

The great sages of antiquity have had fundamental disagreements about the problems of human existence. As Bertrand Russell so accurately expressed,

> There are many questions—and among them those that are amongst the profoundest interest to our spiritual life—which, so far as we can see, must remain insoluble to the human intellect. . . . Yet . . . it is part of the business of philosophy to continue the consideration of such questions, to make us aware of their importance, to examine all the approaches to them, and to keep alive that speculative interest in the universe which is apt to be killed by confining ourselves to definitely ascertainable knowledge.[1]

What helps make these philosophical approaches so valuable is their diversity and distinctness. Were there only one appropriate response to each human challenge, human beings would be nonautonomous and machinelike. If philosophy is to enrich the spiritual life of most of us, it must be as diversified and variable as human beings themselves.

This said, there are still some common denominators, things to which most philosophers would verily nod assent. In the first place, there is a consensus among philosophers that the eleven cardinal fallacies addressed in this book really *are* fallacies. Philosophers have struggled to make rational sense of the universe, especially the conditions of human happiness. This is why these fallacies have been a prime philosophical target. As this book suggests, a substantial part of the history of philosophy can be viewed as an attempt to construct rational antidotes to these fallacies.

Second, in assenting to a fallacy, the philosophers have impliedly assented to a truth. No doubt you are familiar with the Ten Commandments, which, according to the Old Testament, were delivered to Moses on Mount Sinai. These deliverances of truth spoke in the negative language of "Thou shall not," such as Thou shall *not* kill, commit adultery, steal, covet thy neighbor's wife, and so forth. Each tells you *not* to do something that is presumed to be morally wrong. For each of the eleven cardinal fallacies, there is also a "Thou shall not" that rings true. I present to you the *eleven commandments of human happiness*: Thou shall *not*

1. Demand that this imperfect universe or any part of it be perfect or flawless.
2. Deny the inherent worth of a human life or of the universe itself.
3. Discount the relativity of bad by rating it as worst.
4. Act, speak, or think like a programmed machine in blind conformity.
5. *Can't*stipate autonomous control over emotion, behavior, and will.
6. Distress over problems of living as though a solemn moral duty.
7. Manipulate and deceive others to get what you want.
8. Expect external reality to bow to personal beliefs, preferences, desires, and values.
9. Oversimplify reality by perceiving it in black-or-white, all-or-nothing, or stereotypical ways.
10. Make generalizations and judgments about the future that are not probable relative to the evidence at hand.
11. Advance explanations of the whys and wherefores of existence on the basis of preference, fear, superstition, magic, or other manner of unscientific thinking.

Are there any philosophers who would have a bone to pick with one or more of these? Yes. For example, Machiavelli thought manipulation was an excellent political strategy. But this book is itself a testament to the abundant support that philosophers have historically given to these cardinal precepts.

Are these commandments as "binding" as the Ten Commandments? If people went around killing and plundering, you couldn't hope to live happily. But it is also true that if you habitually demanded perfection in this earthly world; damned yourself, others, and the universe; thought the absolute worst; and so forth, then you couldn't live happily.

This suggests another important parallel to the Ten Commandments. Just as not killing and plundering are minimum conditions of morality, so too are these eleven commandments of human happiness *minimum* conditions of human happiness.[2] No person who abstains from killing his neighbor is deserving of an award for his high moral deeds. This would require going that extra mile, such as sacrificing time or money or even risking your life for a noble cause. In like manner, becoming *profoundly* happy would take more than complying with the eleven commandments of human happiness. For example, it is one thing to perceive misfortune in a relative light. It is another to grow and prosper from your misfortunes, as Nietzsche recommended.

Similarly, it is no small matter to stop stereotyping people, no less than it is a small matter to respect their material property. But you go even further when, as Kant would say, you come to see your fellow humans as one "community of ends" or, as Buber would say, you begin to "I-Thou" them. To stereotype someone is to prejudge them, to unfairly discriminate against them. Ceasing such behavior is clearly a precondition for treating others with dignity and respect, but it takes more than just this to build solidarity and community. This is where the real potent philosophical stuff kicks in.

In contrast to the eleven commandments of human happiness, which speak in the language of "Thou shall not," *philosophical antidotes* tend to be affirmative in character—they tell you what *to do* rather than what not to do. This is because, as you have seen, they address *virtuous* living, not merely minimum conditions of human happiness. Thus, in proclaiming that "profound suffering . . . makes noble," Nietzsche was telling you to look on suffering as a gateway to fulfilling your higher human capabilities, not merely as something to avoid. In the language of logic-based theory (LBT), it's a way to attain transcendent virtue, in particular to cultivate courage in the face of evil. As in the case (discussed in chapter 3) of the woman who was brutally assaulted and left for dead, triumph did indeed come from adversity, and this woman became *stronger* than she ever was before.

For someone in the circumstances of this woman, Nietzsche's antidote might have been more potent than say one prescribed by Epictetus, who emphasized the attainment of serenity.[3] This clearly shows the value of having more than one philosophical antidote up your sleeve for addressing the same fallacy. As you travel through life, your relative circumstances will inevitably change. Stocking up on potent philosophical antidotes for the future, even if you have less need for certain ones today, may prove abundantly useful tomorrow.

Are you up for the challenge? Human flourishing is definitely something you will need to work at. It is a lifetime pursuit. As Aristotle so eloquently stated, "One swallow does not make a summer, nor does one day; and so too one day or a short time, does not make a man blessed and happy."[4] Backsliding is part of the human scene too—being as we are imperfect. But the potential to attain transcendent virtue through philosophy and therefore to become profoundly happy is not reserved for sages or saints. It's a *human* potential. If you are reading this book, then you are a candidate for this forward-moving journey of spiritual growth.

I hope you can now see clearly why I have chosen to call this book *The New Rational Therapy*. If you have acquired several of the antidotes assembled in these pages, then you have probably come away with some very useful ideas that you would not ordinarily have gleaned from conventional therapy.

In fact, the conventional approaches tend to go to extremes. Some emphasize "positive" psychology to the neglect of looking at the irrational thinking that generates human problems in the first place. Others dwell largely on irrational thinking to the exclusion of helping you to construct dynamic, forward-moving, antidotes. In contrast, LBT both addresses irrational thinking (the eleven cardinal fallacies) and offers you a carefully articulated set of philosophical antidotes. Moreover, unlike *any* of these other approaches, LBT systematically and comprehensively keys in on the vast stock of philosophical resources to help you ascend to the higher reaches of human capability (the eleven transcendent virtues).

This is not to say that standard approaches are not useful and important. Nor is it to say that you should substitute this or any other self-help book for professional therapy. But, as you have seen, the truth typically lies somewhere between the extremes. Moreover, how much you can derive from *any* approach will depend largely on how hard you are willing to work.

If your goal is the modest one of feeling less anxious, less down, less guilty, or less angry—in a word, less stressed—then you can attain this by treating yourself with the modest antidotal powers of the eleven "Thou shall *nots*" listed earlier. Classical rational therapy has indeed done an excellent job in building a repertoire of cognitive and behavioral techniques toward this more modest goal. On the other hand, if you want more out of your life—no, not just more, a *lot* more; then why not go for the gold? Against the irrational emotional and behavioral currents that stifle your spirit and squander your creative, human potential, I say treat them with philosophy. With this, I wish you well. No, not just well: I wish you serenity, success, and *profound happiness*.

NOTES

1. Bertrand Russell, *The Problems of Philosophy* (New York: Oxford University Press, 1972), 156.

2. They belong to the "morality of duty" as distinct from the "morality of aspiration." See chapter 1.

3. Said Epictetus: "Do not seek to have everything that happens happen as you wish, but wish for everything to happen as it actually does happen, and your life

will be serene." Epictetus, *Encheiridion*, in *From Plato to Derrida*, 4th ed., ed. Forrest E. Baird and Walter Kaufmann (Upper Saddle River, N.J.: Prentice Hall, 2003), 260.

4. Aristotle, *Nicomachean Ethics*, trans. W. D. Ross, in *The Basic Works of Aristotle*, ed. Richard McKeon (New York: Random House, 1941), bk. 1, chap. 7, 943.

SELECTED BIBLIOGRAPHY

Allport, Gordon W. *The Nature of Prejudice*. New York: Perseus, 1979.

Aquinas, Thomas. *Introduction to St. Thomas Aquinas*. Edited by Anton C. Pegis. New York: Random House, 1965.

Arendt, Hannah. *The Human Condition*. 2nd ed. Chicago: University of Chicago Press, 1998.

Baird, Forrest E., Walter Kaufmann, eds. *From Plato to Derrida*. 4th ed. Upper Saddle River, N.J.: Prentice Hall, 2003.

Beck, Aaron. *Cognitive Therapy and the Emotional Disorders*. New York: Penguin Books, 1979.

Belenky, Mary, et al. *Knowledge, Difference, and Power*. New York: HarperCollins, 1996.

Bok, Sissela. *Lying: Moral Choice in Public and Private Life*. New York: Random House, 1989.

Burtt, E. A., ed. *The English Philosophers from Bacon to Mill*. New York: Modern Library, 1977.

———, ed. *The Teachings of the Compassionate Buddha*. New York: Penguin Books, 1991.

Cohen, Elliot D. *Caution: Faulty Thinking Can Be Harmful to Your Happiness*. Mason, Ohio: Thomson Custom Publishing, 2003.

———, ed. *International Journal of Applied Philosophy*. Philosophy Documentation Center, Charlottesville, Virginia.

———, ed. *International Journal of Philosophical Practice*. Journal of the American Society for Philosophy, Counseling, and Psychotherapy. Online periodical (http://www.ijpp.net).

———, ed. *Philosophers at Work: Issues and Practice of Philosophy*. Fort Worth, Tex.: Harcourt, 2000.

———. *What Would Aristotle Do? Self-Control through the Power of Reason*. Amherst, N.Y.: Prometheus Books, 2003.

Cohen, Elliot D., and Gale S. Cohen. *The Virtuous Therapist*. Belmont, Calif.: Wadsworth, 1999.

Cooper, John M., ed. *Plato: The Complete Works.* Indianapolis: Hackett Publishing, 1997.

DaMasio, Antonio R. *Descartes' Error: Emotion, Reason, and the Human Brain.* New York: Avalon Books, 1994.

Ellis, Albert. *Feeling Better, Getting Better, Staying Better.* Atascadero, Calif.: Impact Publishers, 2001.

———. *A New Guide to Rational Living.* Hollywood, Calif.: Wilshire Book Company, 1975.

———. *Overcoming Destructive Beliefs, Feelings, and Behaviors.* Amherst, N.Y.: Prometheus Books, 2001.

———. *Reason and Emotion in Psychotherapy.* New York: Citadel Press, 1962.

Epictetus. *The Art of Living: The Classic Manual on Virtue, Happiness, and Effectiveness.* New York: HarperCollins, 2004.

Frankfurt, Harry G. *On Bullshit.* Princeton, N.J.: Princeton University Press, 2005.

Frankl, Viktor E. *Man's Search for Meaning.* New York: Pocket Books, 1984.

Fuller, Lon L. *The Morality of Law.* New Haven, Conn.: Yale University Press, 1974.

Gilligan, Carol. *In a Different Voice: Psychological Theory and Women's Development.* Cambridge, Mass.: Harvard University Press, 1993.

Hamilton, Edith, and Huntington Cairns, eds. *Plato: The Collected Dialogues.* Princeton, N.J.: Princeton University Press, 1961.

James, William. *Pragmatism.* New York: Dover Publications, 1995.

Kant, Immanuel. *Groundwork of the Metaphysics of Morals.* Translated by H. J. Paton. New York: HarperCollins, 1964.

Lehav, Ran, and Maria Tillmanns, eds. *Essays in Philosophical Counseling.* New York: University Press of America, 1995.

Martin, Mike W. *Everyday Morality: An Introduction to Applied Ethics.* Belmont, Calif.: Wadsworth, 2000.

McKeon, Richard, ed. *The Basic Works of Aristotle.* New York: Random House, 1941.

———, ed. *The Basic Works of Aristotle.* New York: Modern Library, 2001.

Metcalf, Franz. *Just Add Buddha.* Berkeley, Calif.: Ulysses Press, 2004.

Mill, John Stuart. *On Liberty and Other Essays.* Edited by John Gray. New York: Oxford University Press, 1998.

Nietzsche, Friedrich. *Basic Writings of Nietzsche.* Translated by Walter Kaufmann. New York: Modern Library, 2000.

Popper, Karl. *The Open Society and its Enemies.* Princeton, N.J.: Princeton University Press, 1971.

Raabe, Peter. *Philosophical Counseling: Theory and Practice.* Westport, Conn.: Praeger, 2000.

Rogers, Carl. *On Becoming a Person.* Boston: Houghton Mifflin, 1989.

Russell, Bertrand. *A History of Western Philosophy.* New York: Simon & Schuster, 1945.

———. *The Problems of Philosophy.* New York: Oxford University Press, 1972.

Sartre, Jean-Paul. *Existentialism and Human Emotions.* New York: Philosophical Library, 1985.

Schuster, Shlomit C. *Philosophy Practice: An Alternative to Counseling and Psychotherapy.* Westport, Conn.: Praeger, 1999.

Seligman, Martin E. P. *Authentic Happiness.* New York: Simon & Schuster, 2002.

Stumpf, Charles Enoch, and James Fiesler, eds. *Philosophy: History and Problems.* 6th ed. New York: McGraw-Hill, 2002.

Wittgenstein, Ludwig. *Philosophical Investigations.* Translated by G. E. M. Anscombe. New York: Macmillan, 1968).

INDEX

ABOUT THE AUTHOR

Elliot D. Cohen, Ph.D., Brown University, is a principal founder of philosophical counseling in the United States and the author of numerous books and articles, including his recent book, *What Would Aristotle Do? Self-Control through the Power of Reason.* Dr. Cohen is an advisor to the Albert Ellis Foundation, president of the Institute of Critical Thinking, a founder and executive director of the American Society for Philosophy, Counseling, and Psychotherapy, and professor and department chair at Indian River Community College. He is also ethics editor of *Free Inquiry* magazine and editor-in-chief and founder of the *International Journal of Applied Philosophy* and the *International Journal of Philosophical Practice.*

Made in the USA
Lexington, KY
09 January 2015